The M of Mo.... Cyprus

from obscurity to statehood

Dr. Stavros Panteli

Introduction by
Professor
Robert Browning

INTERWORLD
PUBLICATIONS Ltd

First Published in England in 1990
by Interworld Publications Ltd
12 The Fairway, New Barnet,
Herts EN5 IHN — England

ISBN: 0 948853 09 3

Designed and prepared by Tophill Designs, Barnet, Herts. England
Typeset by PRINTCO LTD — Nicosia
Printed in Cyprus by F RINTCO LTD — Nicosia, Cyprus

History cannot pass judgement.....
it is simply an experience of the past,
possibly a pointer to the future.

INTRODUCTION

Cyprus is among the youngest of nations. Yet it has a longer history than most. Looked at in one way it is a history of rule by foreigners – Assyrians, Egyptians, Persians, Macedonians, Romans, Byzantines, French, Venetians, Turks and British. But in another way it is a history of the meeting and often fruitful mingling of different cultures. Geography and history make the island a bridge between the Mediterranean, Asia Minor and the Fertile Crescent. From the arrival of the Mycenaeans more than three thousand years ago Greek has been the predominant language and Greek culture the predominant culture. I have deliberately not said 'dominant', because the question of domination rarely arose. For most of the time Greeks and Phoenicians, Greeks and Latins, Greeks and Turks have lived peaceably together, sharing the same cities and villages. Zenon of Kition, the founder of the Stoic school of philosophy and one of the most influential thinkers of the ancient world, was a Phoenician who wrote in Greek-and doubtless thought in Greek. Some of the later Lusignan Kings spoke Greek better than French. During the three centuries of Ottoman rule Greek and Turkish Cypriots not infrequently joined in protest, or even in revolt, against the government of the Sultan.

Perhaps because of their cosmopolitan background, Cypriots have never been stay-at-homes. Two of them became Ecumenical Patriarchs and heads of the Orthodox Church. From the fifteenth century many Cypriots settled in Venice. Among these was Thomas Flanginis, who in 1626 founded what was for two centuries the most celebrated Greek school in Europe. Haji Baki Agha, an illiterate Turkish woodcutter from a village in Cyprus, rose, after a not entirely reputable career in the service of the Sultan, to become Governor of his native island. Today the Cypriot diaspora stretches from California to the Persian Gulf, and many Cypriots have made their mark as men of affairs or men of science in their adopted homes. In particular the Cypriot community in Great Britain, which includes Turkish as well as Greek Cypriots, has grown immensely since the Second World War, and London is probably the second Cypriot city in terms of population.

Dr. Panteli in this, his second book on the history of Cyprus, concentrates his attention on the period of British rule (1878-1960) and the years of Cypriot independence. There are many paradoxes in the recent history of Cyprus. It has a higher proportion of graduates in its population than any country in Europe, yet it has no university. Happily, serious measures are now being taken to found one. A long struggle, the avowed objective of which was union with Greece, resulted in the establishment of an independent republic. A country with a millenary experience of polyethnic living together has since 1974 been divided by a barrier as impenetrable as that which separates North and South Korea. Dr. Panteli guides his readers through the jungle of tendentious statement and counter-statement, of unrealistic rhetoric and face-saving compromise, of conscientious negotiation and naked exercise of power which marked the gestation and birth of the nation. Fair-minded in his judgements, at home in the sources, both published and unpublished, scrupulous in his handling of them, he provides an admirable introduction to the complex of problems surrounding Cyprus, some of which will not go away, but fizzle away like time fuses, ready to detonate an international crisis. The problem of Cyprus is the problem of all of us.

The demand for union with Greece was traditional and strong in its appeal to the Greek Cypriots. That it was not realised was due in part to the skill — or the good luck — of successive British governments, who from being the foreign ruler who must be got rid of, gradually transformed themselves into the mediator, and perhaps the arbitrator, between ethnic groups in Cyprus and even between their Greek and Turkish backers. In so doing they helped to create and encourage separatist feelings among the Turkish Cypriots, which soon led to the breakdown of the new constitution. Perhaps it never could have worked. Thus the scene was set for the tragic events of 1974. Some blame for these must fall on the Greek Cypriot people and its leaders, who did not, until it was too late, make a serious attempt to understand and respond to the aspirations and fears of their Turkish fellow-citizens, but tended to regard them as a tiresome minor nuisance. But it was above all the indescribable folly of the military dictatorship in Athens and the eagerness of a weak government in Ankara to show its muscle that led to the invasion and partition of the island.

So today Cyprus has sovereignty, but only over part of its territory. Its rise to full nationhood has been interrupted and flawed. If present difficulties are to be overcome — and the key to their solution probably lies far from Cyprus, as far away as Washington and Moscow — it will once again play its historic role as a bridge between east and west. Whether some kind of association with Greece will eventually be sought is a matter for the Cypriot people, Greek and Turkish, to decide. It is no one else's business.

In the meantime British readers need reminding how by its actions — or lack of action — as colonial power, and later as joint guarantor of the independence and territorial integrity of the Republic, their own country has contributed to the present disastrous impasse. Dr. Panteli's book will help them to understand how things came to be as they are, and perhaps to discern what must be done to put them right.

Professor Robert Browning

CONTENTS

PREFACE

The period covered by the book extends from the earliest years to the last few months of 1989 — from *"obscurity to statehood"*. The latter years, especially, have not been easy to write. Contemporary history presents many pitfalls to anyone rash enough to record it; Cypriot history incurs extra hazards. In the first place, fewer sources are available than in the case of some other countries. The Turkish invasion of 1974 for example, has been instrumental in either destroying both private and public records or keeping them far away from researchers and writers. Secondly, valuable Cypriot sources either appear years after the event or are simply kept from the public —ostensibly at times, to protect an individual or a group. Thirdly, the problems of statehood and internal strife are certainly not conducive to the presentation of good archival material. There are other reasons which are too numerous to even consider.

What the author has tried to present is not a strict narrative history, following the course of events year by year. Hence at all times statistical data, tables, appendices, maps and photographs have been added to assist the reader. It is not intended therefore to be a textbook giving the facts, all the facts and, nothing but tiring details necessary for passing an examination in Cypriot history. It is an unbiased, easy-to-read account aimed at everyone who cares to learn and understand the problems which faced and, still face, this tragic island. This is in the main a political history. The economic, religious, cultural and social sections make no pretence to comprehensiveness: they are intended merely to provide the minimum framework within which political events become intelligible.

The reader is invited to read on and pass his own judgement.

ACKNOWLEDGEMENTS

Acknowledging people who have been instrumental in the production of this work is certainly extremely difficult. I have received much help and encouragement during the writing of this book, and I wish I could find new words to express my gratitude. It is impossible to acknowledge them all, and many, may be unaware of the help they have given because it came as a result of my recollections of discussions amongst friends and colleagues over a period of several years.

In a more formal sense I am indebted to my associates Mrs and Mr Lavithis for reading and making useful comments on the entire typescript and also for providing the maps and photographs.

Above all, I am indebted to Professor Robert Browning who read the whole draft and made some penetrating and helpful criticisms. The Introduction bears witness to his great wisdom, experience and scholarship.

I am forever grateful to my sister Thesbo for her most efficient typing.

Next, I wish to record my deepest gratitude to my wife Floria, not so much for helping me in completing this study but more for her sense of understanding, respect and patience during my many years of research in Britain, Cyprus, Greece and elsewhere.

To conclude, however, I wish to reiterate that the responsibility for any errors or shortcomings in what appears in print is entirely mine.

CHAPTER ONE

THE FORMATIVE YEARS

**c. 10,000 BC
to 1570 AD**

Cyprus, nobly described as a 'paradise par excellence' is situated in the northeastern corner of the Mediterranean Sea. It is its third largest island after Sicily and Sardinia and has an area of some 3,572 sq. miles or 9,250 sq. kms. Its greatest length up to Cape Andreas is 140 miles (233 kms) and its greatest breadth is very nearly 60 miles (98 kms).

At all times Cyprus has been what she is now - the watchtower and outpost of three continents: Europe, Asia and Africa. Consequently, the advantages of its strategic location have made her the envy of more powerful neighbours who had, from most ancient times, practiced a policy of territorial expansion at her expense. Cyprus was always important both for its geographical position linking East and West and for its rich resources of copper, other metals and timber.

According to the Holy Scriptures[1] the 70 nations of the earth may be classified as descended from one or another of Noah's three sons: Shem, Ham and Japheth. From the latter's descendants we find the Cypriots Elishah and Kittim. In general therefore the Bible refers to Cyprus as the *"land of the Kittim"*. Flowery literary epithets include, *'Cerastes'* because of the many promontories it thrusts into the sea like horns; *'Asperia'* from the roughness and unevenness of its soil; *'Collinia'* from its numerous hills; *'Aerosa'* or *'Aeria'* because of the mines of copper and brass which were first said to be found there; *'Makaria'* ('blessed') because of the fruitfulness of the soil and happiness of the climate; as *'Amathusia'*, *'Paphia'*, *'Salaminia'* and *'Lapithia'* from the towns of Amathus, Paphos, Salamis and Lapithos. It was also known as *'Alashiya'* and *'Elishah'* by ancient oriental scholars and described so in sources of the 2nd millennium BC. It was also called *'Iatanana'* and *'Iadnana'* by the Assyrians of the 8th century BC., whereas the Greek settlers and traders of the end of the 2nd millennium preferred the name 'Makaria'. An unjustified name was *'Ophioussa'* (abode of snakes), which was acquired in late antiquity.

So much about location and terminology. To date it has been customary to record that human occupation in Cyprus starts rather belatedly in the **Neolithic** (or New Stone) **Age** around the 7th millennium. The earliest settlers probably arrived from the Syro-Palestinian coast. It is also suggested that they came from the Balkans (Thesally-Macedonia) or even from Cilicia.ı.

---

[1] Genesis xx: 2-4

However recent findings[2] from Akrotiri Aetokremmos ("Eagles Cliff") suggests a much earlier occupation - in fact, a very late Mesolithic presence c 10,000 BC. What is not disputed is the fact that settlements at Khirokitia and Kalavasos around 7,000, Sotira around 4,500 (divided by the so-called *"Dark Age"*) with others (much later), at Erimi, Petra tou Limniti and Ledra (Nicosia) show that Cyprus' Neolithic culture lasted for over 3,500 years and was developed locally with little apparent influence from abroad. This, of course is not altogether surprising considering that mastery of the seas lay far into the future, as did also the technological advances which were to drive these self-sufficient food-raisers into a position of dependence upon their neighbours for certain rare and precious commodities. During this period the inhabitants lived in low circular-domed stone huts, similar to igloos, and were very fond of hunting. Their settlements were usually near the coast or near streams and were mainly found along the north coast and in the south. The Cypriot 'economy' was based (apart from hunting) on mixed farming and fishing. It also appears that grapes and olives, both characteristic Mediterranean products were now gathered.

The **Chalcolithic** (or copper-stone) **Age** which spanned the years c. 3900 to c. 2500 denotes the period when metal first appeared but was still uncommon. Features of the period include: the western end of the island seems to have been inhabited for the first time; the increasing use of metal; changes in burial customs; a new type of miniature sculpture is developed, and Cyprus, henceforth increasingly takes part in international - in fact, regional commerce.

The transition to the **Early Bronze Age** (c 2500 to c 2000) shows an unbroken development from the earlier cultures, with an infusion of new and foreign ideas. Paramount amongst these is the knowledge of metal-working while the West Anatolian[3] strain in some pottery shapes indicates the source of these new traits. Settlements, which were at first spread around river valleys (e.g. Philia and Vasiliko), soon spread right across the island. The long sequence of red polished pottery which spans the period 2500 to 1650 is remarkable for its variety and power of expression. Furthermore, tools and weapons made from copper and bronze show the importance of smelting as a

---

[2] Nature: Volume 333. 9 June 1988.

[3] Anatolian settlers arrived in Cyprus c 2300 - following the disasters which afflicted their homeland.

main source of income for the people. Therefore, a thriving economy supplemented by an emerging metallurgical industry led to better provision for the dead. They were henceforth buried in rock-cut chambers approached by an open passage known as a *'dromos'* and the cave-like chamber was sealed by a large stone slab. And, in common with most of the ancient world the Cypriots believed in life after death. Hence, even humble burials were equipped with pottery vessels containing food, drink and ointment. The wealthier ones also received utensils, tools and weapons.

Towards the end of the period a small number of imports reached the island and Cypriot products reached Egypt and the Near East.

Commercial and cultural contact was continued into the next phase called the **Middle Bronze period** c.2000 to c.1650. Settlements, with the exception of the most mountainous regions, were now found right across the island. Trading relations (especially with countries close by) reached new heights and Cyprus became known as the 'trading emporium' of the region. A pottery style known as 'White Painted II' — burnished vessels decorated with dark paint applied in linear motifs direct to a light background — characterises this phase which is often described as "an epilogue to the Early Bronze Age and the prelude to the Late Bronze period". Agriculture, copper-mining and pottery-making continued to be the cornerstones of the Cypriot economy.

The **Late Bronze** phase c.1650-c.1050 is characterised by various events that can only be described as "climacteric". Firstly, Cyprus traded freely with neighbouring countries — copper and pottery being major items. This must have been the heyday of the cosmopolitan coastal towns such as Enkomi, Kition, Hala Sultan Tekké and Maroni. Secondly, and probably the most important event of the Bronze Age, was the arrival of the Achaean-Mycenaeans around 1200 BC. At about the end of the 13th century many of the Mycenaean settlements were afflicted with disaster, in the course of which Pylos was overwhelmed and Mycenae grievously harmed. A considerable dispersal of the mainland population took place, which resulted in the establishment of refugee settlements at widely separated points, from the Ionian Islands and Achaea in the west to Chios in the east. At least one substantial group of these people (the actual number is unknown), fled to Cyprus where their establishment in a number of places (including Enkomi, Kition and Kouklia) was of incalculable significance for the future development of the island.

The arrival of the newcomers was important in two respects: firstly,

Cyprus' civilization was transformed and eventually the ethnological composition of the population changed. From their Peloponnesian home, the Achaean settlers introduced into the island not merely a language but names of places, institutions and cults. Secondly, the island turned towards the west and began to draw away from the east. This colonization, it must be stressed, was a slow, peaceful process, achieved through successive waves of newcomers from the Aegean (including Crete, Chios and Asia Minor), and by the close of the 12th century Cyprus was developed into an integral part of the Hellenic world, where Greek was spoken and Greek culture was familiar. Both historians and poets spoke highly of the wealth and culture of the island under kings such as Kinyras, Pylagoras, Onasagoras and Philokypros, King of Soloi who entertained Solon, the famous Athenian statesman and lawgiver in 570 BC. Thirdly, while the process of Greek settlement was under way, the Mediterranean experienced troubled times. During the late 13th and 12th centuries adventurers known as *"Peoples of the Sea"* were roaming the coasts; Cyprus did not remain unaffected.

The **Geometric (Iron) Age** c.1050-750 which witnessed another so-called "Dark Age" between 1050 and 850, also saw the coming of new settlers. The Phoenicians arrived in the mid-9th century. Called *"Canaanites"* they were great seafarers and traders who were probably the first to explore, colonize and trade in the Mediterranean sea — they came from the Syrian/Lebanese coast. Kition and Amathus were to become Phoenician strongholds. Their temple of Astarte at Kition is one of the largest of its kind in the region. The mid-9th century therefore, saw a substantial revival of Cypriot culture and an increase in population.

The **Archaic Period** (750-475) witnessed the further prosperity of the island due to, amongst other factors, continued and extensive trade with the east and the Greek world. Salamis was probably one of the largest and most prosperous cities of the region, with a cosmopolitan culture (Greeks, Jews, Phoenicians and others) combining the exuberance and wealth of the Near East with Greek undertones.

One point that has to be stressed at the outset is the fact that due to the influx of the **Greeks** (especially) and **Phoenicians,** the older Cypriot inhabitants i.e. the indigenous population, called *"Eteocyprians"*, played only a secondary part in the life of the island. Yet, their culture and language was never completely wiped out. The Archaic period was also marked by a swift succession of foreign over-

17

lords: Assyria (c.709-c.660), Egypt (c.560-c.545) and Persia from 545 to 333.

The **Assyrian** occupation proved very brief — it was aimed primarily at the defence of its western borders along the coast of Syria and southern Asia Minor. It appears that political subjugation was not intended. The **Egyptian** hold was even shorter. Yet they hold the destinction of being the first to capture the island by recourse to war.

The destiny of Cyprus was henceforth to depend on the rising Persian empire. At the time of the expedition of King Cyrus II the Elder, against Babylon in 538, the Cypriots voluntarily placed their forces at his disposal. The island soon became the western seaward link of the great Persian empire. The Cypriot kings were obliged to pay tribute to the Persians and to supply them with an army and ships for their foreign campaigns.

Internally, the island was organised (during the Archaic period) into autonomous city-kingdoms; 7, and later 10 (Salamis, Kition, Soloi, Paphos, Kourion, Lapithos, Kyrenia, Marion, Amathus and Tamassus), are mentioned in Assyrian documents. They grew prosperous and had wide-ranging commercial connections; moreover, towards the end of the 6th century they began to strike their own coinage. However, **Persian** domination was another turning point in the development of the island. During the whole of the 5th century Cyprus joined in a panhellenic struggle for freedom, an event which had far-reaching political effects. The Greek consciousness of the Cypriots was awakened and closer political and cultural contacts developed between the Greek mainland and Cyprus. It was in this atmosphere that the great king of Salamis **Evagoras I,** appeared on the scene of Cypriot politics, as an advocate of the panhellenic ideals of freedom and Greek culture. For 40 years (from 411 to around 371 BC), Evagora's fate was also the destiny of Cyprus. He fought the Persians (circa 390 to 380) with exceptional bravery against vastly superior odds. Yet, like the earlier Onesilos revolt of 499-498, internal discord (in part due to the cosmopolitan composition of Cyprus' cities) and fighting against a more powerful opponent proved decisive.

A point that needs to be mentioned is that under the Persians, satisfactory progress was made in the arts and general culture of the island. In fact, a particular style in sculpture, the so-called "Cypriot character", appeared and made some headway.

Also, some explanation of the island's religious beliefs and practices should be given. The beliefs of archaic Cyprus remain obscure, but the concept of fertility (as shown by the scores of human figurines) was evidently paramount. Greater foreign influence is evident during the late Bronze Age when a Syrian type of female figurine is often described as the 'Astarte' type, taking the name of the eastern mother goddess. Sanctuary remains are also of this period. During the years 750 to c.325 (the Archaic and Classical eras) the principal deity was the Great Mother Goddess. She was identified above all with **Aphrodite the Cypriot** goddess par excellence, who was already described as *"the Cyprian"* in the 8th century poems of Homer and in the later works of Hesiod. Aphrodite's sanctuary at Old Paphos was the chief religious centre of the island and famous throughout the ancient Mediterranean world. Dedications to her indicate that she was also known as *"the Paphian" "Wanassa"* and *"the lady"*. From the many female figures found it is clear that the worship of a fertility goddess remained supreme in Cyprus. Hylates and perhaps the deified Kinyras, the legendary founder and the first king of Paphos, were male gods much revered in the island.

The **Phoenicians** also introduced their own deities — the goddesses Astarte and Anat and the gods Baal, Eshmoun, Reshef, Mikal, Melquart and Shed. Egyptian cults were also initiated into the island by the Phoenicians — long before the time of Egyptian rule.

It must be noted that in the Archaic and Classical periods the sanctuaries were hives of activity. Here the gods were believed to be and even participate in the sacred banquets accompanied by ritual dancing celebrated in their honour. The priests wore animal and humanlike masks, animals (and at times humans) were sacrificed, libations were offered and incense burnt. During the 4th century Greek cults became widespread in the island. Also around this time Cypriot and Phoenician gods and goddesses started to become identified with Greek deities. Thus the Cypriot Hylates and the Phoenician Reshef became identified with the Greek Apollo. It is also probable that Zeus became the principal god — at least this was the case at Salamis. Nevertheless, towards the close of the 4th century some kings made great efforts to Hellenise their kingdoms and in so doing propagated Greek cults.

Ptolemaic rule (294-58 BC) naturally affected Cyprus' religious institutions. For 200 years or so of this rule the governor or *"strategos"* (general) received the title of High Priest. This enabled him to collect the revenues from all the sanctuaries and so enrich the royal treasury. The worship of the ruling Ptolemy, the *"Dynastic-Cult"*, became of prime importance and a special organisation known as the **"Koinon ton Kyprion"** (confederation of Cypriots) was set up to

19

promote it. Being Greeks themselves the Ptolemies promoted Greek cults. Moreover, existing practices were rarely interfered with and worship continued at many of the traditional open sanctuaries and rustic shrines.

With the arrival of the **Romans** (58BC-330AD) the dynastic cult gave way to the *"Imperial Cult"*. The "Koinon" became an officially recognised national organisation (centrally based at the sanctuary of Aphrodite), whose principal function was to promote the worship of the Roman Emperors. Some of the traditional rites survived as did the worship of Greek deities. The cult of the Paphian Aphrodite the Goddess of Love and Beauty, remained pre-eminent. Aphrodite, was identified as Venus by the Romans. Of paramount importance was the spread of Christianity during the 1st century AD. The apostles **Paul** and **Barnabas** (a native of Cyprus named Joseph), attended by the latters' young relative **John Mark,** proceeded in 45-46 AD on a teaching mission to proclaim the message of salvation to Jews and Gentiles. From Seleucia they crossed to Salamis and they eventually arrived in Paphos presumably via Kition, Amathus and Kourion. It was in Paphos that the Roman Governor was converted to Christianity. An aristocrat from Rome he was a highly educated person and a very influential man. He was an authority in matters of physical sciences, open-minded and well-disposed towards philosophy and theology.

According to tradition and before meeting **Sergius Paulus,** Paul had received from the town's Jews[4] the customary 40 stripes save one. A column of white stone about seven feet high is still pointed out to travellers as being the one to which he is said to have been tied for the occasion. From the Holy Bible we learn that the apostles encountered a sorcerer or magus, a Jew who posed as a prophet, called Bar-Jesus. He withstood them and sought to turn aside the governor from the new faith. Paul's anger reached boiling point and calling him "an enemy of all righteousness" he cast a spell on Bar-Jesus and blinded him. The Governor was truly converted and following the conversion of Constantine the Roman Emperor in 313 AD, christianity was henceforth fully embraced by the Cypriots. In the late

---

[4] Excluding 'Hellenized' and 'Crypto' Jews the Jewish community in Cyprus, about this time, numbered around 15,000.

4th century it became the official religion of the Roman Empire, and c. 488 the Church of Cyprus was declared autocephalus (independent), a position maintained to this very day. So much for the development of religion. We must now revert back to the 5th and 4th centuries BC. Throughout the Classical period (c. 475 - 325 BC), Cyprus was poised between Greece and Persia. The failure of the Ionian revolt (499-498), the activities of the Athenian statesman and commander Kimon (485-465), and the heroics of Evagoras I of Salamis all failed to wrest Cyprus permanently from the vice-like grip of Persia. That honour belonged to **Alexander the Great**, King of Macedonia, leader of the Greeks and eventually conqueror of the world. Following Alexander's victory over the Persians at Issus in 333 BC, the Cypriot cities voluntarily submitted to him. Then they helped Alexander to take Tyre in 332; this finally set the seal on any hopes the Phoenicians had of dominating Cyprus. Persian control over the island was finally brought to an end. Alexander left the Cypriot kings (pro-Persian and Phoenician were restricted) in undisputed possession of their little kingdoms, honoured them with his friendship and, later on, entrusted them with important duties. Thus Stasanor of Soloi became governor of the Persian province of Drangiana, and other kings were well spoken of. The only administrative change of any significance was that Cyprus became part of the huge system of Alexandrine coinage. Another point of major importance was that commercial relations between the Greek mainland, particularly Athens, and Cyprus were very active. The island's economy reached new heights.

Following Alexanders' premature death in 323 BC, his generals struggling to inherit his empire, used the island as a battleground and a number of the city kingdoms were destroyed. After 29 bitter years, Ptolemy who triumphed over Antigonus, annexed Cyprus in 294 BC and claimed Egypt also as his share.

During this period (it lasted for 236 years) Cyprus achieved a fairly high degree of culture and prosperity, with the cities perserving a certain amount of autonomy — similar to the duties performed by local government bodies or communal chambers today. In practice therefore, the masters of the cities were the commanders of the garrisons (strategoi) who gave their orders to the elected organs of native government. The island was however administered by viceroys and regarded as one of the most valuable possessions of the large Hellenistic monarchy of Egypt. The revenues which the Ptolemies drew from Cyprus were enormous. Hence came the copper and corn that Egypt needed so much; here too were built many ships for the Egyptian navy and mercantile fleet. The point that needs to be emphasised is the fact that even though the city kingdoms finally disappeared the Cypriots participated in the regulation of their cultural affairs. Besides "To koinon ton Kyprion", the "League of the Cypriots", a federation of semi-autonomous communities, was a powerful force making for cohesion. The Phoenicians and all other minorities were tolerated but Cyprus became artistically-orientated to the Hellenistic world. This was understandable since the rulers were Macedonian Greeks themselves.

For nearly 400 years (58 BC - 330 AD) the **Romans** were the island's rulers although for a brief period, probably from 47 BC to the death of Cleopatra in 30 BC, Cyprus returned to Ptolemaic rule. It is interesting to recall that Mark Anthony, who met Cleopatra at Tarsus in 41 BC and married her at Antioch four years later, presented Cyprus to his wife and her sister Arsinoe because it was, he explained, "supreme in beauty and well above all other places".

Cyprus became part of the province of Cilicia[5] (on the southern coast of Asia Minor, now modern Turkey), itself Roman since 103 BC and governed by a proconsul. Porcius Marcus Cato became Cyprus' first administrator. During Emperor Octavian's reign (called Augustus from 27 BC) the island became first an imperial province (27 BC) and then, in 22 BC, a senatorial province again governed by a proconsul. Administratively, Cyprus was organised in four districts —Paphos in the west, Amathus in the south, Salamis on the east, and Lapithos on the north. Salamis was regarded by the Romans as the commercial centre of Cyprus whilst Paphos was the seat of government (as it had been since early in the 2nd century) under the name of *"Augusta Claudia Flavia"*.

As already pointed out the conversion of Sergius Paulus the Roman proconsul to christianity by the apostles in 46 AD marked the beginning of the penetration of the new religion into the Roman administration. This was an important event which was thereafter accompanied by radical changes in the life of the Cypriots. The island's history, so deeply affected by the new faith, was to be dominated thereafter by religion. In spite of the evident difficulties (for example, the island's Jews were faithful to their religion and system

---

[5] In 58 BC.

Above: Remains from the Neolithic settlement of Khirokitia.
Below left: A four-sided bronze stand. This side shows a worker carrying an ingot of copper, a main trading commodity in ancient Cyprus.
Below right: Two coins of different periods - showing the Temple of Aphrodite in Paphos. In the centre is the sacred cone.

Above: Limestone sarcophagus from Amathus c460-450BC showing a military or ceremonial procession. Below: Ivory draughts box from Enkomi – late bronze age – showing a hunting scene.

COINS: Left:
Silver Tetradrachm of Alexander the Great-Paphos mint - C330-320 BC
Right (next page): Bronze coin of Emperor Vespasian — AD69-79 — On the reverse it shows the statue of Zeus of Salamis-issued by the Community of Cypriots (Koinon Kyprion).

24

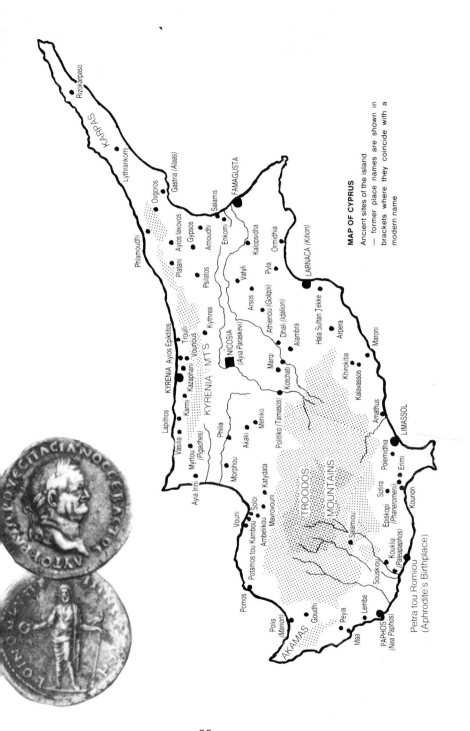

MAP OF CYPRUS

Ancient sites of the island — former place names are shown in brackets where they coincide with a modern name

KARPAS

Rizokárpaso

Lythrankomi

Phlamoudhi

Ovgoros

Gastria (Alaas)

Ayios Iakovos

Platani

Psilatos

Gypsos

Arnoudhi

Salamis

FAMAGUSTA

Enkomi

KYRENIA Ayios Epiktitos

Troulli

Kazaphani

Vounous

Kythrea

Vatyli

Kalopsidha

Ormidhia

LARNACA (Kition)

Pyla

Lapithos

Karmi

KYRENIA MTS

NICOSIA
(Ayia Paraskevi)

Arsos

Athienou (Golgoi)

Dhali (Idalion)

Alambra

Hala Sultan Tekke

Arpera

Maroni

Vasilia

Myrtou
(Pigadhes)

Philia

Akaki

Meniko

Marqi

Kotchati

Khirokitia

Kalavassos

Amathus

LIMASSOL

Ayia Irini

Morphou

Politiko (Tamassos)

Polemidhia

Erimi

Vouni

Soli

TROODOS
MOUNTAINS

Sotira

Episkopi
(Phaneromeni)

Kourion

Potamos tou Kambou

Ambelikou

Mavrovouni

Katydata

Salamiou

Koukila
(Paleapaphos)

Souskiou

Pomos

Polis
(Marion)

AKAMAS

Goudhi

Peyia

Maa

Lemba

PAPHOS
(Nea Paphos)

Petra tou Romiou
(Aphrodite's Birthplace)

25

Above: The reconstructed Theatre of SOLOI – of the Roman period, 2nd century AD. Below: Salamis – The greatest of all Cypriot Kingdoms. The picture shows the Gymnasium and public baths – (Soloi and Salamis are under Turkish occupation).

of worship and the Greeks and Phoenicians had their own deeply entrenched deities and methods of worship), the spread of christianity continued steadily during the first three centuries of our era. By the fourth century the new faith had an undisputed dominance. Among those who contributed to this triumph were: Lazarus, who according to religious writings was raised from the dead by Jesus Christ, and later became the patron saint of Larnaca; Spyridon of Tremithus, who took part in the First Ecumenical Council in 325 AD; and St. Epiphanius of Constantia (Salamis) who though not a native of Cyprus distinguished himself as a scholar and played an important part in the various church controversies of the 4th century.

The religious zeal of the Cypriots expressed itself in the establishment of monasteries, the building of churches and the beautification of both with frescoes and icons of the highest artistry. The Byzantine period (330-1191) and the years immediately following are notable in this respect. Important frescoes survive in the island dating from the 11th century: St Nicholas of the Roof (tis stegis) in Kakopetria; St Mary of Araka in the Pitsilia region; St Neophytos Monastery in Paphos, and so forth.

If we carry the religious theme further it must be stressed that Barnabas visited Cyprus again — once more accompanied by Mark. He was martyred by the Jews in Salamis. Did Elymas, still bitter over his earlier defeat by Paul, incite the Jews himself? Evidence is scanty but the possibilities are certainly there. What is not disputed is that Mark buried his 'uncle' with a copy of the Gospel of St. Mathew, which Barnabas always carried with him. The discovery of the tomb by Anthimius, Archbishop of Constantia, in the reign of Zeno (474-491) proved to be a unique blessing to the church of Cyprus.

The island was found to be, like Syrian Antioch, an apostolic foundation and hence in c.488 its church became autocephalus (independent). The Cypriot church therefore is one of the oldest "autocephalus and isotimous" (independent and equal) constitutent bodies of the Holy Orthodox Eastern Church. It is senior by some 1000 years to the church of Russia, by 14 centuries to that of Greece and junior only to the four earlier Patriarchates of Constantinople, Alexandria, Antioch and Jerusalem. To this day the Archbishop signs with red ink (a distinction which none but the Emperor enjoyed), wears a purple cloak at church festivals and carries an imperial sceptre instead of a pastoral staff.

Religion and survival undertones were written all over the Jewish rebellion of 115-117 AD. The first signs of the rising consisted of clashes between Jews and Greeks in Alexandria and Cyrene. The revolt soon gathered momentum to the extent that it became an open war encompassing Libya, Cyrenaica, Egypt, Cyprus and Mesopotamia. Cyprus where the Jews were numerous (around 15,000) and wealthy, the revolt was headed by one named Artemion (or Arteminius), a person whom we know nothing about.

The causes of the revolt in the island are not entirely clear: apparently, it was due in part to the friction between Jews and non-Jews (gentiles) and not necessarily to their relations with the Roman administration. Yet, in none of the references to the Cypriot Jews during the 1st century is there any hint of friction at any time between them and the Greeks. However, covert hostility must have existed and seems to have been as old as the Apostle's missionary journey to Cyprus in 45-46 AD. Dio Cassius[6] whose father was governor of Cilicia (which included Cyprus), wrote that the Jews were strong enough to massacre their neighbours. His assertion however, that the number murdered amounted to 240,000 is without doubt a ludicrous exaggeration. What is not disputed is the fact that Salamis was destroyed and for a time Artemion controlled a large part of Cyprus. Moreover, there must have been heavy losses on both sides. If we say that around 24,000 died then perhaps it will be nearer the truth. Obviously, the margin of error in such guesswork is enormous. We cannot even be certain of the exact number of Jews in Cyprus since the literary evidence is spotty and the archaeological data almost nil. Dio Cassius of course, is supported by another ancient source (Orosius and Eusebius' Chronicle) which points out that the Jews massacred the inhabitants of Salamis and destroyed the city. In fact, horrible scenes had desolated the peaceful island of Cyprus. Salamis was a great city and it has been calculated that the then existing aqueduct could serve some 120,000 inhabitants. So, was the death toll higher than our estimated figure? Moreover, towns and villages, especially in the northeastern part of the island, suffered extensively. Lapithos and the Karpass district witnessed several bloody clashes, and at Soloi, where a sizeable Jewish community was found, the dedication of a statute to Emperor Trajan between 115 and his death suggest that he had inaugurated the repair of damage caused by the revolt. In another honorific inscription Hadrian was hailed as 'Benefactor of the Salami-

---

[6] Greek historian born c.155 who became a Roman Senator and Consul. He died in 235 AD.

28

nians and Saviour of the World'.

The revolt therefore appears to have come out of the blue without prelude or reason. It was put down with bitter severity by the able General Marcius Turbo. A law was passed according to which no Jew might approach the island even if he suffered shipwreck on its coast. The apparent slaughter and consequent emigration must have reduced the island's Jewish population by over 50%. After the rebellion there followed a period of repression and probably the virtual end of the great period of Jewish history in Cyprus — the next distinct stage is in the early 1570s. No details are preserved of the severity or measures taken against the insurgents. We can only surmise that the Romans repeated their practising methods and exacted reprisals. No doubt the Jewish population in Cyprus was depleted. Yet a thriving Jewish community still lived peacefully in towns and villages — with the exception of the district surrounding Salamis. It is also important to note that some called "Crypto or Hellenised Jews", may have embraced the christian faith in order to save their lives but in practice they adhered to their own religion.

The suppression of the Jewish insurrection was the sole recorded military operation in the history of Roman Cyprus. The tranquility of the island was again disturbed in 269. The Goths, a Germanic people from the Western Black Sea area, for centuries harassed and proved an embarassment to the Roman Empire. After their failure in Moesia (part of present day Bulgaria), a section of their fleet made a series of raids through the Aegean, attacking Greece, the Cyclades, Crete, Rhodes and then Cyprus. The damage to the island however was slight and the expedition, ravaged by disease, eventually came to a sudden end.

Further minor incidents with several Byzantine rulers, failed to bring any significant changes to the island. However, its cities were repeatedly ruined by seismic convulsions. Especially serious were those of 15BC which destroyed Paphos, and 76-77 AD when several cities, amongst them Salamis and Paphos, suffered extensive damage.

Like their predecessors the Romans exacted great booty from the island. However, the material lot of the Cypriot showed a slight improvement. As in their other provinces the Romans paid great attention to the building of gymnasia and theatres and of course, road making. Thus they encircled the main part of the island with a road running from Salamis in the east diagonally to Kyrenia in the north and from there roughly following the west and south coasts round, and so back to Salamis. Administratively, the cities had their own municipal institutions and were, generally speaking, composed of a *'vouli'* (council) a *'demos'* (popular assembly) and a *'gerousia'* (council of elders).

Before we proceed with the Byzantine period we must round-off our historical introduction by saying something about the 'Cypriot agriculturalist' or 'Cypriot food-raiser' — enough has been written on other issues such as religion, commerce, system of administration and the problems faced by all incoming rulers: In Cyprus' early days the inhabitants were largely self-sufficient, drinking water rather than wine and growing for themselves all they needed to survive. In later years the principal cereal crop grown was wheat, with barley, mainly used for animal fodder, the next largest. Peas, beans, onions and cabbages were also extensively grown. Olives were very important providing not only the principal edible fat but also soap and lamp oil. The honey of Cyprus had a great reputation and its wax was valued as a filler in ointments and remedies for medicines, cooking, cosmetics, perfumes and many other purposes.

Flax was usually raised for manufacture into linen. Cattle were used mainly as draught animals, though some cows were kept for milk and cheese; goats were raised mainly for milk, meat, skin and hair; sheep for their wool, though some mutton was eaten and pigs were the main meat producers.

Ownership of land was very widely dispersed but agriculture remained on the whole in a flourishing condition during the first centuries AD.

However, a sizeable number were landless and could not therefore furnish their basic necessities. During the Roman ascendancy, at least, cattle and vegetable markets (forums boarium and holitorium), were of great importance. In this situation craftsmen and shopkeepers flourished by providing manufactured articles of necessity. Hundreds of other things were also needed by a farming community. Someone had to build houses, temples, bridges, others had to kill animals and sell the meat (where domestic animals were not available), while others had to make and sell cooking utensils, shoes, carts and so forth.

From 330 to 1191 Cyprus was part of the **Byzantine** complex, Several events are worth recording:

(1) The earthquakes of 332 and 342 which destroyed Salamis, Paphos (not rebuilt for some time) and the other cities and the 30 to 40 — odd year drought and famine of the first half of the 4th

century, when Cyprus was depopulated, left their ugly scars on the island. Salamis was rebuilt a few years later through the material aid given by Constantine, the son and heir to Constantine the Great, who renamed the city, Constantia. The new city replaced Paphos as the island's capital and became the seat of the first bishop who thus became Archbishop of Cyprus. His name was **Epiphanius** (later to be called Saint Epiphanius) and he led the Cypriot church from 368 to 403.

(2)   Around the year 488 Emperor Zeno the Isaurian declared the Cyprus Church *autocephalous*. We have already mentioned the privileges pertaining to the Archbishop. After two centuries the independence of the Church of Cyprus was again confirmed. Justinian II, in his struggle with the Arabs, broke the compact of 689 between Byzantium and Islam by which the tribute of Cyprus was divided and in 691 removed a large proportion of the island's population to the Hellespont (Dardanelles) and other districts in the south and west of Asia Minor. Just as Justinian I had founded the city Nova Justiniana in the previous century, so in 691 Justinian II founded the city of Nea Justinianoupolis for the Cypriots. The synod[7] of the same year recognised the Metropolitan of Cyprus, now Bishop of Nea Justinianoupolis, as Metropolitan of the Hellespont and enacted that he should enjoy the same independence of the patriarch as in Cyprus. Once again therefore the autocephaly of the Church of Cyprus and the prerogatives of its Archbishop were recognised and definitely asserted.
Before the close of the century Cyprus was repeopled when most of the inhabitants of Nova Justinianoupolis were sent back to the island by Leontius, the new Emperor.

(3)   Under the Byzantine Empire Cyprus was a proconsulship and it enjoyed considerable prosperity. However, the **Arab raids** of the 7th to the 10th centuries brought great destruction and the island's development was retarded. Especially severe were those of 632, 647-9, 653, 726, 743, 747, 772-773, 790 and 806. Very briefly the raid of 632 was presumably led by Abu Bakr (father-in-law and successor of the Prophet Mohammed), and he obtained temporary possession of Kition. The one of 647-49 was led by Muawiya, the Emir of Syria, who commanded a large fleet.

---

[7] Called the Trullan Council.

31

In his entourage was Umm Haram, a kin of the Prophet. Alleged to have been attacked by local bandits she fell from her mule and died. Her burial place now a shrine called *'Hala Sultan Tekke'* has become one of the most revered sanctuaries of the Islamic faith. So much so that the wife of King Husein of the Hejaz[8] who died in 1930, was buried within its precincts.

In, 653, Muawiya despatched a second but smaller force under Abu'l-Awar. The raiders carried out a systematic policy of senseless cruelty, brutality and destruction. A garrison established in the island was eventually withdrawn around 682 by Caliph Yazid, but it appears that Cyprus continued to pay some form of tribute. From 653 on and for about a generation, very little is heard about Cyprus. It is probable that the island, having been twice plundered within a few years, offered little prospect of further booty; moreover, the tribute seems to have been continuously collected by the Arab authorities. However, there were fresh raids in 726,743, and 747. In 772-773 it is recorded that the raiders carried off the governor whom they eventually ransomed. Of the 790 raid few details are preserved; one however, records a battle which took place in the gulf of Attalia.

Perhaps the most destructive was the one led by Khalif Harum-ar-Rashid in 806. Alleging that the Cypriots had violated the treaty of neutrality which for years had regulated their relations with both Byzantium and Islam, the Arabs landed in Cyprus, laid waste the island and took back to Raqqa (a town on the Euphrates) several thousand prisoners, including the archbishop *('Bishop of Cyprus')* other ecclesiastics and many archons. Once the neutrality treaty was renewed most of them were allowed to return. It is interesting to record that the bishop was ransomed for 2,000 dinars.

In 965, **Emperor Nicephorus Phokas** sent General Nikitas Chalcutzes to Cyprus to repel the Arab raiders once and for all. The Byzantine fleet achieved the final conquest of the island and the defeat of the Egyptian fleet in August 965. Cyprus soon recovered from the suffering inflicted on her by the Arab raids and was turned quietly into a Byzantine *'theme'* or military province.

---

[8] Region of west Arabia, encompassing Mecca and Medina-centre of Islam.

The Arabs it may be noted, never made any organised attempt to become permanent rulers of Cyprus. They were content with the loot and prisoners their raids yielded. The attacks however caused a marked movement of the population from the coastal towns to the interior of the island, where they sought refuge in caves and fortifications. Thus the three principal castles on the Kyrenia range, St Hilarion, Kantara and Buffavento were erected during the Arab raids as a defence against the 'barbarian' onslaughts. Yet, in spite of all these difficulties, Cyprus was still considered a place of refuge by the Christians of Syria and Palestine.

(4) Cyprus was often used as a place of banishment by both the Roman and Byzantine Emperors — not that it hasn't been practiced in later years! During their long hegemony the Romans made Cyprus a place for 'probationary correction'. Morally corrupted (or perverts) nobles and senior citizens of Roman society, having disgusted the not-to-sensitive susceptibilities of their professed morality were sent to Paphos "to finish their sensual studies". The sanctuaries of the capital were certainly notorious for such moral issues.

Similarly, during the iconoclast persecutions, Cyprus became a place of refuge for iconodule monks. In fact Constantine V given the nickname of 'copronymous', gave icon-worshipping monks and nuns the alternative of marrying or being blinded and sent to Cyprus. It must be noted that the veneration of icons, previously encouraged was first prohibited by Emperor Leo III (founder of the Isaurian dynasty) in 730 and the resulting persecutions reached their peak in the 740s under Constantine V. Following an acute conflict the final restoration of icon veneration, promulgated in 843, is still celebrated as the Feast of Orthodoxy in the Eastern Church.

(5) The two risings of 1042 and 1092 and the attack on the island which began in 1156 were also significant events. Both risings were attempts by local governors to proclaim Cyprus independent. The first was led by Thephilos Eroticos and the second by Rhapsomates. Both revolts had been planned in collaboration with Tzachas, the Emir of Smyrna who had been raiding the Aegean islands and both had been vigorously suppressed by the Grand Duke John Ducas, brother-in-law of Emperor Alexios Comnenos. Nicosia, which played an important part in the second revolt, became the island's capital in the 11th century.

In 1156, Reynald of Chatillon (since 1153 husband of Constance, Norman Princess of Antioch), together with the Armenian Prince Thoros, led a devastating and unprovoked attack on Cyprus from Armeno-Cilicia in southern Asia Minor. It failed. Further raids by Arab bandits in 1158 also proved abortive.

The year 1184 was to prove a turning point in the fortunes of Cyprus. **Isaac Ducas Comnenos,** great nephew of the old Emperor Manuel Comnenos, arrived on the island with a small body of armed men and on the basis of forged documents claimed to be its first governor — just sent out from Constantinople. His deception was highly successful and he established himself under the high-sounding title of *'Emperor of Cyprus'.* He ruled the island with great cruelty. His reign ended — more by accident that by design — in 1191.

Meanwhile in 1189 **Richard I** was annointed King of England and in 1190 he set out for the Holy Land in that remarkable endeavour, semi-feudal, semi-religious but wholly adventurous, known as the Third Crusade. From Lyons they moved to Sicily and after a delay of around six months the crusaders set sail for Jerusalem on 10 April 1191. When they dropped anchor at Crete on 17 April, it was found that 25 transport ships were missing —due to a storm five days earlier. On 18 April they set off for Rhodes where Richard made enquiries about Isaac Comnenos the self-styled emperor of Cyprus. Richard was told that Isaac did everything he could to hold up supplies to the Holy Land and that his missing ships had been driven by the great storm to the island. And so they were.

Among the ships unaccounted for were the three dromonds that carried his affianced bride **Berengaria of Navarre,** his favourite sister Joan, widow of William the Good of Sicily, the greater part of his treasure and the Great Seal. As it turned out the missing ships had been wrecked trying to put into the port of Limassol (then west of Amathus), and Roger Malcael, the Vice-Chancellor, had been drowned with the Seal hanging round his neck. Those who managed to struggle ashore were disarmed, robbed of their possesions and imprisoned but the ship carrying the Royal ladies had managed to ke p clear of the rocks and had put out to sea again in fear of Isa. c.

Richard *'Coeur de Lion'* who stayed ten days in Rhodes set sail for Cyprus and the island was sighted distinctly on Sunday 6 May

1191. On the following day Richard sent a courteous message to Isaac requesting him to make amends for all the evil done to the shipwrecked pilgrims. His messengers were insulted by Isaac who then amassed his troops on the shore between Richard's fleet and the fortified town beyond. The King's order was *'Aux Armes'* (To Arms). After a brief skirmish the Anglo-Normans marched into the town and on the following day Richard and around 50 knights made a surprise attack on Isaac's camp. The islanders were poor soldiers, badly armed and badly trained and were certainly no match for Richard's men. The *'Griffons'* (a Crusader-Latin term for Greeks) were annihilated but Isaac escaped on his fleet Arab courser 'Fauvel'. The chase of Isaac and the conquest of Cyprus, which was regarded as a fait accompli by the crusaders, was temporarily halted.

On 11 May allied crusaders, including Guy de Lusignan who later helped Richard defeat Isaac, had arrived to do homage to Richard and to seek his support against the political manoeuvres of Phillip II 'Augustus' King of France. On 12 May, the king celebrated his marriage to Berengaria in the chapel of St George in the Limassol area. The ceremony was conducted by Nicholas, Richard's chaplin, and then, Berengaria was crowned Queen of England by John Fitz, bishop of Evreux. It is worth noting that this was the first and last time (to date) that a queen was crowned whilst away from Britain.

By the end of May, Isaac capitulated after suffering a humiliating defeat at Tremethousha — the ancient Trimythos principal town of Mesaoria. The whole island, including the mountain fortresses of Buffavento, Kantara, Kyrenia and St Hilarion (called "Dieu d'Amour" or "Castle of Love", by the Franks), and Isaac's stronghold (Kolossi Castle) were now in the hands of the English King.

Richard imposed a capital levy of 50% on the inhabitants and the government was then put in the hands of two Englishmen, Richard of Canville and Stephen of Turnham, who were instructed to send regular supplies of Cyprian wine, barley, wheat etc, to the Holy Land. The traditional laws and customs of the island were confirmed but as a sign of the new order all loyal 'Griffons' were required to shave-off their beards ensuring that they looked like westerners. The booty extracted from Cyprus was vast and amongst the horses taken was *'Fauvel'* — Isaac's unmatched steed. On his return to England, it may be added,

Richard dedicated Isaac's imperial standard to the memory of St Edmund — Suffolk's martyr prince.

Our story soon takes a further twist. In early June, Richard sailed from Famagusta en route to Palestine. However, a revolt was brewing in the island and a relative of Isaac's, a monk, was being put up as the new *'emperor'*. Stephen of Turnham crushed this so-called rising and hanged the 'emperor'. Some time after he reached Palestine, Richard, once more in need of money sold Cyprus to the Order of the **Knights Templars** for 100,000 byzants (or besants, the great gold currency of Europe in the Middle Ages), of which 40,000 was to be paid at once and the remainder by instalments.

The Templars however, soon found their new burden a heavy one. The war with Saladin was already absorbing all their energies in Syria and the small garrison they were able to maintain in Cyprus could barely cope with the impoverished Cypriots. Accordingly, in May 1192 (following the Easter massacre in Cyprus), they begged Richard to buy back the island on the same terms as he had sold it but the King, who was not prepared to lose the cash he had received, induced **Guy de Lusignan** to acquire it as some compensation for the loss of his kingdom of Jerusalem. He took possession of his realm towards the end of May and for 297 years Cyprus became a **Frankish Kingdom**. Around 300 French noblemen, a personal guard of 200 and many soldiers accompanied Guy and settled in Cyprus — mainly in or around Nicosia.

The Lusignan coat-of-arms seen on the east side of Kolossi Castle, Limassol. The centre shield depicts the emblems of the kingdoms of Jerusalem, Cyprus and Armenia.

Before we proceed with a brief discussion of the next epoch it must be emphasised that it had always been the fate of the island to be governed by a succession of rulers who were, generally speaking, different in race and religion from the bulk of the inhabitants. Taking the year 1192 (the beginning of the Frankish dynasty) as an illustration we find the following: By far the largest racial and religious element which went to make up the population of Cyprus was of course the Graeco-Cypriot; the Arabs in spite of their frequent incursions, did not settle in any great number (Arabic place-names are Kantara and Komi Kebir); the Syrians, were entirely fused with the Greeks (Syrianochori near Morphou bears witness to their presence even though it may have been an agricultural settlement); the Armenians, to this date, have never lost their national identity; the Maronites are still present in Cyprus; the Jacobites, Nestorians and Jews were also of some importance. Thus many races and languages were represented in the island. It has been said that *"the tongues of every nation under heaven are heard, read and talked and are taught in special schools"*.

In economic terms the Cypriots, like the rest of Europe's peasantry, were harshly taxed and the peasants were not allowed to leave the land on which they worked. They were simply neglected by their imperial masters. Some managed to keep their land while others prospered as craftsmen, doctors or men of commerce. The majority toiled in the fields for long hours — they simply existed for there was no *'life'* for them. Politically, the situation was very much the same: only the rich and the professionals had any say in the running of the country and even then only on a local level. However, at least up to 1250, these were few and far between.

The Lusignans ruled the island on a feudal system — all privileges belonged to the nobles, with the masses reduced to serfdom. There were 3 main classes of landless native Cypriots:

(a) The lowest was that of the *'paroikoi'* who usually paid an annual tax and rendered a corvée (angaria) of two days' labour a week to their lords, who also took one third (triton) of their produce (excluding the seed) of the fields.

(b) Slightly higher in status were the *'perperiarii'* who were originally 'paroikoi' but had since become freemen. They also paid a similar tribute — a "landshare".

(c) At the apex were the *'lefteri'* (freedmen) or *'francomati'* who had been emancipated either on a lump payment to their lord or by his mere grace. Their lands and crops were free save for a small proportion, varying from 1/5 to 1/10, which was taken by their master.

Two other classes but in a different category to the three mentioned above were the *'White Venetians'* and the *'White Genoese'*. These were usually of Greek, Italian or Syrian origin who enjoyed the fruits of their labours and who usually paid only an annual tax to the island's overlord.

Another tax that should be pointed out is the *'stratia'* or hearth-tax. Although inherited by the Lusignans it was kept by them even though they suppressed the *'stratiotai'* (soldiers) for whose payment it was originally established.

It appears therefore that in post-1192, the Cypriots were even worse off than before. The land was distributed among the barons and the knights to whom most of the Cypriots were attached as serfs. In the words of Porcacchi, a Venetian historian *"the tyranny of the masters grew so fiercely insolent that some bartered their slaves unblushingly for dogs and other animals"*.

Ecclesiastically, the policy of the Franks was to effect the subordination of the autocephalus Orthodox Church of the people to the Church of the ruling race. Roman catholic sees were endowed with the property taken from the Orthodox bishoprics and a series of acts of oppression culminated in 1260 (3 July), in the issue by Pope Alexander IV of the famous *'Constitutio Cypria'* or *'Bulla Cypria'*, whereby the Latin Archbishop was made the supreme acclesiastic, chief of Latins and Orthodox alike. The Latins therefore persecuted the already established Greek Orthodox Church of the island, robbing it of its revenues, controlling its ordinations and 'burning' its bishops as heretics. Hence in 1231, thirteen Greek monks were condemned to death at Kantara because they refused to accept certain Catholic beliefs. Yet, the Orthodox Church thrived under persecution and its monasteries, particularly those in the remote mountain ranges where the painted churches may still be seen today, continued to prosper. The Church had undoubtedly become a focus for the islander's obstinate sense of Greekness in an alien Latin world.

To summarise the above, it may be said that in 1192 Cyprus commenced nearly 400 years of western rule which saw the introduction of western feudalism and of the Latin Church into a land which had hitherto been Greek in its institutions and Orthodox in its religious beliefs. At every level Cyprus was horizontally divided into two separate and distinct sections. At the apex were the feudal class,

Above: 14th century icon from Ayios Nicolaos tis Steyis – showing the presentation of Christ in the Temple – Right: A copper engraving of Saint Epiphanios the Cypriot. Below: St. Barnabas monastery, first built in 488 AD. One of Cyprus' most important and revered Greek Orthodox Churches.

Above: Bellapais Abbey – founded in the 12th century by the Lusignans.
Below: The formidable Kantara Castle as seen by travellers in the 18th century
Both are now under Turkish occupation.

Holy Roman
Empire

Venice

Hungary

Belgrade

RICHARD THE LIONHEART
ON THE 3rd CRUSADE 1191

Black Sea

Adriatic Sea

ROME

Kingdom
of
Sicily

Brindisi

BYZANTINE
EMPIRE

Philippopolis

Adrianople

CONSTANTINOPLE

ASIA MINOR

CORFU

Laodicia

Antioch

Seleucia

Messina

SICILY

Route of Richard's Crusade

RHODES

CYPRUS

Tripoli

Famagusta

Tyre
Acre

MEDITERRANEAN   SEA

CRETE

Jaffa
Jerusalem

Ascalon

Kyrenia

St. Hilarion

Abbey of   Buffavento
Bellapais

Kantara

Famagusta

EMPIRE OF SALADIN

NICOSIA

Scale: 0   100   200   300 miles

Polis,

Pyrga

Kouklia   Kolossi

hos

Limassol

Larnaca

CYPRUS MEDIEVAL CENTRES
★ Castles before & after Richard

The Abbey of Bellapais,
also known as the
monastery of Cozzafani.

41

Above: Berengaria, Richard I's bride reluctantly departs from Cyprus.
Below: Venetian Cyprus under naval siege by the Ottoman Turks; a copper plate engraving.

mostly of French origin and the foreign merchants (the vast majority being Venetian and Genoese) who resided in the island (especially in Famagusta and Paphos), and at the bottom were the local Greek inhabitants who were serfs and labourers. The ruling class belonged to the Catholic church and the Greeks to the Orthodox one. The elite spoke mostly French and the masses spoke Greek.

Nevertheless, the lot of the Orthodox Cypriot was improved in the 15th century by the passionately Orthodox queen of John II, **Helen Paleologa.** Helen was the daughter of Theodore II Paleologus, ruler of the Morea. Helen's daughter Carlotta also followed a pro-Hellenic policy. Futhermore, rulers such as Hugh II and Hugh III (called 'the Great') in the 13th century, Hugh IV and Peter I in the 14th century, contributed immensely towards the stability and financial prosperity of the island. In fact, Peter I, a benevolent monarch, attracted scores of Egyptian Jewish traders to the island by promising equal treatment to all minorities. However, rivalries, claims and counter-claims, feudal disputes and the inefficiency of other rulers, disturbed the island's growth.

And, there was worse to come. During the reign of Peter I (1359-1369), Turkish vessels twice attacked the island. Taking advantage of the seriousness of the plague (the so called 'Black Death' of 1348-49 took the lives of something between 1/4 and a 1/2 of the inhabitants), and of the king's absence in France, these vessels landed near Pentayia and then near Rizokarpaso. Looting and senseless destruction followed. The Cypriots retaliated and pursued their attackers across the seas to Anemouri. The place, directly to the north of Kyrenia, was pillaged and many hostages were taken, just as the Turks had done earlier.

Another significant event occurred in 1374. Following a quarrel dating from 1364, Famagusta, one of the richest cities of the Mediterranean, was taken by the Genoese from Peter II. The *emporium of the near east'* continued to be a colony of that commercial republic until 29 August 1464, when it was reconquered by James II, the illegitimate son of John II.

Further disasters were to follow in the 15th century. It was ravaged successively by plagues (the one of June 1438 resulted in many deaths and lasted for 17 months), locusts and droughts. In the midst of such misfortunes the Sultan of Egypt, accusing the Cypriots of allowing the roaming Christian pirates to pillage the Saracens and then buying the booty declared war and invaded the island in 1424. The Cypriot forces were defeated at Khirokitia; King Janus was taken prisoner and carried to Cairo in 1426. He obtained his freedom by consenting to a ransom plus an annual tribute of 5,000 ducats to the Sultan. To this day the site of the battle can be seen. It is called *'Kremmos tous Frangous'* — the cliff of the Franks. The island was then overrun by the Egyptian troops; Nicosia, the capital was occupied, its fortifications destroyed and its palaces almost reduced to ruins. The churches, monasteries and houses of Christians were pillaged and many of them were taken prisoner by the Saracens. All this was followed by the so-called *'peasants insurrection'* when many rose in rebellion and plundered property belonging to the Christian inhabitants — many were also killed. Leontios Machairas, secretary to King Janus, gave an excellent account in his 'Chronicle of Cyprus' of the fortunes of the Lusignans from 1359 to 1432. He wrote that *'they did many ill deeds which God would not endure''.*

The apparent negative aspects of Frankish rule, which were in essence the norm for those years, were on the whole outweighed by the positive elements of Lusignan rule. To say that the period 1192 to 1489 was the most brilliant epoch of Cyprus' varied history is not very far from the truth. Sir Harry Luke in his remarkable study of 'Cyprus under the Turks' explains that in every aspect of medieval civilization the tiny island of Cyprus played a distinguished part — its remarkable achievements in every domain of human activity invested it with an importance among the nations of Europe wholly out of proportion of its small size and population. For example:

(a) its constitution was the model of that of a medieval feudal state;

(b) the great legislative monument, the 'Assizes of Jerusalem', drawn up for Cyprus set the standard of medieval jurisprudence;

(c) its men of letters, like Philippe de Novare and Philippe de Mézières, were real pillars in the realm of literature;

(d) in King Peter I (1359-1369) Cyprus possessed one of the greatest crusader warriors the world has ever seen and in his Order of the Sword the most perfect expression of chivalrous ideals;

(e) works were dedicated to its Kings by writers such as Thomas Aquinas and Boccaccio. Moreover, there was a parallel literary beginning, albeit on a small scale, by the islands Greek inhabitants;

(f) after the fall of Acre in 1291, Cyprus became the outpost of Latin Christendom in the East;

44

(g) in the realm of commerce Famagusta vied in importance with cities such as Venice;

(h) the wealth and luxury of its inhabitants, especially in the 14th century, was the envy of all other peoples; and

(i) Cyprus abounds in western medieval architecture — thanks to the Lusignans. The impressive Bellapais Abbey, the cathedrals of Nicosia and Famagusta and the castles of St. Hilarion, Buffavento and Kantara are excellent examples of Gothic architecture. However, it is a curious irony of history that nearly all such monuments are situated in what is, since 1974, the Turkish occupied zone.

The **Venetians** were the next masters of Cyprus. The island became first a *'protectorate'* in 1473 and then it passed into direct rule from 1489 to 1571. How did the 'protectorate' come about?

By a stroke of diplomatic craft the Venetians succeeded in inducing James II to marry **Katherine Cornaro,** daughter of the Venetian patrician Mark Cornaro. James did not long survive his marriage. After his death, which was attributed to poisoning, the republic managed to place Queen Katherine under a most humiliating tutelage. The crafty senators futhermore, did not limit their acts to this unjustifiable interference. In 1489, having poisoned her son James III, they compelled Katherine to yield to them the kingdom of Cyprus.

Especially in the early years Venetian rule was characterised by total disinterestedness. The island's treasury was in a chronic state of depletion. This meant that all sorts of devices were used to 'ease' the situation. Thus, serfs could purchase their freedom if the price was right and whole villages belonging to the royal domain were sold to private persons. These practices were also true of earlier administrations. Both instances gave ample opportunities for corrupt dealings by officials. Droughts, locusts, floods and earthquakes added to the distress caused by misgovernment.

Trade languished, manufactures practically ceased and all who could afford to do so emigrated. By the turn of the century there was a fall of around 15% in the island's population. Martin von Baumgarten, returning from his pilgrimage to the Holy Land and Mount Sinai, visited Cyprus from 8 February to 28 March 1508, and wrote that *"all inhabitants are slaves to the Venetians".* The persecution of the Orthodox Church was intensified and culture on the island sunk to very low depths. According to a rather harsh statement by a Christian abbot, *"the Cypriots escaped from the grasp of the dog to fall into that of the lion".*

Towards the end of the Venetian era the administration became benign and tolerant. Population figures confirm that by 1570 the estimated number of inhabitants was 150,000. It must also be noted that since Cyprus was regarded primarily as a military post the Venetians built magnificent fortifications at Nicosia, Famagusta and elsewhere. They also added to the island's architectural heritage — built in 1530, the monastery at Ayia Napa is dedicated to the *'Holy Veil of Santa Veronica'*. It is believed that the original church, cut into a rock and partially underground, dates from the 8th or 9th centuries. A noble octagonal marble fountain surmounted by a dome, beside a sycamore, occupies the middle of the courtyard.

A balanced and carefully considered evaluation of the 82-year Venetian epoch shows that the island was seen primarily as a military outpost against the rising Ottomans[9], and that the new rulers made no real effort to help conciliate the inhabitants to whose welfare it was virtually indifferent. The Venetians who obtained the island mainly by extortion, shamefully lost it by their negligence, jealousy and cursed pride of those to whom the preservation of it had been entrusted. One in particular, Sir Eugene Sinclitico (Count of Roucha and probably a Westernised Hellene), commanding the land forces, was described by Alexander Drummond (a British diplomat) as *"a brave but empty madman"*.

---

[9] The capture of Constantinople in 1453 which signalled the end of the Byzantine Empire, sent cold shivers across the Christian states.

CHAPTER TWO

THE ARRIVAL OF THE OTTOMANS

1570 — 1878

The Ottoman Empire under Suleimãn I (1520-1566), its benevolent and far-sighted ruler, justifiably called *'The Great'* and *'The Magnificent'*, had reached the summit of its power and splendour.[1] He was however succeeded by a prince to whom his own national historians have given the epithets *'Selim the Sallow'* (Sari Selim) and *'Selim the Drunkard'* (Sarhos Selim). To western historians he is known as *'Selim the Sot'*. Selim II the eleventh Sultan of Turkey (1566-1574) coveted Cyprus while he was the governor of Kütahya[2] in his father's lifetime. It seems that he found the attraction of Cyprus' wines and liqueurs irresistible. He was consumed therefore with a feverish desire for the possession of the island; a feat which he accomplished in 1571.

The causes of the so-called 'Cyprus War' need no thorough examination here. Suffice to say that amongst these were the Turco-Venetian relations which showed a turn for the worse; palace friction at the Porte between the hawks (e.g., Joseph Nasi, a Jew who held in fief the island of Naxos and hoped also for the investiture of Cyprus) and the doves (e.g., Mahomet Sokolli, the Grand Vizier); and economic issues etc.. In February-March 1570, an emissary from the Porte arrived in Venice and threatened that if the island of Cyprus was not voluntarily surrendered it would be seized by force. The Venetians replied on 27 March that they were firmly resolved to defend their legitimate possessions and trusted in the *'justice of God'*.

By late May 1570 the Ottomans carefully prepared a well-equipped fleet at Constantinople. Under the command of **Mustapha Pasha** (*'Lala'* or *'Tutor'*), with Piale Pasha as admiral of the fleet, the Turkish invading force, which consisted of well over 220 long vessels of which 160 were galleys, the rest galliots and about 80 ships of burthen of various kinds, set sail on 27 June. By 1 July 1570, Turkish troops began to disembark in Cyprus. The port of Limassol was soon overrun and on 8 August, after a siege of 48 days, the island's capital was captured. Thousands of Nicosia's inhabitants were put to the sword. In Famagusta, **Marco Antonio Bragadino,** the town's leader and governor-general, led a desperate resistance against overwhelming

---

[1] In brief, Constantinople was captured in 1453 (the siege lasted from 6 April to 29 May), Syria in 1516, Egypt in 1517 and Rhodes in 1522.

[2] Anatolian province in northwest Turkey — west of Ankara and south of Constantinople.

odds. The city did not capitulate until nearly a year later, on 1 August 1571, after a blockade of ten months.

The peace terms appeared to be generous. All Italians were to be allowed to embark, with colours flying, for Crete together with any Greeks, Albanians or others who wished to accompany them. Greeks who elected to stay behind would be guaranteed their personal liberty and property and would be given two years in which to decide whether they would remain permanently or not; those who then decided to leave would be given safe conduct to the country of their choice. The document, setting out these terms, was signed by Lala Mustapha Pasha and authenticated with the Sultan's seal. It was then returned to Bragadino and Baglioni, the two heroic leaders of the ten-month resistance, with a short note complimenting them on their courage and on their magnificent defence of the city. On 5 August, Bragadino sent word to Mustapha proposing to call and formally to present him with the keys of Famagusta. The Turkish leader replied that he would be delighted to receive him — and so he did! Suddenly however, his face clouded and his manner changed. In a mounting fury, he began hurling baseless allegations at the Christians accusing them of murdering Turkish prisoners, of concealing munitions and of not respecting the peace terms. Bragadino's lieutenants (Baglioni, Martinengo and Quirini) were executed in his presence but the treatment meted out on him topped all atrocities. After being subjected to the most excruciating public tortures, which he bore with great fortitude (Mustapha three times made him hold out his neck under the axe; he cut off his nose and ears; stretched him on the ground and trampled on him using all kinds of insults), he was flayed alive: his skin was stuffed with straw and suspended to the yard-arm of a vessel it was sent to Constantinople. His skin was then exposed in the prison in which the Christian prisoners and slaves were confined. It remained there for 25 years until redeemed by his brother Antony and his three sons, Mark, Hermolaus and Antony, for a great price and laid in its present resting place in the Church of Saints John and Paul at Venice.

Now that the killing had begun it was very hard to stop it. The island was sacked and plundered. Paolo Paruta[3] in his most lucid account of the sieges of Nicosia and Famagusta recorded that the Turks destroyed whole villages and hamlets, churches and monasteries

---

[3] See C.D. Cobham 'Excerpta Cypria' 1908. Pages 107-119.

and committed other bestial and cruel acts — even against the dead! The undisciplined soldiery (at times on their own initiative) were spurred on to even greater atrocities because the siege of Famagusta was unpredictably costly;[4] amongst those killed were many prominent nobles and commanders.

It is worth noting that even though the whole island was henceforth under firm Turkish control, the Ottoman navy suffered a crushing defeat at Lepanto[5] on 7 October 1571, from the united fleet of the League — Venice, Spain, the Papacy and several smaller ssociated states. Don John of Austria (not yet 25 years of age), commanded the Christian fleet which overrun the enemy in one of the greatest naval battles since Roman times. The legend of Ottoman invincibility at sea was shattered once and for all. Worse still, it had become clear that Sultan Selim had failed as leader of Islam against the 'unbelievers'. Cut off by the Shiite schism from its Persian and central Asian religious and cultural roots, the Ottoman Islamic empire, with its universalist claims, was becoming a limited Turkish empire — no more that one of the several great military powers in Europe and Asia.

The League however secured a moral rather that a material victory in 1571. Following the abortive campaign by the Christian armada (a light-hearted and disjointed effort to reverse the Ottoman advance) in 1572, a treaty was signed at Constantinople on 7 March 1573. Besides paying a large indemnity and making various miscellaneous concessions, Venice ceded the island of Cyprus. Consequently, only Crete, Paros and the Ionian Islands remained in Venetian hands. The Cyprus War of 1570-73 was over. The Ottomans had lost the battle (Lepanto) but they had won the peace.

Cyprus remained in Turkish hands until 1878 — it was then conditionally ceded to Great Britain. For 307 years the Cypriot masses fared badly under their new rulers. Yet for a substantial section of the upper or ruling classes (especially those who acquisced with the new administration) and of the higher clergy there were benefits (especially after 1660, as we shall see below) beyond their wildest expectations. Those who collaborated with the new regime (often called

---

[4] Venetian, other Christian and Islamic sources differ greatly over the number of men lost. It has been said that the Turks lost around 50,000. What is not disputed is that the death toll, on both sides, was very high.

[5] Now known as Navpaktos in the Corinthian Gulf.

cryptochristians or *'linobambakoi'*) were duly rewarded — some retained their land, others made successful false claims to land and property and others were simply *'moslemised'*.

What were the effects of conquest and settlement? We have already seen that a cross-section of Cypriot society either co-operated with the new regime or simply accepted it as a necessity which they hoped may have resulted in an improvement in their overall standard of living. Such hopes never materialised. We have also seen that the upper echelons (or 'archons') of Frankish, Italian and Greek society not only co-operated but were kept in their positions by the Turks in order to establish and solidify their regime. Secondly and often forgotten is the following: the ruin caused on some Venetian families was frightening. The Turkish war which consumed much Venetian wealth, underlined the hazards of engaging in trade in the Levant which was close to enemy territory. Some patricians (e.g., the large Cornaro, Pesaro and Giustinian families), experienced not only grave financial losses, but also the indignities of enslavement and were forced to cut into their surviving resources by ransoming themselves and their families. Those who did not have the financial resources (just like a lot of Greeks) were reduced to extreme poverty and had to make a living as muleteers or pedlars.[6]

The third and vital issue concerns the demography of the island. Following the conquest, Cyprus' population showed a marked decline. Thousands were put to the sword and entire villages and hamlets were wiped out. Moreover, the Turks forced a large number of Greeks to resettle in Anatolia — mainly near Antalya. These were considered as hostages for the good behaviour of their compatriots. Other Greeks, rich enough to afford it and lucky enough to escape, fled to France and Italy. As though this was not enough the Turks carried their plan of transplanting the island's population a step further.

The Porte issued a decree on 9 April 1571 aimed at sending mainland Turks to Cyprus. The system applied was styled *sürgün* (exile) but this population transfer was not generally speaking, imposed by force; in reality, it was affected by selecting those willing to be transplanted. Another document dated 7 January 1581 informs us that 8,000 families (out of 12,000) arrived in Cyprus and were duly registered.

---

[6] Sir G. Hill: A History of Cyprus (4 Volumes). Volume 4. 1952. Page 1.

According to the *tahrir* (census) of 1572, the new settlers numbered around 20,000. This included the permanent garrison — infantry *(janissaries)* and cavalry *(spahis)* —which numbered approximately 3,780. Bernard Lewis[7] a prominent historian, stresses that Ottoman records for the period immediately following the conquest contained several 'deportation' orders for the transfer of populations to Cyprus. They included Turkish peasants so that the countryside should not be exclusively Greek and Christian but partly Turkish and Muslim. There were also orders to transfer Turcoman tribes (Turkish pastoral nomads) from Anatolia, so that stock-raising and the supply of animals for food and transport should be safely in Muslim hands.

The Turks proceeded to institute a policy which directly created the so-called *'Cyprus Problem'*. It was very similar to that which the English government was pursuing, about the same time, in Ireland, and it had similar results. This was the policy of *'transplantation'* —importing Moslem Turks, speaking a foreign language and practising a different religion, to form an ascendancy and help keep the native Greeks — the majority — under control. And, from about 1576 onward we find orders to send Jews to Cyprus — presumably in order to restore the commercial prosperity of the island following the departure of the Venetians. In reality, the purpose was mainly to consolidate Turkish rule by counterbalancing the Christian element in the island's population.

In addition, the Moslem population of Cyprus originated from the Franks and to a smaller extent from the Greeks who, in order to escape the massacre or enslavement which ensued, adopted Islam in order to enjoy greater quiet but continued secretely to observe the numerous customs of the Greek Orthodox Church. They were called renegades, cryptochristians or simply *'linobambakoi'* (linen-cottoners). Niven Kerr, the British consul in Cyprus, observed in a letter dated 4 June 1844, to Sir Stratford Canning (a prominent British politician), that there were several villages whose inhabitants, although professedly mussulman, secretly embraced the Greek religion and attended the services of that church.

What of the Island's form of administration? Cyprus was divided into 17 cadelisks, or administrative districts (reduced to 6 during the 19th century), each having its *agha* or governor and *cadi* or minister of

---

[7] The Jews of Islam. 1984. Page 123.

justice. Turkish administration and personnel varied tremendously over the years. Favouratism and corruption, the twin cankers of Ottoman rule, determined the choice of the highest officers in the state. At the top, the administration of the island was, generally speaking, in the hands of the governor *(Mutassurif)*, assisted by a council over which he presided. It was composed of the *Mufti*, or - highest mussulman religious authority, the Greek Archbishop and or Dragoman (or interpreter, especially in the post 1660 period), the *Evcaf-Nazir*, or administrator of mussulman religious property, 3 mussulmans and 2 christian notables. The council usually met once a week and its decisions were embodied in documents called *'musbatas'*, which were signed by all the members present. From its membership it can be seen that all initiative came from the mohammedan majority.

The fifth issue that needs brief comment is the following: Serfdom[8] disappeared and after the expulsion of the Latin priests the Greek Orthodox Church was restored. The island's Greeks were henceforth recognized as a *'millet'* or nation under the leadership of the Church of Cyprus and its Archbishop who was, especially after 1660, the *'millet bashi'* or ethnarch. The Church in fact, was the upholder and protagonist of the continuous existence of a well-defined Greek Cypriot national community. Moreover, for many years of Turkish rule (especially from the 1660s to 1821) a certain measure of 'autonomy' was granted to the Christian population — the non-moslem element, often called *'dimmis'* (tolerated infidels) who were virtually guaranteed their lives, liberties, property and religion.

Another point that needs elucidation is the institution of the office of the *'dragoman'*[9]. During times that were very difficult for the local population this institution, which provided the link between state and people, took on great importance both economically and politically. The relevant Porte decree in the middle of the 18th century reinforced this institution. Moreover, it gave the Archbishop, together with the bishops and the dragoman, the authority to apportion and collect taxes. This meant that the dragoman, who could communicate directly with the Sultan, achieved the second highest political position in the island after the Pasha or Governor. At the same time it

---

[8] Human beings 'attached to the soil' like chattels or other goods.

[9] Dragomans were usually chosen by the Bishops or by the notables and their election was confirmed by the Sultan.

made him a target for the schemes of the Turkish administrators who wanted a free hand to amass a fortune, at the expense of the people. The most famous dragoman was perhaps **Hadjigeorgakis Kornesios** (born in Kritou-Terra Paphos around the middle of the 18th century), who married the sister of Archbishop Chrysanthos and who for a time (c. 1780 - 1805) became the most important person in Cyprus.

The problems and hardships associated with an alien regime and its strange governmental institutions were further accentuated by natural disasters. Thus, the pestilence of 1624 was so severe that the number of villages and hamlets were reduced by one third. The plague of 1691-92 was responsible for the death of around 30% of the island's population. As if these disasters were not enough the economy and general well-being of the inhabitants were further paralysed by unjust taxes. Successive changes in the administration meant that the people were harassed with exactions of all kinds, enough to reinburse its rulers after one year in office. Both mussulmans, christians and other ethnic minorities had equal cause to be dissatisfied with the maladministration that continued unhindered. Insurrections and mass protests were therefore joint affairs.

The rebellions prior to 1680 were minor events yet were highly significant with long-term effects. Those of 1578, 1580, and 1593 of which we know very little about were instigated by the surviving members of the old ruling class[10], who tried to incite the masses against the existing regime. Thousands perished. In 1617 the flag of revolt was raised by one called Vittorio Zebeto. This was another failure[11]. What were the effects? These defeats led to a superficial moslemisation of many rural families especially in the northern parts of the island. Extreme poverty was also a significant factor in the acceptance of a new religion. Also important is the fact that the activities of the crypto-christians led to a Cypriot mentality which may be termed *'tolerant and hesitant'*. Tolerant because they accepted, at least in practice, the new regime and hesitant because by accepting it their Greekness was dampened and hence were less eager to participate in rebellious activities. They were also suspected on many occasions as being spies and informants. Another study perhaps, can prove or disprove this allegation.

---

[10] Usually aided and abetted be western powers.
[11] Also a failure was the one of 1607-08 which was to be led by the notorious Norman corsair Jacques Pierre, known for his great experience as 'the Captain'.

There were other mass protests or rebellions which were much more serious. The first uprising occurred in 1680 under the leadership of **Mehmed Agha Boyadji-Oghlu** and lasted for 7 whole years. It was a mass protest against harsh taxes and maladministration. It was also a protest brought about by petty rivalries and jealousies amongst the various lords of the land. After some difficulty the rebellion was crushed and Oghlu, together with some of his closest followers, was executed. After this uprising the island became for some time the personal possesion of the Grand Vizier. This led to further exactions and then a band of armed men from the Turkish fleet attempted in 1712 to usurp the authority of the existing administrators. They stated that they were acting on direct orders from the Sultan; they were soon found out and were executed.

Another protest in 1745 was easily dealt with. However, the revolt of 1765-66, had wider repercussions. As soon as **Chil Osman** had entered on his post as agha in July 1764, he issued an order compelling the payment by each christian subject of $44^1/_2$ piastres and by each moslem of around 22 piastres. Within a few months he had managed to extort 350,000 piastres over and above the legal assessment. A special mission to Constantinople, believed to have been led by Hadji-Vasilis of Mia Milia, was successful in persuading the Sultan to order Osman not to demand the half of what was collected. A special envoy was also sent to the island to see that the order was enforced. The bishops and around 300 other leading personages arrived at Osman's palace on 25 October 1764 to hear the order read. The assembled crowds suspected that Osman was plotting to kill all the notables in his own residence and when part of the floor actually collapsed they rushed the palace. Osman and about 18 others were murdered. The incident was patched up but a commission was sent by the Porte to inquire into the events that led up to it.

A considerable amount of money was thus required to cover the expenses of the commissioners, compensation for the victims, the rebuilding of the Saray, thefts from the treasury and other demands. Hafiz Efendi was left behind to arrange for the entire settlement. Because of his greed however, the expenses were overestimated. This placed the tax collectors in an unenviable situation and when they visited the Mesaoria villages they were forced to run for their lives. The exactions were however pressed and open rebellion ensued. Events moved at a steady pace: On Easter Tuesday April 1765, around 300 Turks from the Mesaoria and Famagusta districts seized Kythrea with its water mills and thus cut-off the capital from its supply of flour. Concessions were granted but the tax continued to be collected. Some months later, at a fair (panigyris) in Myrtou, **Khalil Agha,** commandant of the fortress of Kyrenia, was chosen to lead the rebellion against tax injustices. All religious and socio-economic strata of Cypriot society supported Khalil and by August over 3,000 armed men were under his orders. The authorities completely lost control of the situation but Archbishop Païsios and the bishops of Paphos and Kyrenia escaped to Constantinople to plead for help.

Khalil withdrew to Kyrenia. The authorities then promised that excessive taxes would not be levied and that all the insurgents would be pardoned. But, it was not long before Hafiz decided once more to collect the taxes. Khalil reacted by making attempts at both Famagusta and Nicosia. The men under his command grew and grew and it appeared that the island was within his grasp. Perhaps if he were a more decisive person that would have been the result!

Meanwhile, the Porte despatched Ibrahim Bey to Cyprus to deal with the rebellion. In June 1766 Kior Ahmed was also sent to the island this time with a far superior force (2,000 troops, 500 horse and 16 ships), and Kyrenia was blockaded. After a three-week siege Khalil surrendered and by August the revolt was over. Khalil was garroted; his lieutenant Emir Ahmed was impaled and around 200 were beheaded. According to custom their heads were sent to the Sultan.

The cost to the islanders was crippling. Half a million piastres fell on the heads of around 15,000 tax payers. More was to follow. In 1771, one named **Hadji Baki,** believed to be a native Turkish peasant, managed to get himself appointed as chief of the treasury. Four years later he poisoned the new Turkish governor, Hadji Ali Agha, and several others including the governor's deputy. By 1777, this quite illiterate woodcutter who was banished from the island in 1767[12] was appointed governor calling himself Hadji Abdul Baki Agha.

The same story is repeated many times in the annals of Turkish rule over Cyprus. Even the Turkish troops mutinied in 1799 but in 1804 the results were very serious. Stirred by rumours of a shortage of foodstuffs, the troops together with the Turkish civilian population of Nicosia, raised the flag of revolt against the governor, archbishop and the dragoman (Hadjigeorgakis), who was at the time perhaps the wealthiest person in the island. The insurgents gained possession of Nicosia but following the dragoman's appeal to the Porte, the revolt

---

[12] On charges of trickery, deceit, treachery and many others.

56

was suppressed. The Turks however resented the powers of the dragoman and in 1806 enlisted the help of Altiparnak *('six fingers')*, a colonel at Tarsus, to champion their cause. Christian life and property suffered greatly. However Altiparnak was soon taken prisoner and flayed alive. In 1809 and 1810 Cyprus was to lose two intellectual and cultural benefactors. Hadjigeorgakis was executed in Constantinople on charges of corrupt behaviour, and in 1810 Archbishop Chrysanthos was exiled to Euboea.

A brief summary of events to the 19th century is not out of place: Despite the protests and revolts outlined above it must be emphasised that Turkish rule, thanks to the co-operation of large sections of Cypriot society, was firmly entrenched. Taxes raised crippled the inhabitants; apart from the 'garrison tax' and 'produce tax' raised by the Sultan there were taxes raised by the governor-general and local governors. And there were taxes collected by the Greek bishops — a responsibility entrusted on them in 1660. This practice was in accordance with the customary procedure of the Porte in using the leaders of a country's majority to act as tax collectors and thereby keeping the displeasure of the people in manageable bounds. Despite their enhanced and omnipotent position, the status of the church leaders was difficult and delicate. They often became victims of intrigue, plots and rebellions. The events of the 19th century were indicative of that trend.

Another characteristic of the Turkish administration which brought much controversy was the creation of the position of dragoman. With the dragoman directly in control of affairs and the archbishop enjoying immense prestige, the Greek population became, in effect for many years, self-governing. This was a unique experience for the islanders.

As if these anomalies were not enough the inhabitants were further 'punished' by acts of nature. A severe pestilence in 1624 resulted in thousands of deaths and the plague of 1691-92 wiped out a large proportion of the population. The two earthquakes of 1741 and 1756 (the former damaging the cathedral of Saint Sophia), brought great material destruction. The dearth of 1757-58, being the outcome of the drought and the locusts, meant that a slice of the island's population fled to Syria and Asia Minor. The year 1768 was also one of famine. To those misfortunes was added the stark reality that the mohammedan lords, who possessed considerable areas of land, seldom engaged in farming but simply drew what they could from the impoverished Cypriot. The island's peasants were further tested by the

57

greedy, senseless and self-motivated activities of the newly-rich mohammedan and other lords[13] like Hadji Baki who 'fought' to control larger and larger areas. More and more exactions were therefore added to the already long and multi-form tax list.

We may also add that the widely-expected collapse of the decadent Ottoman empire never materialised. The Ottomans succeeded in crushing every revolt against its authority. Hence for the Cypriot and the other middle eastern and Balkan nationalities the dream of an Ottoman breakdown never really came about.

The 19th century was dominated by five major events:

1. Cyprus benefited slightly from the reforms promulgated by the, Sultans Selim III and Mahmoud II. The two liberalizing charters, Hati-Sherif of 1839 and Hati-Humayun of 1856, which applied to all their dependencies were practically meaningless albeit, a step in the right direction.

As regards Cyprus the annual tribute was finally fixed and the practice of leasing the island to the highest bidder was abolished. Moreover, a salaried governor was appointed and was to be helped by a council known as the *'divan'*. Thus relative prosperity showed mild signs of emerging and a sizeable increase in population[14] was the outcome.

2. The disturbances of the 1820s associated with the Greek rising. On a charge of conspiring with the insurgents in Greece, the Turks on 9 July 1821 hanged Archbishop **Kyprianos** and **Meletios,** his archdeacon, beheaded three bishops (**Meletios** of Kition, **Chrysanthos** of Paphos and **Lavrentios** of Kyrenia) and many laymen. Its worth noting that the archbishop issued an encyclical on 16 May 1821 advising his flock to remain calm. Even though revolt in the island never materialised in any form or shape, a number of Cypriots were members of the **'Philike Hetairia'**, the Hellenic revolutionary society, and fought at Messolonghi, Roumeli and the Morea. Cyprus, it may be added, was known to Hetairia members by the secret code number of 13.

---

[13] Often referred to as 'Ayans' or 'Ayianides'. The 18th and early 19th centuries bear witness to their detrimental activities.

[14] From around 105,000 in the 1820s it increased to 125,000 inhabitants in the 1850s.

What exactly led to the killings? The Porte was in great dissaray at the time and did not approve of **Kutchuk Mehmed's** (the island's governor) intentions of putting to the sword leaders of the so-called *'Greek insurrection'*. It finally sanctioned the killings and the seizure of property belonging to the accused. G.I. Kepiades, in his 'Reminiscences of 1821 in Cyprus' described the massacre (followed by looting, rape and other atrocities) as *"the most monstrous spectacle ever seen"*. Vasilis Michaelides, perhaps the finest of the Cypriot dialect poets, described the events in his magnificent 560-verse narrative poem *'The Ninth of July 1821'*. The common grave erected at Phaneromeni church in Nicosia in 1872-73 honoured the victims of the purge. The killings did not stop with prominent people: monks, priests, young and old, innocent peasants and other laymen did not escape the sword. Those able to flee the island disguised themselves and embarked for Genoa, Marseilles and elsewhere.

There were other atrocities. Scores of villages and hamlets (mainly) had entirely disappeared. Many churches had been turned into mosques and a few into stables. General Thomas Gordon, a British historian of some repute, wrote in 1832 that *"the whole of Cyprus was converted into a theatre of rapine and bloodshed"*.

3. The revolts of the early 1830s[15] were protests not only against maladministration and unjust taxes but the two Greek-led ones had enosist aspirations. Following the success of the Greek insurrection, **Count Capodistria** who had come to power in 1828, immediately expressed a desire for the union of Cyprus with the new state. The rising led by **Nicholas Theseus** (nephew of Archbishop Kyprianos) was easily put down. The *'Ides of March'*, as one writer commented, were fatal for the Cypriots. Theseus, with the help of Bottu, the French consul, managed to escape on board a Greek ship to Rhodes. The renowned French poet Lamartine, who spoke of Theseus as being "good-mannered and intellegent" took him to Constantinople to plead his case. Having failed in his mission he left the Ottoman dominions. In 1839 he returned to

---

[15] One in 1830 was easily erased from human memory. However, the three protests in 1833 were rather different. Those led by Theseus and Ioannikios were motivated by the Greek Cypriot aspiration for union with motherland Greece.

Greece and was appointed consul in Beirut — a post which he held for a few years.

The second revolt of 1833 was led by **Giaur Imam**, a well-to-do Turk of Trimithousa (situated around 10 miles southeast of Polis in the Paphos district). It was a massive protest against the payment of unjust and exorbitant taxes. For a time he managed to *'rule'* Paphos and made plans to attack Limassol and Larnaca. After several months of highly successful disobedience the revolt was crushed around July[16].

The third rising of 1833 (July) had a much stronger enosist element than the one led by Theseus. At its head was **Ioannikios,** a fiery monk born at Ayios Elias and said to have fought in the Greek War of Independence. From rather patchy historical evidence we find that *'o kalogeros'* was encouraged by leading Cypriots, by several European consuls in the island and helped by Albanian troops to whom he promised lavish prizes. He proceeded to raise the insurgent's flag at Trikomo but the revolt fizzled out and was crushed within four days. The defeated received no mercy. Many were hanged, others were tortured and the countryside was devastated. The impoverished peasant was left to foot the tax bill. The three rebellions were costly.

4. The fourth major event of the 19th century was the so-called *'archaeological sin'* which was committed at the expense of the island's heritage. In Cyprus, as elsewhere, mischievous digging (tomb-robbing) had a venerable history. The widely-travelled Edward Daniel Clarke who visited Cyprus in 1801 refers to the English consul, an Italian called Signor Peristiani, digging up statues and figurines in Larnaca and to goldsmiths of the island who traded in antiquities. He is certainly backed-up by other writers and travellers. Under the Ottoman domination, chance finds by Cypriot peasants were exploited by officials who followed up reports of finds by their own investigations and simply carried away the results. However, this regular and profitable activity was apparently far from being on the scale which it attained in the 19th century.

---

[16] The governor's troops freed after crushing the Karpass revolt (led by Ioannikios), moved on Giaur and defeated him. He managed to escape on board a Greek schooner bound for Alexandria.

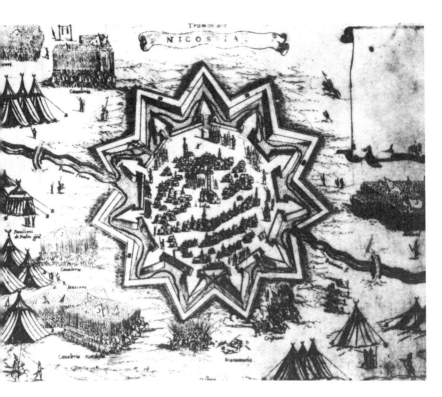

Above: Copper plate engraving depicting the dramatic events of the siege of Nicosia by the Turkish forces. Below: Marco Antonio Bragadino, heroic leader of Famagusta, is tortured by the Turks.

61

Since the 1850s but especially between 1865 and 1875 this trade of antiquities began to develop on a far larger and damaging scale Consuls and local administrators were among the prime movers in this unofficial and usually clandestine antiques trade. Tombs were laid bare and robbed indiscriminately; those of Idalium, Golgoi, Kourion, Kition, Amathus and Paphos were hardest hit. Messrs T.B. Sandwith, R.H.Lang, G. Collona-Ceccaldi and Luigi Palma di Cesnola, competed fiercely and nearly always for personal gain. The latter, who was followed by his brother Major Alexander, boasted in a letter to Sir Henry Layard (Britain's Ambassador to Constantinople), that he had in his possession *"the island's whole history"*.

Thanks to the British connection a high standard of professionalism was brought to the archaeological investigations of the island. Sir **J.L. Myres,** often referred to as the *'father of Cypriot archaeology '* was aided in his task by various societies and by Max Ohnefalsh-Richter. In 1883 the Cyprus Museum was established in Nicosia. Although illegal sales were reported well into the 1880s the problem had virtually ceased to exist.

5. For the second time in its illustrious history the island of Cyprus became a valuable possession of England. It is a significant fact because, to date, the English hold the unique distinction of being the only foreign country to hold Cyprus twice. In 1191 it was acquired by chance and recourse to war and then sold within a few months for a handsome fee. In 1878 (687 years later), it was taken over by diplomatic agency and it remained under the English Crown for 82 years. To protect their commercial and strategic interests the British, according to Lord Salisbury (Foreign Secretary), saw fit to *"erect another dyke behind the shattered Turkish break-water"*. Prime Minister Disraeli (later Lord Beaconsfield) also emphasised that Queen Victoria henceforth reigned over the *"jewel of the Mediterranean"*.

Before we move on to the next distinct phase in the development of Modern Cyprus we must briefly highlight the main issues and characteristics of the years 1571-1878. It must be stressed from the outset that with the advent of the Turks, the island sunk into a *"long sleep"* — from being a kingdom (true of the Lusignan dynasty), renowned throughout christendom, the island had become an obscure Ottoman dependency. Moreover, the behavioural pattern of Turkish

Above: Janissaris – Turkish infantry, constituting the Sultan's guard and chief part of the army, 14th to 19th centuries. Formed originally of renegade prisoners and of a tribute of children taken from Christian subjects.

Below: An old engraving depicting scenic Kyrenia and its formidable castle..

rators was one of unpredictability; its tax gathering[17] (the
of risings bear proof to this injustice) was crippling; its
⹂s policy, generally speaking, was one of tolerance although as
⹂l, it was punctuated by acts of sheer brutality; its administrators
self-motivated and greedy; its 'justice' was riddled by bribery and
corruption; schools were few and far between (most were run by the
Orthodox church) and hence literacy levels were extremely low; the
medical well-being of the people was very poor; public works were
non-existent and Cyprus' heritage was left to rot or as in the case of
tomb-digging exploited. Yet the Ottomans held Cyprus for 307 years
— serfdom was abolished and after the expulsion of the Latin
hierachy the Greek Orthodox Church was restored.

Such were the stark realities of Cypriot life. Yet it cannot be
disputed that throughout history man's way of life has changed
considerably. The evolution of civilization has abolished ethics and
customs that at their time were regarded as indispensable, and has
substituted them with others, which, in their turn, also became
outdated. Their impact however, on the historical events of a
particular period was so great that nowadays it is necessary for us to
study how people lived in those days in order to understand their acts
and attitudes. What is our assessment therefore of the island's
population? The Cypriot peasant, cramped in 'feudal' bonds and
medieval poverty had one method to escape from his material lot
—religion. He became first superstitious then God-fearing and prayed
constantly for the salvation of his soul. To attend church services and
functions (weddings, christenings and festivals) were his only
recreational activities.

Moreover, the social and economic gulf between the rich and the
labouring masses was as wide as the Mediterranean sea itself.
Although not 'tied' to the land, the peasants were 'bound' on it out of
sheer necessity since there was nowhere else to go. The alternatives
were either to starve or seek an existence from charity (rarely
available) which was really beyond the character of the toiling, proud
and respectable Cypriot. The masses were therefore either 'bound' to
the land or to the mines. In such circumstances crime existed but more

---

[17] Taxes were collected for the Sultan, for the government and district
administrators, for the higher clergy of the Greek Church and for the owners of
farm land. On top, there were levies on produce and following a natural disaster or
a rising further exactions were imposed.

importantly youngsters were forced to work extremely long hours to supplement the meagre family income. Consequently, large families were the order of the day and survival was the ethos of the period. Such families ate and slept in one or two rooms — often adjacent to stables. Much of Cyprus even in the late 19th century was still remote and isolated. Most peasants lived and died in their village without even seeing their nearest town[18] Even though the agricultural revolution (new methods of draining, drilling, sowing, manuring, breeding and feeding of animals etc.,) touched the entire European continent (some more than others), Cyprus continued to exist with outdated and primitive methods. The peasants continued to live under conditions of extreme misery and degradation,

And, what about the Cypriot diet? It was very basic and one based on vegetables such as beans, onions, chic peas, lentils, olives and supplemented by as much bread as possible. Red or white meat was rarely eaten: families often resorted to selling even home-reared fowl so that some of their other basic needs could be met. Some wine was drunk however, especially in mountainous areas where vineyards were plentiful.

The picture drawn so far is a depressing one which it may be added also pertained to other dependent countries. In contrast however, the professional classes (e.g. doctors and lawyers, skilled artisans and the few shopkeepers that existed evidently fared much better under such a system. Some had the opportunity to educate themselves and to travel abroad. Some were prominent in providing something for the poor; others were responsible for 'importing' new ideas from other countries.

This leads us to another very important and related point: the period under discussion was one of great cultural decline. The more educated and progressive people of the island were forced to take refuge in other countries, notably Italy, where Greek communities thrived under benevolent rule. Two writers deserve a special mention: **Neophytos Rodinos,** born around the end of the 16th century, wrote extensively in both Greek and Latin. He was a great scholar whose patriotism was beyond question. The other is **Archimandrite Kyprianos** born in the middle of the 18th century, who lived in Trieste and Venice for many years. His work *'Chronological History of the Island of Cyprus'* (Venice 1788) not only marked an important point in the history of the language but was also of historical and literary value. It

---

[18] Communications were practically non-existent. Generally speaking, there were only mule and camel tracks.

may be noted that the cultural renaissance in Cyprus began in the 1870s. As soon as the British had arrived, printing presses were set up, the first newspapers started to circulate and the first books were printed. Communication with Europe became easier and new ideas started to filter through to Cyprus, mainly from Athens.

Lastly, any people living under harsh conditions and denied both material and spiritual welfare, are bound to develop some defence mechanisms for protection and self-preservation. The Church, as already noted, with its privileges accorded to it by the Turkish administrators, was a strong institution and played an important role in safeguarding the national identity of the island's Christian inhabitants. However, the largely poverty-stricken, isolated and illiterate section of the people developed under foreign rule its own folk culture (music, dance, song, tales and legends) in which it expressed itself and its spiritual world. Since this was a period when the Church played an important role, it was only natural that many of the stories were based on religious themes. Place legends and traditions also made up a large category of folk tales.

Of unique importance is the fact that peaceful co-existence and fruitful co-operation between the Greeks and Turks of Cyprus, during the long Ottoman administration, is a precise historical event and beyond any shadow of doubt. Some brief remarks will suffice:

We have already noted that the recurring mass protests and rebellions were joint affairs. Both had cause to complain against harsh taxes and maladministration.

Also noted earlier is the fact that part of the Turkish population of Cyprus originated from the local or Greek-speaking inhabitants.

In the economic sector there existed complete unity and mutual dependence. There were never two separate economies in Cyprus — one Greek and one Turkish. It must be added however that certain trades, such as building and cabinet-making were practised exclusively by Greeks, whilst others such as midwifery, folk-medicine, quilt-making and sackcloth-weaving, exclusively by Turks.

The cultural and folklore relations between the two communities are also deep and presuppose therefore a long and prolific mutual dependence. Thus the Greek folk poets in the prologue to their poems which they used to recite at fairs and other places, called upon both Greeks and Turks (and others) to listen to them because all groups used to take part in such community festivities. It is also worth noting that there were also Turkish folk poets who composed in Greek in the traditional manner.

This successful co-existence and mutual influence of the two groups was shown by the fact that most Turks in Cyprus spoke Greek and in some villages Turkish school children actually performed patriotic Greek plays. Moreover, the close connection between the two languages in Cyprus added a great number of Turkish words and phrases to the Greek spoken in the island.

Many aspects of the folklore of both Greeks and Turks have a common origin. An example is the 'Zeimbekes'. Their fame as sailors for the Byzantines, Franks and the Ottomans and, at times as pirates, spread from coast to coast and both dances and a special costume (the 'vraka' or baggy trousers) had their origin in these sailors. Because of these Zeimbekes, there are many similarities between Greek and Turkish dances and music.

Architecture is also a feature which is common to both groups. The railed balconies, large windows and the broken arch seen in public buildings are typical examples.

A further feature which needs brief comment is the following: The Greek narrative, poems of Cyprus and especially the 'Akritica' (border ballards), the legends about mythical persons and heroes, about old buildings and treasure, spirits and 'kalikantzari' (a sort of goblin or demon), exist equally among the Greeks and the Turks of Cyprus. It has in fact been shown that certain 'akritic' ballads exist in fuller versions among the Turks of Karpasia and Paphos than among the Greeks.

Finally, the customs and traditions of the two groups are almost the same except that the Greeks call upon the Christian God and the Turks upon Allah. Thus, both have the same traditions about predicting the sex of a baby, about spells and nostrums, about votive offerings, about preparations for a wedding, about funerals and about the life of farmers and shepherds. Thus, like his Greek counterpart, the Turkish farmer puts a pomegranate among his seed and turns towards the East before planting it. Similarly, a clay vessel is broken over the grave of both Turk and Greek. Such examples can be multiplied. Suffice to say that these features are clear evidence of a long period of peaceful co-existence and harmonious contact between the two communities in Cyprus.

Above: Archbishop Kyprianos Killed in the Turkish purge of 1821.
Right: The interior of the Latin Cathedral of Nicosia - Ayia Sophia - it then became the Selimieh Mosque.
Below: An old view of Larnaca - towards the end of Ottoman rule.

CHAPTER THREE

THE
BRITISH
CONNECTION
1878 — 1960

(1) Years of Uncertainty 1878-1914

In the 1870s, the fortunes of the Ottoman Empire assume a new dimension. Its demise after nearly 400 years on the ascendancy, the fear of a Russian advance into the Balkans and the Mediterranean, the development of a new European Order based on the emergence of new nations which resulted in a shift in the fragile European balance of power and the surge for new markets and territories by the established and emerging industrialised nations meant that the *"rosy realm of Venus"* became a prized possession. Amid some intra-governmental debate, the secret convention between Britain and Turkey, dated 4 June 1878 and called *'The Cyprus Convention'*, transferred the island to the British Crown. The Convention was later sanctioned by the Berlin Congress of June-July 1878.

The terms were simple but uncertain: In return for the 'protection' of the bankrupt Ottoman Empire, a tribute of nearly £92,800 and as it turned out 4,166,220 okes (or 10,865,416 lb) of salt per annum, Britain was to administer and occupy Cyprus. Furthermore, if Russia at any time restored to Turkey her three Armenian conquests of 1877, then Cyprus was to be evacuated and returned to Turkey. This however, was a hollow provision — as was the one concerning the 'protection' of Turkey in the event of war. Thus, when Ardahan and Kars were transferred to Turkey in 1921 Cyprus was not relinquished by Britain. It was first annexed in 1914 and in 1925 it became a Crown Colony.

As to its strategic importance Cyprus directly commanded the entrance to the Suez Canal[1] the coasts of Palestine and Syria and the southern provinces of Asia Minor. With Gibraltar in the west of the Mediterranean, Malta in the centre and now Cyprus, the process of converting in into a distant **'British Lake'** was complete. And, with Britain henceforth the chief adviser and comforter to the Porte, its moral influence among all the nations of the east, and especially the people of India, was considerably increased. Economically and commercially, Cyprus once more, brought many advantages to its new occupier. For 82 years this *"rosy realm of Venus"* remained one of the most valuable possessions of the British Crown.

---

[1] The British government in November 1875 became the owner of around $^1/_2$ of the Suez Canal Company stock (shares).

Vice-Admiral Lord **John Hay,** the island's temporary guardian arrived at the bay of Larnaca on 4 July 1878. However, Cyprus and its inhabitants were an unknown quantity both to Hay and to his crew. Captain Harry Rawson was sent on shore on the 8th and 9th to test the situation. He was well briefed by Watkins, the British consul, and following his second visit he laid an informative but short report before Hay. He described the townsfolk as *"quiet and sociable, very lazy and given to pleasures of every sort".* He went on to say that *"since they were not fanatical they would not fight"* and though *"robberies, assassinations and brigandage were nearly unknown, drunkeness was not uncommon".*

However, the inhabitants of Nicosia, being chiefly Turkish, were described as *"fanatical, men devoted to their religion and faithful to their caliph; in other words, men who might possibly turn out to fight".* Such fears did not materialise. Driving in a wagonette with no military guard, Hay entered Nicosia by the Famagusta gate at 11.30 am on 12 July. As it was Friday and the hour of prayer at the Saray (the Turkish governor's official residence) nothing could be done until later. The firman was then read and Hay was handed the reins of the administration. In his brief address Hay explained that as a result of the convention that had been concluded between HM Queen Victoria and the Sultan and enforced now by an imperial firman, he was commanded by HMG[2] to occupy the island of Cyprus in the name of the Queen and to assume its temporary administration until a governor was appointed. He went on to promise justice, progress and equality to all the inhabitants. This very plain and businesslike address, spoken in English, was of course not understood[3] by those present. Only the words *'Queen Victoria'* were comprehended and were soon echoed by the crowd amidst tumultuous cheering. All this took place within the Saray and when Hay and his officers emerged on their way to the flagstaff they were followed by large crowds. The marines were drawn up and Captain Rawson hoisted the Union Jack, which was then saluted. As soon as this brief ceremony was over, Hay formally announced to the people that HM Queen Victoria now reigned over Cyprus. The crowds once more applauded enthusiastically. Hay was then followed to the rostrum by George

---

[2] Her Majesty's Government.
[3] There were of course some who could read and understand English — some even spoke French.

Kepiades, a prominent Greek and the historian of the purges of 1821, who expressed the joy of the Cypriots and their hopes for prosperity and full political liberty.

On 22 July Sir **Garnet Wolseley** arrived in HMS Himalaya, landing at Larnaca at around 6.00 pm and accompanied by some 1,500 troops. On the following day he issued a proclamation (in English, Greek and Turkish), in which he gave assurances of the Queen's wishes for the prosperity of the island and her desire to take measures for the promotion and development of commerce and agriculture, and to endow the people with the benefits of liberty, justice and security. Everyone welcomed the British occupation as a break in Cypriot affairs; in fact, the substitution of a christian empire for a mohammedan one was seen as the golden bridge for higher achievements.

The period between 1878 and 1914 (from occupation to outright cession) was dominated by five major issues:

1. Problems of Settlement;
2. The Hellenic ideal or Meghali Idhea (Great Idea);
3. The emergence of the Constitution;
4. The Economic situation; and
5. Church disputation.

Problems of Settlement.

In 1907 Winston Churchill[4] stressed that Cyprus in 1878 came under British rule *"ruined and prostrate from centuries of horrible ill-usage"*.

Consequently, the problems encountered must have been many. Those associated with the Sultan's lands were troublesome since the departing Turkish administration claimed more or less all the land for which the inhabitants showed no title. In the end large areas were ceded by the Turks and a settlement, which took several years to finalize, was reached. Then there were tax problems but more serious was the issue of the tribute.

The process of clearing up the accounts of the administration was

---

[4] He was then Parliamentary Under-Secretary of State for the Colonies.

Above: Captain Swaine and escort enter Lefkoniko village triumphantly.

Left: The hoisting of the British flag at Nicosia which then became the colonial administrative capital.

complicated by the endeavours of the Turks to present as large a balance as possible in the treasury. It was in their interests to do so, since the annual tribute (as per the Cyprus Convention) was to be based on the average surplus of the last five years. Moreover, to meet the expenses of the Russo-Turkish War of 1876-77, taxes had been doubled. This created further problems for the tax collectors, who had the unenviable task of extracting more and more from Cypriot peasants who could hardly make ends meet.

Law and Order was another thorny issue. Wolseley asserted that impartial justice was his motto and mentioned as illustration the fact that he had in his first three months in office, imprisoned one tax collector for robbery, one Greek churchman for refusing to pay tithes and one Maltese antiquity hunter for breaking the law. He also insisted on the immediate deportation of around 314 Turkish convicts whose presence on the island was as undesirable as it was dangerous. Under Turkish rule[5] it may be noted, the island was made the receptacle for the worst criminals in the Sultan's empire. Wolseley was also convinced that Turkish 'cadis' should instantly be removed from their posts as judges although he believed that they should be retained as expounders of the existing law while verdicts should be delivered by a British judge or commissioner. He further emphasised that if they were kept the Greeks — the mass of the population — would never feel satisfied that justice was being done to them.

The question of privilege, which caused a lot of recrimination, was also a matter for deep consideration. While the peasantry were quite satisfied with the way things were going in the early years of the new administration, the privileged classes — those who had exemptions from taxation — lost all tax gathering rights[6] and hence a new grievance was born. This played a major role in increased agitation for union with Greece. The clergy were the biggest losers but other privileged classes such as lawyers, merchants and bankers also lost out.

The problem of corrupt office holders (allied to the one of law and order) was perhaps at the root of many problems which faced the island. Nepotism, bribery and corruption had been allowed to grow and

---

[5] The Romans and Byzantine Emperors also carried out the same policy. The banishment of undesirables to Cyprus was therefore not new.

[6] In 1878-79.

flourish without check. Officials once appointed became untrustworthy, dishonest, greedy and arrogant. Wolseley was convinced that radical changes were needed to stir the island's energies and set forward her welfare. However, following a strong hint from the government at Westminster, he set about purifying rather than abolishing the decadent Turkish institutions. One of his first acts therefore was to nominate 6 British officers — of whom the first was Colonel **Robert Biddulph** (eventually his successor) — to take the places of the *'kaimakans'* who had administered the six districts into which the island had been divided. The British excuse (for keeping things more or less as they were) of course was uncertainty of settlement.

Health was another issue which had to be tackled by the new administration. Obviously acts of nature such as earthquakes could not be prevented but the poor health of the inhabitants and afflictions such as cattle disease (an outbreak occurred in 1879/80) and locust destruction to crops (to prevent which a considerable amount of money was spent between 1881 and 1885) could, with the right men and resources, be alleviated.

Education and language were also major problems. Illiteracy and therefore apathy were the rule rather than the exception. Schools were few and far between (most were run by the Orthodox Church), and towards the end of the 1870s there were only around 170 in the entire island of which most were small and inadequate. The language problem also meant slower progress within government circles. Thus, at the first, and quite successful meeting of the legislative council which met on 9 December, the languages spoken were English, French, Greek and Turkish.

These and many other problems faced Wolseley, in addition to the usual difficulties which always face an incoming administration.

The Hellenic Dream

The ideal of having a greater Hellas encompassing all Greeks who were under the domination of foreign states, was centuries old. In the case of Cyprus it was much older than the British occupation. Attempts were made by the island's Greeks, usually on the instigation of friendly nations, to free themselves and hence to decide their own destiny. In the 16th and 17th centuries such appeals or attempts proved abortive.

During the 18th century the same story is repeated. Yet there was a difference. Following the Russo-Turkish War of 1769-70 two important events for Hellenism took place. First, Cyprus showed some signs of recovery both economically and politically, and second, the concept of Hellenism found political expression in the *'Philike Hetairia'* founded by Constantine Rhigas at Bucharest in the early 1780s. Although the movement received a check with the execution of Rhigas and his 7 associates in 1798, it was revived and expanded in Odessa in 1814. From 1818 onwards several Hetairia emissaries visited the island (known by the secret code number of 13) and the part of Cyprus in the coming struggle was determined. The events of 1821 and the two enosist rebellions of 1833 in Cyprus have already been discussed in the previous chapter.

The movement for union with Greece, therefore, had begun before the British occupation. Furthermore, the provisional character of the Cyprus Convention and the precedent of the Ionian Islands[7] fostered the belief that it was only a matter of time before a similar gesture would be made over Cyprus. Resolutions, memoranda, deputations, protests and riots in favour of union with Greece are to be found with great frequency in the annals of Cypriot history after 1878.

For over 3000 years the **'Greekness'** of Cyprus was beyond doubt — at all times Greeks were in the majority. Thus the struggle to unite Cyprus with the Greek mainland was from the outset a Greek-Cypriot affair. Only certain elements of the Turkish minority[8] as we shall see in later chapters objected. Contrary to what has been written elsewhere, the vast majority of the Turkish population did not support the repressive measures imposed by the British to check the agitation for enosis.

Enosist aspirations were expressed in many ways and forms: In 1880, a wave of enthusiasm swept Cyprus as Greece mobilized for war against Turkey. Scores of volunteers and 107 mules were the Cypriot contribution. King George I praised the islanders and in a sincere letter to the Archbishop, dated 2 December, he re-iterated that this was clear proof of the true strength of Greek feeling — Hellenism — an

---

[7] Britain took them from the French during the Napoleonic Wars of the early 19th century and, following enosist unrest in 1849, ceded them to Greece in 1864.

[8] The biggest minority (around 18%); mainly descendants of the Ottomans who ruled Cyprus from 1571 to 1878.

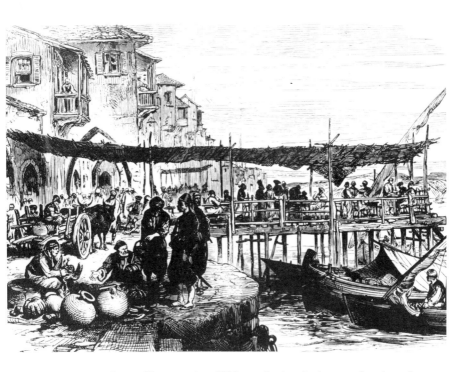

Above: The waterfront of Larnaca, late 1800s, projecting the increased trade under the new administration.
Below: The first British forces land in Cyprus – a wood engraving.

indissoluble bond based on descent, religion and tradition.

Public statements by English politicians, like W.E. Gladstone (the great Liberal leader and four times Prime Minister of G.B. between 1868 and 1894) and Sir Charles Dilke, another leading parliamentarian, in favour of either enosis, cession, or retrocession, were eagerly seized upon by the Cypriots.

In 1897, once more, the Christian element of Cyprus demonstrated yet again their Hellenic feelings by sending around 1,000 volunteers to fight in the so-called *'Thirty Days War'* between Greece and Turkey. They were commended for their heroism, especially at Velestino. Sir Walter Sendall pointed out to his superiors in Whitehall that the chief aider and abetter was the recently appointed Greek consul named **Philemon.** He was regularly greeted by the Greek inhabitants as the representative of *"our king",* but paradoxically enough he was regarded by the authorities in Cyprus as a *'sincere gentleman'* who was *'especially friendly to England and the English'.*

Nevertheless, the High Commissioner issued a proclamation on 23 April calling on all the inhabitants to abstain from acts likely to cause disturbances. He then informed the Colonial Office that the anxiety that still existed arose partly from the composition of the police force. He was of course referring to the loyalties of Christian and Moslem policemen in the event of clashes between the two communities. By 6 May the most perfect tranquility prevailed everywhere. Yet two notable incidents during the Greek Easter celebrations, which very nearly set the patriotic embers of the two sides alight, are worth recalling. The first incident occurred at a Famagusta church where an explosion injured 35 persons and killed a child and an old man. Although several moslems were arrested, the motives, if any, for this reckless act were not established by the authorities.

The second incident took place in a Limassol church and it nearly provoked communal violence. In this case, during the ceremony of the 'Judas bonfire' (lit in the precincts of churches on Easter eve), a native Turkish police officer was seen to enter the church smoking a pipe. Once more the moderating influences prevailed and there was no trouble. In fact, communal violence was a rarity in the island.

The Greek-speaking, Greek-thinking, Greek-feeling Cypriots continued their agitation for enosis by all available means. It was consequently no surprise when a Greek cadet training ship *'Admiral*

Above: The British fleet in Larnaca harbour celebrating and saluting the Duke of
Edinburgh's birthday.
Below: The headquarters and camp of Sir Garnet Wolseley in Nicosia, by the
Metokhi of Kykko Monastery. The church is that of St. Procopios.

Miaoulis' visiting Limassol in 1906 occasioned fervent enosist demonstrations.

Further outbursts resulted from the visit of Winston Churchill in 1907 — he arrived on the morning of Wednesday 9 October and departed on the evening of Sunday the 13th. Churchill received both the Greeks and the Turks. A memorandum from the Greek elected members of the legislative council emphasized the three cardinal issues: union with Greece, abolition of the tribute and wider political liberties for the people's elected representatives. Concerning enosis, Churchill commented significantly that

"such a desirable consummation will doubtless be fulfilled in the plenitude of time and that in the meantime, the people of Cyprus will be content to remain under the British flag".

And, in his reply[9] to the Greek elected members he stressed that it was only natural that the Cypriot people who were of Greek descent should regard their incorporation with what may be called their mother country as an ideal to be earnestly, devoutly and fervently cherished. To Churchill such a feeling was an example of the patriotic devotion which so nobly characterized the Greek nation. His government however had to consider also the views of the island's Moslems and the fact that the British occupation of Cyprus should not lead to the dismemberment of the Ottoman Empire. Furthermore, as to the alleged precedent of the Ionian Islands, they had actually been in the possession of the British government, and Cyprus was not. So ended Churchill's reply.

The Greeks however persisted with further protests, letters, telegrams and deputations. Members of the Royal Family, senior ecclesiastics and parliamentarians were targets for telegrams and memorials. All moves expressed the steadfast desire of the Greeks for national restoration. And, on 28 April 1912, approval was given by the members of the legislative council, who resigned *en masse* on 17 April, to the formation of a central committee under the presidency of the Archbishop, for carrying on the national struggle. The resolution adopted declared that no power in the world, no oppression could alter the national sentiment and will to be annexed to Greece.

The Turco-Italian War of 1911-1912, which brought a Turkish defeat, caused some excitement in certain towns of Cyprus. The distur-

---

[9] C M D (Command Papers) 3996. 1907-08. Volume 71, Page 985.

ances in Nicosia and elsewhere were not at all serious but the 'amouda' (little mosque) incident in Limassol on the night of 27 May 1912 was very serious indeed.

A synopsis of the events is as follows: Some Greeks stoned two carriages full of Turks coming from the village of Malia. At once one of the Turks drew a knife and stabbed two Greeks. The bells of the Catholidgi church began ringing and the Greeks, sensing trouble, arrived in large numbers. A brawl developed but when the police opened fire the crowds dispersed.

On 15 June a three-man mixed commission was appointed to carry out a full enquiry into all matters relating to the Limassol riots. The commission was unable to come to a unanimous conclusion as to the actual cause of the disturbances (the British and Greek members stated that the riot was not premeditated, whilst the Turkish member insisted that it was), but they were all of the opinion that the local police commander was justified in firing on the rioters. The casualties reported by the commission were as follows:

3 killed and 100 wounded, caused by the rioters to civilians;
1 officer and 14 men wounded, caused by the rioters to police; and
2 killed and 9 wounded, caused by rifle fire of the police.

Furthermore, at least 18 persons were sentenced, using the outdated Ottoman penal code, to imprisonment ranging from 9 months to 15 years. These sentences were reduced considerably in June 1913. Disturbances of this nature were rare and caused by certain irresponsible elements, both Greek and Turk, usually flaring up on the spur of the moment. A typical example occurred in 1909 when, following some excitement caused by several meetings of Greeks, around 700 Turks assembled in one corner of Nicosia and armed themselves with swords and knives; nothing happened.

Further delegations and memorials (and sometimes counter-memorials) fill the annals of Cypriot history right up to the advent of the First World War — and beyond. Language, tradition, race and religion prompted the Greeks of Cyprus to struggle for union with Greece. Such feelings, beliefs and attachment was only natural. There was however, another factor that kept this desire alive — the voice of the clergy and of the educated professional classes — ie., the apostles of the **meghali idhea** (great idea). For years the Greeks had been dreaming of a Greater Hellas in which all Greeks, especially those living under foreign governments, would be united under one flag. No Greek thought however of bringing his compatriots in Egypt, the United States or Britain into this Hellenic fold, but nearly every Greek thought in terms of rescuing his enslaved brothers from Turkish rule The most concern was shown for those in the Smyrna district, the Bulgarian littoral, Macedonia, Epirus, the Dodecanese Islands and Cyprus.

This Great Idea, the hope for a Greater Greece, was a national ideal that transcended party lines. Hence the desire to expand, to liberate more and more Greeks from Turkish rule became the motivating force of Greek foreign policy. Indeed, since independence, the Greek people were passionately attached to a foreign policy inspired by the meghali idhea.

Greece obtained the Ionian Islands in 1864; Thessaly and one district of Epirus in 1881; Crete, southern Epirus, a large portion of Macedonia and most of the Aegean Islands came to her as a result of the Balkan Wars of 1912-13. Greece as a result increased its territory by 68% and its population from approximately 2,700,000 to around 4,800,000. This was a powerful incentive for the other Greeks to aspire to join the motherland, aspirations which were greatly encouraged by President Woodrow Wilson's[10] plea for government with the consent of the governed. All subject peoples took new hope.

---

[10] The 28th President of the United States; led that country from 1912 to 1920.

Above: Turkish convicts sent back to Turkey on board HMS 'Black Prince'.
Below: The last Gate of the old Venetian walls of Nicosia also known as the
Famagusta Gate.

The emergence of the Constitution

Less than two months after the arrival of Wolseley, an Order in Council[11] dated 14 September 1878, established a legislative council and an executive council to run the affairs of the island. The latter was constituted as might be directed by instructions addressed from time to time to the island's administrators by the British Government.

The legislative council consisted of the High Commissioner and not less than 4 and not more than 8 other members — half being officials and the others unofficial. At its first meeting on 9 December 1878 it was composed of 4 English, an Italian, a Greek Cypriot and a Turkish Cypriot. It is important to recall that at its third meeting on 1st December, it took into consideration a proposed ordinance regarding the sale of land to subjects of foreign countries. The three non-British members objected but it was finally passed. Hence, the freedom which Britain promised the Cypriots turned out to be the autocratic ('monokratoria') rule of the High Commissioner who possessed practically unlimited powers.

Protests began to pour in — those of 1881 being particularly effective. Soon the British government contemplated changes; moreover, Cyprus was transferred on 6 December 1880 from the Foreign Office to the Colonial Office. An Order in Council dated 30 November 1882 modified the existing form of administration.

The subsequent elections however brought out certain long-standing divisions in the island. For instance, the so-called 'Old Turkish Party' objected at first believing that the elections and the formation of the legislative council would stabilize the British regime thereby giving the non-Moslem majority a chance to impose its will on them.

The 'new' legislative council assembled on Thursday 21 June 1883 and those present were the High Commissioner[12] and 6 British official members, 8 Greeks (one was absent) and 3 Turks. This undemocratic form of colonial administration (communal representation was first formulated in Cyprus) meant that those areas of business not decided solely by the High Commissioner were handed

---

[11] Together with proclamations, writs and ordinances, orders in council are prerogative powers of legislation which are still important in the armed forces, civil service and the colonial empire. They provide a convenient mechanism for implementing important governmental decisions.

[12] He had a casting vote.

BRITISH JUSTICE Above: The British district commissioner and local representatives judging an assault case at Eptakomi – Nicosia. Below: Sir Garnet Wolseley, British High Commissioner, receives a Turkish delegation.

to the legislative council. This however, worked on the principle tha the British and Turkish members at least equalled or exceeded by on the number of Greek members with the High Commissioner havir the casting vote. An Anglo-Turkish combination, therefore, coul carry any measure against the united opposition of the Gree representing around 80% of the island's population. Although son form of representative government was given there was no provisio for majority rule and the constitution was attacked as a *"sha gift"*[13]. This system was maintained, especially after Cyprus became Crown Colony, through a process of privileges for the Turkis members, antagonizing the Greek Cypriots and providing therefo the basis for *'divide and rule'*. In brief, the legislative council after 188 consisted of the High Commissioner and 18 members of whom 1 were to be elected (3 by mohametan voters and 9 by non-mohameta electors) and 6 were to be non-elective. Changes were few and fa between although non-mohametan representation was increased to 1 in 1925.

Local people with traditional holiday dress.

---

[13] The Edinburgh Review. Volume 173 (1891) pages 453-4.

he Economic situation

The Cypriots were assured in 1878 that measures would be taken promote and develop commerce and industry. The inhabitants were ven to understand that ½ a century's peace and good management ould push the island to as high a position as it had occupied in the me of its greatest glory. As *'The Times'* commented on 22 July 1878 *Englishmen will not prove inadequate to the island's development"*. nce more however man and nature combined to inflict vere blows on the already retarded Cypriot economy. In 1877-78 ere was a drought, a plague in 1880 and bad harvests in 1877 and 889. In 1880 and 1892, two floods in Limassol caused nearly 30 eaths and unquantifiable damage.

The inhabitants were asking for material help to provide for chools of agriculture, an agricultural bank, irrigation works, eplantation of trees in the forests and the introduction of new seeds tc. They were also insisting that the tithe (a tax on produce and stock) nd the tribute should be abolished.

A Greek Cypriot deputation, led by the archbishop, arrived in ingland in 1889 to plead in person for some remission of the fiscal urdens facing the inhabitants. The archbishop was received by Queen Victoria and was created Doctor of Divinity by the University of)xford. The deputation however received no encouragement from the Conservative government of Lord Salisbury.

The tribute was perhaps the most important factor in the fortunes of Cyprus. Britain, in return for the occupation of the island, undertook to make good to Turkey the average difference between the sland's revenue and expenditure in its last 5 years as an Ottoman province. Since Turkey had spent nothing on the island but had, on the contrary, taken what it could get out of it, the difference worked out at £92,799. 11s. 3d a year, a sum which was debited annually from its revenue. Usually, British governments had voted a grant-in-aid of a fluctuating amount, which in 1910 was fixed a £50,000 a year.

1928.
Commemorative
Silver Coin of
King George V.

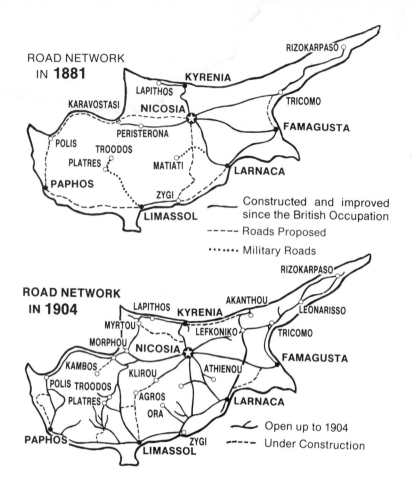

ROAD NETWORK IN 1881

RIZOKARPASO
KYRENIA
LAPITHOS
KARAVOSTASI
NICOSIA
TRICOMO
FAMAGUSTA
PERISTERONA
POLIS
TROODOS
PLATRES
MATIATI
LARNACA
PAPHOS
ZYGI
LIMASSOL

— Constructed and improved since the British Occupation
----- Roads Proposed
•••••• Military Roads

ROAD NETWORK IN 1904

RIZOKARPASO
AKANTHOU
LEONARISSO
LAPITHOS KYRENIA
MYRTOU
LEFKONIKO
TRICOMO
MORPHOU
NICOSIA
FAMAGUSTA
KAMBOS
KLIROU
ATHIENOU
POLIS TROODOS
PLATRES
AGROS
LARNACA
ORA
PAPHOS
ZYGI
LIMASSOL

— Open up to 1904
----- Under Construction

A party of British Government Ministers and Officials leaving Nicosia.

Left: Britons tasting local wine c.1890.

Below: A wood block engraving of a weaving loom and accessories.

This payment evidently retarted the growth of the economy —th Cypriots kept on protesting by all the means available to them: pres pulpit, delegations, memorials, deputations etc., They soon found a influential ally. Winston Churchill insisted that all taxation raise should be used for the benefit of the island's inhabitants. Followin his visit to the island in 1907, he reported to the Cabinet on th condition of Cyprus. He stressed that the payment of the tribute was a

"iniquitous and immoral arrangement ... and a blemish upon Imperial policy ...[14]

Some reforms were certainly passed but Churchill quite rightl stressed that an improvement upon Turkish standards was not sufficient or suitable defence for British policy.

Britain justified the poor economic progress of Cyprus using th argument that the island was held in trust and indeed was the onl British possession in the strange position of not being either inside o outside the British empire. Or was Cyprus simply side-tracked an therefore neglected due to the fact that Britain secured Egypt i 1882?[15] Or can we say that the British authorities lacked the foresigh and the willingness to develop the island? To sum up, the economi story of the island can be described as one of great expectations bu small beginnings.

Church disputation

Another issue which helped to raise Greek passions was the so-called *"squalid schism"* within the Church between 1900 and 1910 brought about by the death of Archbishop Sofronios II on 22 May 1900. Epifanios, the Bishop of Paphos who had precedence over the bishops of Kition and Kyrenia, had died on 5 February 1899 and so the contest was taken up by the two surviving bishops.

The election, organised by the Holy Synod of Cyprus, took place in September 1900, but its validity was disputed and the tranquility of the island was disturbed by disputes between the highest functionaries of the Christian Church. Attempts to resolve the dispute were made —even by the Oecumenical Patriarch — but to no avail. The contest involved the whole Greek population, with charges and counter-charges put forward by the supporters and opponents of the two candi-

---

[14] Colonial Office (CO.) 67/241/4139 H.

[15] In that year G.B. occupied Egypt. Consequently its trading routes to India and the Near and Far East went via Gibraltar, Malta and the Suez Canal.

tes, declarations of support and so forth. At one stage in 1903
arges were brought by 600 persons against the Bishop of Kition for
leged ecclesiastical offences.

Demonstrations and riots were also common with the early
onths of 1908 being particularly eventful. The High Commissioner,
armed at the disturbed state of public feeling in Nicosia, requested
oops to be sent from Limassol. That was in March. The riots of
pril were even more serious and evidence exists showing that they
ere not spontaneous. On the night of the 9th the disorder culminated
a serious riot, in the course of which firearms were freely used. On
e following day the High Commisioner issued a proclamation that,
order to put an end to the disorder, Nicosia would be occupied by
e police and attempts to disturb the peace would be forcibly
ppressed. He warned peacable people to avoid scenes of
isturbance. Although considerable damage was done to property and
ome serious injury inflicted on individuals, it appears that there was
o loss of life.

In April 1909 the Bishop of Kition was elected archbishop under
he Archiepiscopal Election Law, although the Bishop of Kyrenia was
ppointed archbishop by the Church of Constantinople. However, in
arly 1910 the Bishop of Kyrenia at last consented to recognize his
pponent as archbishop and resumed his see with the title 'His
eautitude the President of Kyrenia'.

The dispute was finally resolved in April 1910 following the
lections to the sees of Paphos and Kition. Moreover the Holy Synod
n 1914 drew up a constitutional charter for the Church of Cyprus,
egulating its administration on the basis of the sacred canons and
revailing practice, thus preventing the recurrence of any similar
onflicts. It provided for an electoral body of 66 elected general
epresentatives (22 clerical and 44 lay), voting jointly with the Synod
vhich was reinforced at archiepiscopal elections by 7 abbots and
ertain other dignitaries. The total was to be 77 members. Thus when
Kyrillos II died in 1916 he was peacefully succeeded by his opponent
Kyrillos III who led the Church until 1933.

(ii) From Annexation to the First Major Popula
Protest 1914-1931.

Complacency and near total disinterestedness — this must surel
be our verdict of the years of uncertainty[1]. Yes, Britain was faced with
an awesome task but it was a task she did not attempt to fulfi
Churchill's memorandum to the Cabinet in 1907 categorically asserte
that *'an improvement upon Turkish standards is not a sufficient c
suitable defence for British policy'* — this is certainly the crux of th
matter: **Cyprus had been simply neglected.**

Following the Annexation Order of 5 November 1914, Cypru
formed part, both de facto and de jure, of His Majesty's·Dominions
British citizenship for the inhabitants was finally settled in Novembe
1917 and in March 1925 Cyprus was proclaimed a **Crown Colony**
Once more a long list of customary problems needed to be tackled. I
addition, other issues also dominated Cypriot politics.

The Economic issue:

It is beyond doubt that under British rule Cyprus fared bette
than under its earlier rulers. Cyprus was handed over to Britain by
Turkey in a thoroughly exhausted and ruined condition.
Communications were practically non-existent[2]; post offices,
hospitals, printing presses and schools were hardly in evidence. By the
early 1920s however we find fairly good roads and bridges and a
railway which ran from Famagusta to Nicosia; over 70 post offices
with around 200 rural mail stations dealing with over 3 million letters,
cards, newspapers, books and parcels; hospitals were found in all the
districts; around 15 newspapers were published — showing eloquently
the material and educational advancement of the Cypriots; also we
find nearly 800 schools with well-trained teachers. This was labelled
'unexampled prosperity'.

Yet, there were many negative aspects and complaints were
regularly included in the memoranda sent to the governing authorities.
Cyprus was predominantly an agricultural country and it was here
that least progress had been made. Furthermore, the people

---

[1] 1878-1914: From Occupation to Annexation.

[2] Sir Samuel and Lady Baker, during their travels in Cyprus in the early months of
1879, explained that they were "stuck continuously in the mud" and that only
"animal tracks existed in some places".

ffered high levels of taxation: the tribute and the Imperial Defence ıx were imposed over and above the usual taxes. Living standards ere low, and poverty, accentuated by the malpractices of the money-nding few over the ignorant and uneducated, was widespread. There as a mass exodus from the villages to the towns, children worked ıng hours under intolerable conditions[3], and wages were generally ıw.

Much can be learnt about the island's economic ills if we simply ımmarise the contents of a letter sent by A.J. Cunningham[4] to the Colonial Office in 1917. He was at pains to stress that Cyprus was eing exploited by a handful of *'blood sucking advocates'* or *'legalized oiders'* and several wholesale merchants, who not only controlled the egislative council but in practice also controlled ecclesiastical ecisions, school and village councils. Amongst other things he uggested the opening of an agricultural bank to make advances to illagers at low rates of interest. Cunningham saw the current socio-conomic condition of the island as an affront to human existence and lignity. His suggestions, although noted, were not acted upon. However, in 1925 the tithe was abolished and in 1927 the tribute also eceived the same fate. Moreover, co-operative credit societies ncreased in number from 28 in 1925 to 326 in 1930, catering for about !/3 of the villages. Also, an Agricultural Bank was established in June 1925 under the joint auspices of the government and the Ottoman Bank.

No one however can shy away from the facts: According to the Survey of Rural Life in Cyprus[5], conditions of living were roughly equivalent to those which prevailed in England during the 15th and 16th centuries. The rural population according to the Survey constituted 80.5% of the total yet only around 3/5 of the land was under cultivation, the rest being held by the government and the Greek and Turkish religious institutions. The Survey, which fixed a very conservative minimum level of subsistence, found that over 25% of the rural population lived below that level, some 50% around that scale and the rest above it. Most peasants were illiterate and over 70%

---

[3] It seemed as though Britain of the 17th and 18th centuries was 'transplanted' onto 20th century Cyprus.

[4] He was for some time the Assistant Island Postmaster. His paper was entitled 'England's Duty to Cyprus'.

[5] Prepared in 1927-28 on the instigation of Sir Ronald Storrs, the Governor. Its findings were published in booklet form in 1930.

were chronically indebted to usurers and merchants whose actions f
recovery afforded lucrative employment for numerous advocates. S
Ronald Storrs explained that when he assumed the governorship i
1926 he found on the legislative council 8 advocates three of whor
were money-lenders; one landowner who was also a money-lende
one bishop of the Orthodox Church; one merchant and one farme
He went on to say that even though the real interests of Cyprus wer
those of the peasant producer, the interests represented in the counc
were exclusively those of the *"numerically insignificant class o
parasites who made a living out of him".*[6]

The Cypriots also suffered from that monstrosity of feudal an
manorial domination — forced labour[7]. Hence, what the heroi
French revolutionaries fought — in the name of liberty, equality an
fraternity — to abolish in 1789 still persisted in Cyprus 142 years later
Legislation was enacted in 1931 to put an end to compulsory labour.

The island's inhabitants therefore had to endure excessive an
unfair taxation, forced labour, exploitation, court actions, and the
world economic slump especially of the late 1920s; additionally, they
suffered an unworkable constitution and political persecution. The
above issues, needless to say, give weight to the criticism that Cyprus
was merely occupied rather that administered or developed. They also
illustrate the fact that the island, not being on the direct route to India
(Britain, Gibraltar, Malta and Suez), was slowly acquiring the status
of a second-class colony; hence, the government was not particularly
interested in its development. The British failure to cure the evident
economic grievances of the island was continually attacked by the
press — a medium which assumed great significance in Cypriot
politics. Economic and political unrest was rife in the 1920s. The
political outlook of the people was undergoing change and the labour
movement was beginning to make its voice felt. The formation of
trade unions added a further dimension to the island's history —
stoppages and strikes were henceforth better organized and well
supported.

---

[6] Orientations. 1937. Page 570.
[7] Mainly for village road construction.

Above: Prosperity depicted by the manner of the dress. The "Aristocracy" of Nicosia. Below: A pottery workshop in Nicosia.

The Constitution:

The annexation of the island on 5 November 1914 was n
accompanied by any change in the constitution; in fact, the deman
for wider political representation continued unabated. However, a
Order in Council dated 6 February 1925 increased the membership
the legislative council. It was to consist of the Governor, 9 official an
15 elected members of which three were to be elected by mohameta
voters and twelve by non-mohametan voters. From the brief tab
below it can be seen that an Anglo-Turkish combination could carr
any measure against the united opposition of the Greeks wh
represented around 80% of the island's total population:

	1882	1925
High Commissioner (Governor)	1	1
British non-elective members	6	9
Mohametan elective members	3	3
Non-mohametan elective members	9	12
Total	19	25

The elections of October 1925 duly provided a legislative counci
with 15 elected members and the reconstituted chamber met for the
first time on 6 November. However, in addition to the increase in the
size of the council, a unique restriction was imposed on its powers
The provision, which was contrary to the Colonial Laws Validity Ac
of 1865, stated that the council, despite its representative character
might make no law to alter the constitution. In fact, these so-called
'new arrangements' were no different from those which already existed
— the council had no more power than before and the issuing of
Orders in Council was often used to override its decisions. In 1927
alone, 7 such orders were passed. It was therefore a non-democratic
form of colonial rule since only those areas of business not decided
solely by the Governor were handed to the legislative council; and
even then, there was the threat of passing laws by the use of
prerogative powers.

Political issues:

Enosis agitation, the offers and promises made by Britain to give
up the island and Cyprus' contribution to the war effort of the allies
(1914-1918) will be dealt with in this section.

Firstly, we must explain the so-called *'offers and promises'*)etween 1912 and 1919 and Cyprus' war efforts on the side of Britain ind her Allies. Amongst several more general pronouncements, there were two *offers* in 1912 and 1915 and two *promises* in 1919. After the 'irst phase of the Balkan Wars the combatants met in London (from 6 December 1912 to 6 January 1913), to discuss peace terms. At the 1ead of the Greek delegation was the *'maker of modern Greece'*, **Eleftherios Venizelos,** who holds the distinction of being the first Greek Prime Minister to raise the question of Cyprus in an .nternational gathering. Lloyd George, an influential political figure who was at the time Chancellor of the Exchequer and who had .ntimated on several occasions that Greece should be given Cyprus, 1sked Venizelos whether Britain could use the naval facilities provided 1t Argostoli (Cephalonia) in return for Cyprus. This unofficial request ind offer was accepted in principle by Venizelos, yet neither Athens nor London pursued the proposal to any sort of conclusion in 1912 or 1913. In Cyprus however, the archbishop who chaired a meeting of 1otables and provincial delegates on 7 January 1913 *'proclaimed'* the union of the island with Greece. On 18 January, *Eleftheria,* a Greek-Cypriot newspaper, published an article to the effect that Cyprus was shortly to be handed over to Greece and that Constantinos Papamichalopoulos had been designated by the Hellenic government as its first Governor of Cyprus. The Turkish Cypriots were alarmed but the High Commissioner assured them that their interests would be safeguarded if and when such a change occurred.

Further offers of territory were transmitted to Greece in 1914 and 1915 — in return for immediate participation in the war effort on the side of the allies. Offers of territory were also made in November 1914 and January 1915. In October 1915 Cyprus was the *'bait',* in addition to other concessions in western Thrace and Asia Minor — both it may be noted inhabited mainly by Turks and not British sovereign territories. Furthermore, there was no mention of naval facilities nor any talk of the Turkish minority in Cyprus being an obstacle. In Athens the pro-German establishment was adamant. The opportunity of acquiring Cyprus was lost. Greece eventually entered the war on the side of the allies but by 1917 they were already on the road to victory and there was no reason to change the island's administration.

Nevertheless in 1919 Cyprus was again *'promised'* to Greece. A record of a conversation[8] between Lloyd George (Prime Minister of

---

[8] On 13 May during a Council of Four (Britain, USA, France and Italy) Meeting.

Great Britain) and Woodrow Wilson (President of the USA) went like this:

LG   — *It is my intention to give Cyprus to Greece.*
WW — *Excellent idea.*
LG   — *(referring to the Turks). They have no right in a
          country which they had converted to mere desert.*

Amongst the various reasons as to why this *'promise'* was not kept was the one put forward by military tacticians who argued, very forcibly, that there were strong strategic reasons for not giving up the island. The second *'promise'* was made by Ramsay McDonald, the leader of the Labour party, in February 1919. Speaking at the Socialist International Conference (held at Berne, Switzerland), he emphasised that his party supported Cypriot self-determination and that, if he ever came to power, he would do everything possible to carry out this commitment. McDonald however, who led the short-lived Labour government of 1924 (22 January to 3 November), failed to honour his pledge.

Within the context of such offers and promises we must pinpoint Cyprus' overall contribution to the allied war effort — for so small an island it was simply phenomenal. Approximately 13,000 men, between the ages of 18 and 41, were recruited as muleteers for the British Salonica Force; approximately 47,000 animals (goats, mules, donkeys and horses); around £9,000 was raised for the British and Belgian Red Cross Funds; large quantities of foodstuffs and timber were exported for the use of the Expeditionary Forces. Moreover, the island was used as a place of detention for prisoners of war and as a convalescent depot. Cyprus' contribution was certainly massive. As a result the resources of the island were being strained to the utmost. It may be added that the Cypriots acquitted themselves well in many fronts and were commended highly for their heroism and work-rate under difficult conditions.

With such a favourable atmosphere (the euphoria created by these offers and promises and the island's massive and highly successful involvement during the course of the First World War), the educated proponents of the *meghali idhea* intensified their efforts to achieve national self-realization. They were also spurred on by the Cretan example of 1913. In that year Crete proclaimed its union with the mainland — an ction which was legalized when Turkey abandoned her suzerain rights in a clause of the 1913 Treaty of London. In fact, the political consciousness of the inhabitants had been awakened and had expressed itself in a growing desire of the

Christian majority to realize its nationality. They also believed that the Moslem preference for the status quo and antipathy to union should not prove permanent; they pointed out that in Thrace, amongst other places, the Turkish minority lived happily within a Greek majority. Memoranda, petitions and deputations, once more, fill the annals of Cypriot history. The effects of the 1918 deputation deserve some comment.

On 5 December, a deputation consisting of the archbishop and the 8 Greek members of the legislative council left for London to press their demands on the British government. After meeting Venizelos in Paris the deputation arrived in London on 3 January 1919. They were then received by Viscount Milner, the Secretary of State for the Colonies, on 3 February. Milner listened carefully; even though he appreciated and respected the aspirations of the memorialists he was not prepared to give a definite reply. The Christian delegation on 5 May also appealed to parliament, church, press and nation at large. For nearly two years the Cyprus delegation laboured in London without success.

What were the effects of this initiative and consequent failure? *Firstly,* memorials by the Moslem population of Cyprus recorded the customary protests. They pleaded against the union of Cyprus with Greece and prayed for the continuance of British rule over the island. More importantly however, there were signs of unrest among the Moslems of Nicosia. In 1919 a small party[9] advocating the return of the island to Turkey was formed. It was led by Dr Mehmed Essad and Dr Hussein Behije. Sir Malcolm Stevenson[10] described Essad, who had arrived in Cyprus as a refugee in November 1914, as one of the leaders of the *"anti-Greek section"* and Behije *"a local practitioner who was generally drunk"*. And associated with Essad and Behije was Hasan Karabardak, a *"rowdy individual and leader of the hamals"* (local porters), who took a leading part in the disturbances of 1912.

The expected Moslem agitation did not take place and by May the symptoms of unease had disappeared.

Secondly, the failure of the delegation to London, led to bitterness, resentment and frustration. A new dimension was added to the Cyprus problem. Events moved very fast. There were public meetings and protests and on 8 December 1920, the Christian members

---

[9] It had very limited support and was called the 'Union with Turkey Party'.
[10] At the time he was the Officer Administering the Government of Cyprus but was later appointed High Commissioner.

of the legislative council resigned en masse and unanimously decided to initiate new forms of struggle. The year 1921 was not only the centenary of Greek independence but the year in which a new political organization was set up to direct the enosis struggle. It also witnessed disturbances in Nicosia, the imposition of martial law and the deportation of **Catalanos.**

On 6 and 7 April, Greek Independence Day was the occasion for a disturbance in Nicosia which the police with difficulty succeeded in putting down. Fresh disorders were feared during the Greek Easter —with the prospect of racial riots. The enlistment of 90 ex-policemen and the call for troop reinforcements by the island's authorities were in the end not needed. Further festivities which may have culminated in riots were abandoned by the organizers.

Meanwhile the colonial administration imposed martial law and tightened internal security. On 24 April the deportation of N. Catalanos was ordered by the High Commissioner. It was alleged that he addressed an inflammatory speech to a number of persons at the New Hellenic Club. The charge was denied and his deportation provoked numerous protests.

Soon a new organization to direct the enosis struggle was set up. On Sunday 23 October, a meeting of representatives, known as the **National Assembly** was held in Nicosia under the presidency of the Archbishop. Further meetings took place on 4 and 5 December and on the latter date a new political organization, known as the **National Council,** was set up. It replaced the Central Committee of the National Cause and was to be responsible to the National Assembly and thence to the people for its actions. Petition followed upon petition — *enosis and only enosis* — was the motto. Yet one failure followed another failure. Moreover, the tightening of internal security resulted also in the deportation of **F. Zannetos** in December 1922. Zannetos was the Mayor of Larnaca, for many years a member of the legislative council and a doctor much loved for his philanthropic activities. On the day he left Larnaca a very mixed crowd openly wept for *'their'* doctor. Zannetos left with chants of *'union and only union'* ringing invitedly in his ears.

It may be added that if this action by the authorities was designed to repress national sentiment then it had precisely the opposite effect. The Greeks vowed to coⁿ ʿinue the struggle for enosis — using all the available means at their ɑisposal. The coming to power of the second British Labour government on 5 June 1929 prompted the delivery of a long memorandum on 20 July. Several months later a three-man deputation led by Bishop Nicodemos arrived in London to put their case direct to HMG. Amongst other meetings and contacts they had an hour-long interview with Lord Passfield, Secretary of State for the Colonies, on 25 October. The essence of the Minister's reply was that what Cyprus needed were fewer opportunities for political discussion and more occasions for constructive work. *'Nothing doing'* was the polite government response. Protests and counter-protests were triggered off by the British response. New forms of political expression were discussed. A decisive step was taken in Nicosia on 26 January 1930, when the Pan-Cypriot National Assembly voted for the establishment of a **'National Organization'** the object of which was to promote the cause of enosis. Good use was made of the press in Cyprus, Greece, the USA and Britain. Letters and articles appeared regularly and the movement seemed to be gaining ground.

Cyprus however, was already in very deep waters: On 25 November 1926 the elected members of the legislative council by a unanimous vote of 13 to 9, threw out the Appropriation Bill and ipso facto the Colonial Estimates for 1927. On 7 February 1927 the estimates etc., were passed by an Order in Council. The same method was repeated in 1928. Such action by the authorities caused widespread disapproval and consequently unrest.

Education was also brought into the arena of controversy. For years it was dominated by the Church and its unionist supporters. The Elementary Education Bill of 1929 stated that the control over the appointment, promotion, transfer, dismissal and discipline of elementary teachers of all communities should pass from the *'political'* committees to the government. Even though the Annual Report for 1928 stated that education was functioning satisfactorily, within a year it was *'found'* that the schools were inefficient and functioned only for the purpose of glorifying Greek and Turkish ideals!

The crisis sunk even further. We have already discussed the negative attitude and declaration of Lord Passfield in 1929. Now it was the turn of Philip Snowden to cause further dissatisfaction. The Chancellor of the Exchequer informed the House of Commons on 8 July 1931 that the tribute was henceforth disposed of. The Cypriots consequently expected taxation to be reduced; instead, the governor proposed increases. Meanwhile, the world economic blizzard of the late 1920s and early 1930s was causing new problems. Because of the general fall in commodity prices the customs tariff was in need of readjustment and revision in order to safeguard the island's revenue. A seven-man committee[11] proposed a temporary levy of 5% on official salaries over £100 a year and the substitution of specific[12] for ad valorem[13] customs duties. These recommendations were unanimous and were duly accepted by the governor who proceeded to introduce a bill in the legislative council. The elected members however, refused to agree to any legislative measure involving fresh taxation.

The governor knew that so long as the 3 Turkish members remained loyal to him the wishes of the Greek majority could be overriden. But the activities of Assaf Bey, the Turkish consul, the anti-colonial mood that prevailed in the island and perhaps more importantly, the formation of labour organizations for all peasants and workers ensured the election of **Misirlizade Nejati Bey,** who could not be counted upon to support the government. When the vote for the revised tariff was taken in the legislative council the Greeks solidly opposed it and Nejati Bey voted with them. He was called '*the 13th Greek*' and in effect possessed the casting vote in the debating chamber. The measure was thrown out but the governor imposed it by an Order in Council. The already creaking constitutional machinery now threatened to break down completely. The governor informed his superiors in Whitehall on 4 June 1931 that the loyal Turkish community which had always been regarded as a useful safeguard in troubled times '*cannot at present be guaranteed*'.

The British '*trump card*' had finally lost its value. Moreover, there were other issues which helped to bring the embittered Cypriots and the colonial administration towards the confrontation arena. One such issue was the formation of political groupings like the National Council or National Assembly[14] in 1921-22 and the KKK (the Communist Party of Cyprus) in 1925. We have already discussed the activities of the former. The latter, which was succeeded in 1941 by AKEL (the Progressive Party of the Working People), aimed its work at solving the problems of the working class and impoverished peasants;

---

[11] Composed of 3 British officials, 3 Greeks and 1 Turk.

[12] Duties based on the quantity purchased.

[13] Duties in proportion to the value of goods purchased.

[14] It was eventually succeeded by the National Organization in 1930. Another unionist organ was EREK (Ethniki Rizospastiki Enosi Kyprion — the Cyprus National Redicalist Union), which was set up in 1929 as a secret organization, but officially formed on 18 October 1931. Its organ was the newspaper Irreconcilable (Adiallaktos).

RURAL CONSTABLE
WITH BADGE AND STAFF

PRIVATE
SUMMER UNIFORM
(KHAKI)

PRIVATE
WINTER UNIFORM
(BLUE SERGE)

DISTRICT SERGT.-MAJOR
SUMMER UNIFORM
(KHAKI)

The Police Force under the British Administration — uniforms and ranks.

TURKISH INSPECTOR
WINTER UNIFORM
(UNDRESS)

TURKISH INSPECTOR
SUMMER UNIFORM
(FULL DRESS)

TURKISH INSPECTOR
WINTER UNIFORM
(FULL DRESS)

LOCAL COMMANDANT
WINTER UNIFORM
(UNDRESS)

it also called on all the inhabitants to fight for the island's self-determination. The authorities were alarmed, and they proceeded to ban many (mainly leftist) publications. In 1928 internal security was tightened even further and on 1 January 1929 the KKK went underground; its newspaper *Neos Anthropos* (New Man) was forced to close down only to be replaced by a bi-weekly one called *O Neos Ergatis* (The New Worker). Court actions were also brought against leading leftists.

The aggrieved and *"humorous Cypriots"* (Sir Ronald Storr's favourite description) were now in the mood to see the introduction of radical changes. On 12 September 1931, three days after the publication of the Order in Council which introduced a new customs tariff, the Greek elected members of the legislative council were summoned by the Bishop of Kition (cousin of Archbishop Kyrillos) to a meeting at Saitta (a summer resort near Troodos) to decide on future policy. There were further meetings on 3, 10, 11, and 17 October. Agreement however, on a common front eluded the participants. Yet, at the last meeting the Bishop of Kition, **Nicodemos Mylonas,** read a manifesto which advocated resistance to British rule and demanded its immediate overthrow.

The bishop was now at the centre of a crisis as his advocacy of illegal measures was hailed by the extremist elements. On the 18th he addressed a crowd at Larnaca, advising them not to be afraid of Britain's fleet and not to obey the laws, for in the quest for union *'blood should flow if necessary'*. Two days later the bishop arrived in Limassol and raised what is now customarily called the *'fiery cross'*. He addressed a crowd of over 3,000 at the sports ground and he declared the union of Cyprus with Greece — he proceeded to do the same at the enosis club. At the stadium similar appeals were addressed to the people by **N.K. Lanitis** and **Zenon Rossides.**

Despite the polemical speeches, the crowd dispersed quietly. Nicosia was henceforth to be the focal point of discontent. The secretary of the National Organization received a telegram from Lanitis which concluded that *"never before has there been a more panegyric approval"* of the bishop's activities. The effects of the telegram were instantaneous. The events of **21 October** sparked the first outbreak of major violence in the island. Politicians and leading enosists spoke for union and only union; the members of the legislative chamber resigned en masse; the church bells began ringing to summon the people and shopkeepers were told to shut their shops. The assembled crowds repeatedly shouted *'to Government House'*.

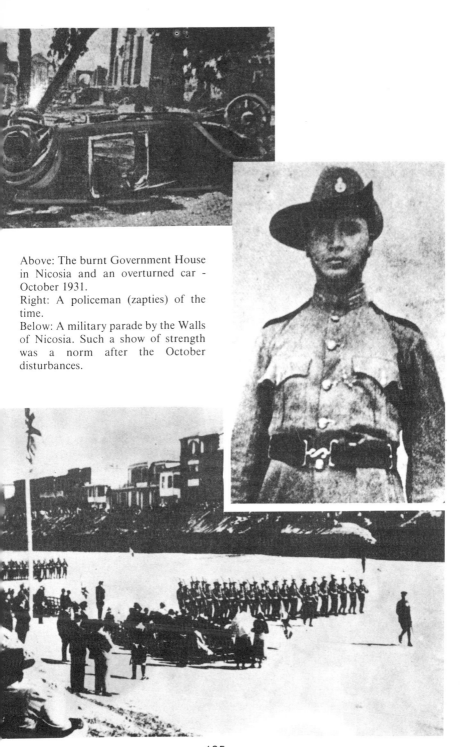

Above: The burnt Government House in Nicosia and an overturned car - October 1931.
Right: A policeman (zapties) of the time.
Below: A military parade by the Walls of Nicosia. Such a show of strength was a norm after the October disturbances.

At that juncture **Dionysios Kykkotis,** chief priest of Phaneromeni, the most important church in Nicosia, stepped forward and declared revolution. A Greek flag was handed to him and he abjured the people to defend it. One more speech was made, the speaker kissed the flag and the cry *'to Government House'* was renewed with frenzy. The leaders seized the flag and at around 6.45 pm began to lead the crowd in the ½-mile trek to their declared destination. Passing the government timber yard, the crowd which was composed mainly of youths, helped themselves to sticks of various sizes and by 7.45 pm the *'exit'* gate of Government House was reached. By 8.00 pm the crowd broke the police cordon at the exit gate and moved into the grounds and within a stone's throw of the wooden building. At around 11.00 pm Government House, an inflammable mid-Victorian military bungalow, was set on fire.

By the end of the evening 15 civilians were injured of whom an 18-year-old youth, Onoufrios A. Clerides, died shortly afterwards. The excitement caused by the Nicosia disturbances spread to the other parts of the island. In Limassol, the commissioner's house was burnt down; in Famagusta, police and troops from HMS Colombo (arrived on 25 October and landed 30 marines), opened fire and Haralambos Fili, an 18-year-old from Lefkoniko was killed; in Paphos and Larnaca demonstrations took place mainly outside police compounds.

Though the towns, especially Nicosia, were the main centres of discontent scores of villages were also active. W. Lunn MP., addressing the House of Commons on 22 April 1932 correctly pointed out that conditions of extreme poverty will ferment disturbances in any community and Cyprus was no exception. Yet, within a week of the *'first outbreak of violence',* order, with the exception of certain minor disturbances in a few villages, was restored.

The Cyprus Gazette

(Extraordinary)
Published by Authority

No. 2167.]   SATURDAY, 24TH OCTOBER, 1931.   937

No. 871.
THE DEFENCE (CERTAIN BRITISH POSSESSIONS) ORDER IN COUNCIL 1928.

REGULATIONS.

RONALD STORRS,
Governor.

In exercise of the powers vested in him by the Defence (Certain British Possessions) Order in Council, 1928, His Excellency the Governor has been pleased to make and hereby makes the following Regulations:—

1. These Regulations may be cited as the Defence of Cyprus (No. 2) Regulations, 1931, and shall be read as one with the Defence of Cyprus Regulations, 1931 (hereinafter referred to as the principal Regulations), and the principal Regulations and these Regulations may together be cited as the Defence of Cyprus Regulations, 1931, to No. 2) 1931.

2. These Regulations shall come into operation on and from the date of their publication in the *Cyprus Gazette.*

3. The following Regulations shall be inserted in the principal Regulations:—

"12. No meeting or assembly of more than five persons shall be held in any place or building without the permission in writing of the Commissioner of the District first obtained:

Provided that nothing in this Regulation contained shall be deemed to apply to any persons being members of the same household.

"13. Any person who takes part in any meeting or assembly held in contravention of Regulation 12 hereof shall be deemed to have acted in contravention of these Regulations.

"14. All officers of the Cyprus Military Police and all officers of His Majesty's Naval, Military or Air Forces and all other persons acting in their behalf or under their instructions shall have power to disperse by force any meeting or assembly held in contravention of Regulation 12 hereof and shall not be liable in any criminal or civil proceedings for having by the use of such force caused harm or death to any person.

"15. No person coming from outside the Colony of Cyprus shall land or disembark in the Colony of Cyprus without the previous permission in writing of the harbour or port authorities of the District in which such person intends to land or disembark.

"16. No person shall print, exhibit or circulate any pamphlet or notice of any kind without the permission in writing of the Commissioner of the District first obtained."

Dated the 24th day of October, 1931

(M.P. 1529/27.)

No. 872.   Telegraphic use of Codes.

With reference to the Order of the Governor in Council No. 1444 of the 3rd day of October, 1931, published under Notification No. 870 in the *Cyprus Gazette* of the 23rd October, 1931, His Excellency directs it to be notified for general information that the use of the following codes is permitted in telegrams:

A.B.C., 5th and 6th Editions.
Bentley's Complete Phrase.
Bentley's Second Phrase.

Messages in private or any other code not recognised will be stopped. In every case the name of the code used must be indicated on the form; no charge will be made for transmission of the name of the code.   (M.P. 829/23.)

By His Excellency's Command,

A. B. WRIGHT,
Acting Colonial Secretary.

Printed by the Government Printer at the Government Printing Office, Nicosia.

The *Cyprus Gazette* may be obtained from the Superintendent, Government Printing Office, Nicosia, post free, on payment of a subscription of 15s. for a year or 8s. for six months, payable in advance; single copies 6cp.

An official record of the post-1931 restrictive measures.

(iii) The 1930s: Repression and Consolidation.

Before we discuss the Cypriot scene of the 1930s certain misconceptions should be cleared up.

Firstly, there is no evidence to suggest that the October outbreak was in any way premeditated or prearranged. It is however probable that the outbreak would not have taken the form it did but for the enosis agitation. The ground for disturbance was prepared by the extreme leaders of the union movement in the hope that the occurrence of general demonstrations would advance the cause of union. Conclusively, it can be asserted that the *'revolt'* was simply a vast popular protest and not a premeditated uprising. The people in fact demonstrated with sticks since they did not plan serious trouble nor did they possess firearms.

Secondly, attempts had been made to lay the blame on Greece for the disturbances. The Greek government had nothing to do with it —its motto was *'strict impartiality'*. In spite of the great pressure brought to bear on Venizelos by the press and organized supporters of the unionist movement, he had flatly refused to give any encouragement to the Cypriot leaders or their sympathizers in Greece. The Premier had clearly done his best to act with propriety and with regard to the obligations arising out of the friendship between Greece and Britain. The agitation however was not obliterated. A manifesto in sympathy with the Cypriot cause, signed by 45 prominent Greeks and headed by Admiral **Paul Koundouriotis,**[1] was published in all the Athenian newspapers on 31 October. The Holy Synod of the Church of Greece issued a statement in the same sense and the Archbishop of Athens telegraphed to his British counterpart. Church masses were held in many districts and at Amarousion, eight miles outside of Athens, 3,000 people attended. Armistice Day (11 November) was celebrated in Athens as *'Cyprus Day'* and a secret committee was formed in Piraeus to equip 1,000 volunteers for Cyprus. In addition to the campaign in the press, practically all the municipalities, chambers of commerce, leagues and local societies passed resolutions in sympathy. Student disturbances at both Athens and Salonica had to be suppressed.

---

[1] Often called *'the grand old man of the Greek political world'*. He was appointed Regent on 18 December 1923 and first President of the Greek Republic on 25 March 1924.

The *third* misunderstanding concerns the **Koundouriotis Circular.** This directive regarding the uprising of the Cypriots and its suppression was received by British MPs and newspapers in the early spring of 1932. It contained allegations of mass killings, maltreatment of innocent civilians, the employment of brutal methods by the security forces firstly to extract the information needed and then to pacify the inhabitants, injuries amounting to thousands (mostly minor) and the confiscation of property belonging to the deportees. The authorities, both in Nicosia and in London, dismissed it as being utterly false and baseless in almost every particular. Although there were certain gross exaggerations it must surely be correct to say, after scrutinising the various reports and documents of the colonial and foreign offices, that some events were certainly sidestepped or misrepresented by the colonial administration.

Fourthly, and contrary to reports by certain uninformed and biased quarters, the use of violence was condemned by all although some speakers both before and during the riots freely mentioned the need for sacrifices and possible bloodshed. Thus in his encyclical of 2 November 1931 the archbishop excluded violence as being one of the ways in furthering and promoting their national aspirations. And, in his letter to the governor on 19 November he expressed the deep grief of the Greeks at what had taken place. Furthermore, the Greek members of the Nicosia municipal corporation, headed by Dervis, its mayor, expressed regret at the burning of Government House[2] in a letter addressed to the officer in command of the military forces and dated 26 November.

The *fifth* misconception relates to the activities of the Turkish inhabitants. It must be emphasised from the outset that the goodwill of the Moslem population and of the other minorities towards the government never wavered throughout the disturbances. However, during the whole period of the disorders there was not the least exhibition of anti-Greek feeling or any single instance of betrayal by Moslems to the authorities of those who had compromised themselves in the disturbances. On the contrary, **Nejati Bey,** a prominent Moslem leader, issued a manifesto during the disturbances calling upon his fellow co-religionists to remain quiet *"because our Greek brethren are only demanding what is their right".* It is also significant to point out that the heartiness and co-operation between Christians and Moslems in

---

[2] The burnt wooden bungalow was replaced by a stone building of outstanding beauty designed by Maurice Webb in a blend of the island's traditional styles.

Left: A local policeman (zapties) in pensive mood.
Below: Police militia on parade.

Cyprus had of late been strengthened by the complete reconciliation brought about in 1930 between Greece and Turkey which had probably convinced the Moslems of Cyprus that the union of their island with Greece would ensure the same absolute equality of political rights with the Greeks as the Moslems of western Thrace enjoyed. Articles in Turkish newspapers also expressed sympathy with the Greeks. These state of affairs alarmed the foreign policy-makers in London.

The *sixth* issue that needs brief comment is the so-called '*non-Cypriot determinant*'. The October outbreak coincided with the world's greatest social catastrophe of recent memory — the unmanageable economic depression which caused the ruin of millions. Economies were shattered, food prices rose, industrial depression multiplied unemployment and the masses of the urban labouring poor were deprived of their modest income at the very moment when the cost of living rocketed. The Cypriot not only faced this economic cataclysm but also had to endure martial law. This led to dissatisfaction, underground activity, a consolidation of political groupings and finally a further eruption. On the economic front it led to strikes and in the 1940s violence.

Some statistics of the events are well worth recording:

In the four months following 21 October the number of trials and convictions were —

Persons tried	2,952
Persons convicted	2,679
Successful appeals	0
Unsuccessful appeals	22
Appeals pending	7
Persons still on remand	304

The major offence was stealing salt: in some districts this misdemeanour accounted for around 90% of all trials. Salt was stolen because it was very expensive owing to the tax on it and an alleged shortage and because the government was piling it up to push the price even higher; moreover, government stores were easy to break into since they were generally not guarded. The next major offence was the theft of firewood from the forest. Very minor offences included the possession of firearms and entering police stations.

The official casualty figures, which are open to question, show that **30 were wounded** and **6 were killed** during the disturbances. There were also many minor injuries.

Altogether 10 **Greeks were deported.** The deportation orders were issued under the Defence (Certain British Possessions) Order in Council 1928 and the Defence of Cyprus Regulations 1931. The deportees were:

Nicodemos — Bishop of Kition

Makarios — Bishop of Kyrenia

Dionysios Kykkotis — chief priest of Phaneromeni Church, Nicosia

Theophanis Tsangarides
Theodoros Kolokasides   ] Radical Union leaders
Savvas Loizides

George Hadjipavlou
Theophanis Theodotou   ] ex-members of the legislative council

Haralambos Vatiliotis — 'Vatis'
Costas Skeleas   ] Communist Party leaders

By 6 November all had left the island on board the steamers *'Franscesco Papale', 'Thurso'* and *'Sicilian Prince'*. The list was later extended to include Evdoros Ioannides, N. Yerolakides and E. Nicolaides, who were living abroad but were henceforth barred from entering the island.

Instead of examining the causes of the mass protest and applying suitable remedies the authorities chose the easy way out — ie., repression. A stern Defence of the Realm Act (D.O.R.A.) was imposed. The legislative council was abolished — a move that was contrary to the Colonial Laws Validity Act of 1865. The press was placed under a harsh censorship; in essence newspapers could publish nothing about local conditions except what the government handed out. Moreover, between 1927 and 1933, 36 publications were prohibited.

Political parties were dissolved and on 15 August 1933, the criminal code was amended with the main object of enabling the authorities to deal effectively with the communists and with all other undesired associations. On the following day the KKK and eight other communist front organizations, including the Cyprus Relief Workers Association, were proscribed.

Trade Unions were forbidden and their members persecuted. Meetings of more that five persons were also prohibited. Municipal elections were abolished and it was only in March 1943 that the first elections were allowed to take place.

Every form of national manifestation was persecuted and other laws even restricted further the liberties of the people. Thus, a law passed in 1939 gave unlimited authority to the police "to place under arrest or banish any person who works, or is likely to work, in such a way, or who might use his relative freedom of movement, for the propagation of ideas detrimental to the defence of the state".

Finally, someone had to pay for the damage caused to government property. The Reparations Impost Law passed on 21 December 1931 implemented the decision that destroyed property estimated at just over £34,000 (around £6,000 was levied on villages) should be duly replaced and repaired. The orthodox community immediately paid up — a tax on land easily recouped the amount demanded.

Briefly, these restrictive measures — the famous 27 *'illiberal laws'* enacted between 1931 and 1937 — did not crush but on the contrary exacerbated the feelings of the inhabitants. Political activity which was driven underground was canalised into a multitude of forms, such as professional and cultural bodies, literary and scientific societies, sports organizations, peasants and workers associations and producer's organizations.

The Cypriot scene of the 1930s was without doubt dominated by six main issues:

(1) A milder enosis agitation fortified by the extension of cultural, social and academic activities. Open agitation for union gradually died down but it was kept alive more by persons and organizations outside the island that from within it. In Greece, the *Cyprus Central Committee, the Cypriot Students' Brotherhood* and other organizations were working very hard for the enosists' cause. In the USA the *Pan-Cypriot Brotherhood of America,* often protested against the suspension of human rights and liberties and demanded amongst other things the abolition of the penal code, the defence and education laws and an end to press censorship. Of particular importance were the activities of Cypriots living in London. The *London Cypriot Committee* formed in 1932, was broadened and renamed the *Committee for Cyprus Autonomy* in 1936; it finally became known as the *Cyprus Affairs Committee* in 1943. It centred its activities on the labour movement and the House of Commons. It dealt not only with the national issue, enosis or self-government, but

with economic problems and with questions concerning civil rights and liberties.

The press outside Cyprus was also vociferous on the side of the islanders and their quest for a more liberal and just regime. Articles in British journals such as the *Economist* and the *New Statesman and Nation* not only urged the initiation and passage of reforms but also the cession of Cyprus to Greece. The *Times Educational Supplement* of 20 August 1932 and another article in *The 19th Century and After* in 1934, were also pro-Hellene and pro-reform. The latter in fact, advocated inter alia the exchange of Argostoli for Cyprus.

In the island itself the general lull was broken on several occasions by a variety of events and by the activities of certain individuals. Heading the list was **Leontios Leontiou,** Bishop of Paphos, who throughout his career, and especially as locum tenens during the vacancy of the archiepiscopal see (1933-1947), was the most persistent and irrepressible of all unionists and a man who threw himself heart and soul into his work. He did not follow the other bishops into exile because at the time of the October *'rising'* he was Archbishop Lang's guest at Lambeth in London. He was not allowed to land in Limassol on 13 November 1931 and he proceeded instead to Constantinople. Yet, he was promised a safe return on the condition that he signed an undertaking to abstain from political activities. The Bishop refused to bind himself in such a way but pursuent to the governments decision to treat agitation for union with Greece as sedition, he was allowed to return. Following the warm welcome given to Leontios on his arrival in June 1932, he plunged into his self-appointed role as leader and demanded union and only union. His actions caused the authorities to retaliate and court prosecutions were served with great rapidity.

The activities of Leontios had attracted the attention of the Athenian press — also that of London and the USA. In Greece all forms of national manifestation were seized upon and discussed in great detail. However, the imposition of a dictatorship in 1936 by General John Metaxas resulted in much less publicity and projection of the unionist cause.

There were also the customary delegations to London. The one of 1937 consisting of D.N. Demetriou OBE, for many years member of the executive council and mayor of Larnaca, G.S. Vasiliades, member of the advisory council and deputy mayor of Larnaca and John Clerides, a lawyer of considerable reputation, returned to Cyprus empty-handed and proceeded to explain their actions in the newspaper *'Eleftheria'*. Its issue of 19 September also included other articles on

Above: The Cyprus Railway. For years the line run from the port of Famagusta to the copper-pyrites region of Karavostasi (Bay of Morphou). It ceased functioning in 1951.
Below: Local competition of ponies—Pissouri Fair 1936.

the same question. As a result the proprietor's permit was suspended for three months.

In 1938 the Colonial Office received another prominent Cypriot — Dr Themistoclis Dervis OBE, mayor of Nicosia, who had an interview with J.B. Williams, a senior official, on 19 October. In addition to the more usual demands, Dervis pleaded for the introduction of more representative institutions and also that clemency should be granted to Theodotou, one of the deportees who was 78 years of age and suffering from arteriosclerosis. In fact Theodotou was allowed to return on 31 December 1939.

Delegations, petitions and other forms of expression had a three-fold target: A commission of some repute to investigate British misgovernment; the restoration of constitutional liberties and ultimately enosis, and an improvement in the economic position of the impoverished inhabitants.

(2) The economic situation created a lot of ill-feeling between different sections of the island's socio-economic stratum and between the entire population and the government. Very briefly, according to the official statistics of the Land Registration Department (covering the interwar period) 18,000 mortgaged properties were sold and 19,500 judgements were given for the forced sale of property which was not mortgaged. The owners consequently remained landless and were obliged to become mineworkers at ridiculous wages, to emigrate or simply to starve.

High taxes were still the rule and had resulted in a serious reduction in the purchasing power of the people. Moreover, the bulk of this enormous taxation fell on the poorer classes, since around 4/5 was indirect (on goods purchased) and only 1/5 direct (on income). This anomaly and excessive taxation in general was regularly pinpointed as being unjust and immoral. With the world slump of the late 1920s early 1930s adding further distress, workers were forced to go on strike for long periods to defend their rights. In the first six months of 1939 a cross-section of employees ranging from blacksmiths to carpenters, tailors and bakers in the Nicosia, Limassol and Famagusta districts went on strike. Some demands were met others were not. The Cypriot working class was ready to explode. Sir Ronald Storrs aptly remarked[3] that *"economic duress is the agitator's meat and the peasant's poison..."* The government was simply reluctant to promote the welfare of the islanders. However, of great importance, to the island's working force was the emergence, following pressure

---

[3] Orientations. 1945. Page 503

Above & Below: Two local pre-war scenes in Nicosia. That above at the Square of the Central Courts. The one below by the entrance of Ledra Street.

from Britain, of trade unions. Legislation permitting the formation of unions was enacted in 1932 by which such bodies, if accepted, could register with the newly created office of the Register of Trade Unions. This and other laws passed on 1941 were largely based on British trade union legislation. Such growth, as seen from the table below, was bound to be reflected in a much greater economic involvement. And, so it was.

	Members	Number of Unions
1932	84	1
1940	3,389	62
1944	10,694	90

(3) The lack of representative institutions was another issue which caused trouble for the authorities. Following the abolition of the legislative council the governor proceeded to set up an advisory body in October 1933. It was established on an informal basis *"to enable the government to keep itself informed of the views and feelings of the community"*. Five prominent Cypriots of whom four were Greeks (three were merchants and landowners and the other a leading advocate) and one a Turkish doctor, were invited to form this council. However, it must be said that due to its composition and limited terms of reference it was highly inefective. The governor, once more, was omnipotent. The feelings or views of the community were totally disregarded. This was a grievance of the greatest magnitude that needed to be tackled. Storrs once more remarked that *"alien rule is not easy to bear, save by the lowest savages..."*[4]

(4) Another prominent issue of the 1930s was the archiepiscopal question. We have already noted the fundamental change in the relationship between the autocephalous Greek Orthodox Church of Cyprus and the state as a result of the British occupation of 1878. Similarly, the crisis in the Church between 1900 and 1910 has already been documented earlier. In the 1930s there was another crisis.

The death from pleurisy at the age of 74 of the peace-loving **Kyrillos**

---

[4] Ibid. Page 477.

III on 16 November 1933, left Cyprus once more without an archbishop. Leontios Leontiou, the bishop of Paphos was unable, owing to the absence from the island of the two other bishops (exiled in 1931), to proceed to the election of a successor. Consequently Leontios, as locum tenens, became the de facto head of the Church of Cyprus. However, when the bishop of Kition died in Jerusalem on 13 September 1937, a renewed agitation developed in the press and elsewhere about the vacant archiepiscopal see.

The government hurriedly passed four laws[5] which attempted to deal with this problem. In essence they struck at the very roots of Cypriot orthodoxy and independence and alienated the clergy even further. The laws approved in 1937 (forming part of the 27 *'illiberal'* laws passed between 1931 and 1937) dealt a heavy blow to the Church. Furthermore, they provoked the resentment even of those Cypriots who were normally little endeared towards their church. Plans for an election were shelved in 1939 with the outbreak of the Second World War. Eventually, the above laws were repealed in 1946 and the first elections since 1916 were held in 1947. The winner was Leontios Leontiou who became archbishop on 20 June. Being a chronic diabetic he died of typhus on 26 July and Makarios II, Myriantheus, succeeded him.

(5) The behaviour of the Turkish element also deserves some comment. As already observed and apart from isolated minor clashes, relations between the two communities were very cordial. Even when Greece and Turkey were at loggerheads on several occasions since 1878, the two sides in Cyprus behaved well towards each other. During the First World War when Turkey was not on the side of the allies and during the Asia Minor fiasco of the early 1920s, there were no outbreaks of violence. Moreover, during the disturbances of 1931 the Moslems did not connive in any way with the authorities against the Greek demonstrators. As already observed a manifesto was issued supporting the activities of *"our Greek compatriots"*. In addition, the Graeco-Turkish reconciliation of the early 1930s greatly strenghened the goodwill and co-operation between the Greeks and Turks of Cyprus. Nevertheless, the activities of extremist national leaders on

---

[5] Dealt with the investigation of the affairs and auditing of accounts of churches and monasteries in certain cases; elections to the archiepiscopal see; control of the actual election and acceptance of the person elected as archbishop.

both sides caused some concern and on several occasions the authorities took precautionary measures to avert possible trouble. Such fears however, never materialised.

Even so the island's deplorable economic situation in the 1930s and Turkish nationalist propaganda convinced some that Turkey held better prospects for them. Events were to prove the opposite. Those who opted[6] for Turkish nationality and actually left the island soon found that Turkey did not prove congenial enough for them. Many returned disappointed and impoverished. However, the spread of *'Kemalism'* continued and it was directed in the mid-1930s by the Turkish consul in Cyprus and by certain other individuals. The governor was alarmed and he reported to London that the consul had become *"the focus of all that is disloyal amongst the younger Turks"*. Moslem leaders such as **Munir Bey** [7] were incessantly attacked as being too pro-British. Turkish nationalism especially amongst the young, was certainly on the ascendancy by the late 1930s. Like communism, *'Kemalism'* was considered by the authorities as being mischievous but as yet not alarming.

(6) In 1938 the situation in Cyprus was further complicated by the spread of Italian, Jewish and German propaganda. The Italians used all means available to spread Fascist influences in Cyprus. The Zionists, according to the governor, considered Cyprus as being part of the *'Land of Israel'* and were constantly trying to get a footing on the island similar to that which they had already obtained in Palestine. This Jewish objective was well understood in Cyprus and viewed with concern. German propaganda was more subtle and a fair number of converts were secured. A broadcast from Paris on 5 January 1939 announced that a speech had been made in Berlin on the subject of Cyprus to the effect that Germany had realized that the Cypriots were a noble and ancient people who had long desired to rejoin Greece but were being kept under harsh rule by the British government. The authorities in Cyprus clamped down hard on clear-cut adherents of the German ideology.

Following the war hysteria of 1939 all issues of the 1930s receded,

---

[6] As provided by article 21 of the 1923 Treaty of Lausanne. Only around 2,500 out of the 9,000 who actually opted to move to Asia Minor, left Cyprus.

[7] Often described by Storrs as "the indispensable and permanent 'Ataturk' of Cyprus".

albeit temporarily, into the background. The Second World War cast a heavy shadow on all of them. On 1 September 1939 Germany invaded Poland and two days later Britain and France declared war on Germany. The war years between 1939 and 1945, were crucial for the Cypriots and their aspirations.

A typical Cypriot face depicting a rural farmer who toiled for hours to maintain the traditions and lifestyle of the family unit and village.

(iv) The War Years 1939-1945.

Twenty-one years after the end of one major confrontation Europe was embroiled into yet another — more brutal, more devastating and with much wider repercussions. The strategic value of Cyprus and therefore the strength of the British garrison, the overall contribution of Cypriots to the war effort of the Allies and enemy attacks on Cyprus are all issues that need some comment.

From the word go the French were anxious to use Cyprus as an advance base for aircraft on seaward patrols, especially towards the Italian-held Dodecanese Islands, and for giving depth to the air defences of Beirut. The British, on the other hand, did not wish Cyprus to grow into a defensive commitment involving forces that could ill be spared. They agreed however, that the airfields of Nicosia and Larnaca should be improved and that refuelling and rearming facilities should be installed and made available to the French. Moreover, the British garrison had been increased from one company to one battalion and permission was granted to the French to send a contingent to the island. The 50th British Division worked on the defences of Cyprus and stayed until October 1941 when it was replaced by the 5th Indian Division which had been in Iraq. The British presence was lessened in 1942 because it was deduced that the chances of being attacked by the enemy were substantially reduced. The British reasoning was calculatively simple — Cyprus should be denied to the enemy although greater troop emphasis should be given to holding the northern flank ie., Syria. Winston Churchill, in a personal telegram to Menzies, the Australian Prime Minister dated 9 June 1941 confirmed[1] that it was not possible to hold Cyprus without having control of the Syrian airfields. In fact, in October 1943 the army personnel in the island totalled 10,500 of which 1,500 were British, 6,000 Indian and 3,000 Cypriot.

What about the enlistment of Cypriots and their contribution to the war effort of the Allies? Cypriot applications to join the British Army and Royal Navy in 1938-39 were refused due to 'regulations' but approval was given in September 1939 for the formation of a Cyprus Regiment. Recruitment proceeded briskly and the first 250 recruits were sent direct to Egypt to be equipped, clothed and trained as motor transport drivers. To meet an urgent demand for mule transport and,

---

[1] PREM 3/113. Page 42.

in view of the good work done by Cypriot civilian muleteers during the First World War, it was decided to form two Pack Transport Coys from the next 700 men enlisted. To December 1944 the Cypriot contribution (in manpower) was as follows.

	Cyprus Regiment (CR)	Cyprus Volunteer Force (CVF)
Enlistments ¹ts	11,447	4,431
Discharges	2,591	2,658
	8,856	1,773

Of the above, 6,830 and 451 respectively, served out of Cyprus. In addition around 20,000 had been continuously employed by the military authorities on defence works in Cyprus. Moreover, some 4,500 were employed in the civil defence services on a compulsory part-time unpaid basis. And, up to December 1940 around 1,200 enlisted for the Royal Greek Forces and approximately 200 women for the Greek Red Cross. The two latter statistics alarmed British officials; protests through the proper diplomatic channels ensured that by the end of February 1941 such recruitment had virtually ceased.

As in 1914, the total war contribution of Cyprus was massive. Statistics for 1942 reveal that around 10% of the island's population of approximately 420,000 was actively engaged in some capacity or other in the war effort. If only those between the ages of 18 and 32 are included then the percentage is well over 50% — a phenomenon beyond question[2]. The Cypriots were the first colonial troops to take an active part in war operations against Germany and her allies and their gallantry was evident on all fronts. The Cypriot muleteers, doing much of their work by night covered country impassable by wheeled vehicles. In rugged country they stood up to discomfort and cold extremely well. The sick rate was very low and they gained a reputation for the cheerful execution of their duties under all conditions.

Cypriots took part in the historic Dunkirk evacuation of 29 May to 4 June 1940, where they were ordered to destroy their mules — an

---

[2] In addition, around 5,000 Cypriots living in the UK, Egypt, the USA, Greece and Australia, also served with British forces.

order which they very reluctantly carried out. Then they took part in the Abyssinian campaign in 1941 where the successful conclusion of the battle for Keren (situated 4,000 feet above sea level), was greatly helped by the ability of Cypriot pack transport companies to supply units under fire in the most inaccessible places. The presence of these companies shortened the siege by weeks and this campaign in itself justified the formation of the Cyprus muleteers.

The Cypriot presence was also seen during the Italian campaign of 1944. They took part in the battle for Arezzo, the attack on Florence, the advance to the Arno Valley and in the final capture of Faenza. Furthermore, at the battle for Monte Cassino (February to May 1944) the toughest spot and perhaps the most crucial in Italy, Cypriots once more distinguished themselves on its rugged slopes by bringing up supplies and taking down the wounded under a hail of enemy bullets and shells doubled in intensity by the splintering rock. A close scrutiny of foreign and colonial office files for the period reveals that without the untiring help, hard work and devotion of the Cypriot muleteers many of the operations successfully carried out in Italy would either have taken much longer or perhaps would not have been undertaken at all.

Cypriots also served in Egypt, the Sudan and under Lord Wavell in Libya and Palestine. Above all the Cyprus Regiment fought many a bloody contest with the enemy and covered itself with glory on Greek soil. In fact, of the 2,500 or so Cypriot soldiers who were in Greece and Crete some 2,000 were lost — the vast majority becoming prisoners of war. The fall of Crete in 1941 sent fears around Cyprus. It was widely believed that the island was going to be the next prey of the Axis powers. Hitler's losses however were very high. The Cretan resistance upset the schedule of further German offensives. It meant that the opening of the Russian front had to be set back at least another week. In view of the early Russian winter of 1941 this unplanned – for delay deprived the Germans of good campaigning weather just when they needed it most. The experience in Crete made the Führer super-cautious and distrustful of all future airborne operations. Consequently, when it was forcibly suggested that Cyprus should follow Crete in order to provide a jumping-off ground for an air and paratroop attack on the Suez Canal, the proposal was shelved. The Germans, although not yet on the defensive, were certainly losing the offensive.

The Axis powers therefore, did not make any attempt to capture the island even though it served as an invaluable supply and relief station for the Allies. However, it was raided on numerous occasions by the Italians and by other unidentified aircraft. The Axis powers were masters of camouflage and flags of all of them were seen on their aircraft by the islanders. It is highly probable that the famous German 'Junkers' (or dive bombers) with a radius of action of up to 1,500 miles may have been used for attacks on Cyprus using the Italian-held airfields of Rhodes. The Italians probably used the twin-engined 'Savoia' bombers.

The year 1940 was relatively quiet. In July, aerial activity was on the increase but the aircraft were too high for identification. On 22 September, hostile aeroplanes raided the mining port of Xero. Damage was slight. The attacks of 1941 were much more severe. A raid by 8 Italian aircraft on 15 May gave Cyprus its first real taste of bombing. Nicosia, and villages such as Dhavlos and Neokhorio were hit. June was even more severe and more damaging. Paphos, Nicosia airport, Xero and Lemba were hit. In Nicosia, one stick of bombs fell near the cookhouse of the Royal Foresters killing five men and wounding fifteen — two of which later died in hospital.

The attacks in July 1941 were by far the worst. Bombs were dropped at Famagusta, Wolseley Barracks in Nicosia, Larnaca, Nicosia airport and Morphou. Damage was extensive and deaths totalled around ten.

Air attacks on Cypriot landing grounds and harbours although fairly constant were on a small scale and mainly carried out by Italian aircraft based in the Dodecanese. It must be added however, that enemy submarines were lurking around Famagusta harbour and mines were laid at its entrance. Thus, the steamtug 'Alliance' struck a mine and sunk on 29 April 1942. The captain and two of the crew were killed and five were injured.

During the last three years of the war Cyprus experienced peaceful times. Although unidentified aircraft were seen over Cyprus the enemy, under the secret operational code 'Ape A', desisted from further attacks on the island. The threat of a serious raid or an invasion never materialised. The desire for enosis or more representative government and the state of the economy caused more trouble for the authorities. Very briefly, it must be emphasised that most of those Greek Cypriots who fought against the Axis powers risked their lives in the naive view that Britain would reward them after the war by granting union with Greece — the eternal British ally. L.A. Karaphodias, a poet of some local respectability, captured quite succintly the character of the freedom-loving islanders:

Above: 1943. Churchill during a brief visit to Cyprus was welcomed by the keeper of the Archbishop's throne.—Leontios Leontiou.

Below: The first platoon of Cypriot volunteers pose before being posted abroad.

Going to fight for the cause of freedom
To protect you all from our barbarian enemies
To victory against the wild beasts
To victory with Greece and Britain

However, certain elements in Cyprus (a tiny minority), formed the '**Turkish National Party**' (a loose and extremely ephemeral organization), and showed some signs of favouring Germany: they believed that a British victory would eventually lead to enosis whereas the Germans, if victorious, would consider their own and Italian interests and would also wish to placate Turkey. Yet, Greek and Turkish Cypriots lived in the same quarters, fought side by side in many battlefields, were both mentioned in war despatches for their gallantry and were both duly rewarded by the granting of military medals. Thus, private I. Theodoulou received the Distinguished Conduct Medal and the Military Medal was given to sergeant I. Mustafa, corporal O. Shukri and to privates P. Constantinou and T. Georgiou.

As always however, the Greekness of the Cypriots was seen and portrayed everywhere. Enosis was an ideá fixe and its attainment the natural aspiration of the islanders[3]. The war years provided further opportunities to express this ideal. Petitions and memorials were once more regularly transmitted to the British authorities: wider political representation and ultimately union were always at the forefront of their demands.

During the first year of the war there appeared a new welcoming phenomenon for the unionist adherents. Following the heroic Greek resistance to Italy after October 1940, a '*Greater Greece*' movement gained ground. This was reflected in many Colonial Office minutes for 1941 and was indirectly aided by the anti-British comments of several Athenian newspapers, such as the '*Proia*' and '*Hestia*'. The enosis ascendancy of 1941 was helped by several important pronouncements:

1. Winston Churchill's message[4] to the Greek Premier Em-

---

[3] See CO 67/327/16
[4] October 1941 — on the first anniversary of Italy's attack on Greece.

manuel Tsouderos implied that when the war ended *'Pan-Hellenism will be at its peak'*.

2. The *'Joint Declaration'* of President Roosevelt and Churchill known as the **Atlantic Charter** of 14 August 1941. The two world leaders announced that they desired to see no territorial changes that did not accord with the freely expressed wishes of the peoples concerned and that they respected the right of all peoples to choose the form of government under which they would live.

The Cypriots rejoiced and, as a memorandum by the Royal Institute of International Affairs stated in 1941, *"there seems little reason to doubt that the demand for union will grow rather than diminish"*. Freedom of speech and assembly, the legalization of political parties and economic assistance were also demanded by the islanders.

3. On 2 June 1941 the War Cabinet discussed the future of Cyprus. Two documents, one from Lord Moyne and the other from Anthony Eden[5] were before it on that date. Eden's memorandum [6] emphasised that *"quite apart from the necessities of the present crisis, there is a strong prima facie case for ceding Cyprus to Greece, subject to safeguards after the war.."* The Royal Institute of International Affairs also stressed that Britain's interests would best be served by such a cession before the end of the war or at whatever moment promised the greatest political advantage.

The War Cabinet concluded that it was best that the future of Cyprus should be discussed with the Greek government after the war as part of the general peace settlement.

Enosist aspirations showed a fluctuating trend in 1943. On 31 January, Churchill visited the island for the third time. In his address to the island's leading personalities he pointed out that when the war was over the *"name of Cyprus will be included in the list of those who have deserved well.."* This gave new hope to the island's Greeks who believed that questions of territorial readjustment were to be settled after the war. Consequently, at the municipal elections of 21 March all candidates freely gave

---

[5] Respectively, Secretary of State for the Colonies and Foreign Secretary.
[6] See FO 371/29846/198

undertakings to advance the cause of enosis and public celebrations of all kinds were taken as an excuse for demonstrations in favour of union.

On 31 March however, Lord Faringdon who often spoke in glowing terms about Cyprus, suddenly expounded the theory, in a House of Lords debate, that Cyprus was not really a part of the ancient classical Greek world and that only British mismanagement provided the strength to the movement in favour of enosis. He pleaded that Cyprus should become a self-governing Colony within the British Empire. Cypriot aspirations were dented even further when in the same debate, the Duke of Devonshire, Parliamentary Under-Secretary of State for the Colonies, expounded his theory of the two pitfalls. He warned the government not to be complacent and the opposition to be on their guard and to avoid making the mistake of readily believing that a very limited number of agitators, not perhaps very responsible persons, really represent the aspirations of a nation rightly striving to be free.

The two speeches evoked a cascade of telegrams from Cyprus – the majority addressed to the Prime Minister. Associations and newspapers outside Cyprus were also annoyed; the American 'Atlantis' and 'National Herald' were especially vociferous. Moreover, 'The Pan-American Committee on the Cypriot National Question' was set up in New York to co-ordinate activities and to work towards achieving the ultimate Cypriot goal.

Other reports also spoke in favour of union. One in particular is worth a brief mention. A Foreign Office memorandum[7] in 1943, deduced that there were three areas in which Greece would claim territory beyond its 1939 frontiers. In order of importance they were the Dodecanese, Southern Albania (Northern Epirus) and Cyprus. The Greek claim on Cyprus it said rested on two arguments: First was the offer of 1915. The other argument was the ethnic one that 4/5 of the population of the island was Greek. Others argued that the eventual cession of Cyprus to Greece would be an act of generosity and wisdom.

---

[7] See FO 371/37248/9151.

ove: A group of Prisoners of War
Germany. Amongst them, pointed
h an arrow is Mr Glafkos Clerides
o later became, and still is, a
minent politician.

ht: One of many Cypriot women
o joined the R.A.F. (Mrs Stella
iliotou who later became
orney General of the Republic).

posite page shows Cypriots in the
tish Army.

p: Inspection of a Cypriot Unit.

ddle: Recruits on parade.

wer: An inspection parade by the
vernor of Cyprus.

The visit of Sir Cosmo Parkinson[8] to Cyprus on 11 August 1944 provided another opportunity for all sections of the population to put their case to him. He received delegations and heard all points of view. The question of enosis was at the forefront. Yet, Sir Cosmo explained that this was a subject he was not authorised to discuss — his mission was simply to acquaint himself with local conditions and problems.

Problems on the political front were often overshadowed by economic ones. Labour relations and the rising cost of living were thorny issues for the authorities. Cyprus suffered considerable economic disturbance on account of the war. The mines, for example, lost their principal market (Germany) and lack of shipping and the contraction of world outlets affected other industries. In order to protect their rights a wide spectrum of the Cypriot working force went on strike.

On 23 February 1940, electricians and mechanics employed in the public works department workshops went on strike and demanded higher wages, shorter hours and improved conditions. A general strike was considered but it was decided to limit it to 24 hours. Meanwhile, on 29 February, part of the labour force engaged on relief work in Nicosia left their employment and endeavoured, early in the morning, to demonstrate at the district commissioner's office. The police arrested 40 of whom 10 were subsequently released. The remainder were brought before the courts and cautioned as to their future activities.

Protests, processions and demonstrations continued right through the 1940s. In 1942 alone there were approximately 30 industrial disputes. In December, workmen employed by the government on defence and other work in Nicosia held a 10-day strike for higher pay. The workers pointed out that the cost of living index had risen to 246 from its August 1939 base of 100. A simple comparison will illustrate this alarming increase:

	1939		1942-43	
Bread per oak (=2¾ lb approx)	2	piastres	4½	piastres
Broad Beans per oke	2½-3	,,	18	,,
Potatoes per oke	1	,,	5	,,
Onions per oke	½	,,	8	,,
Eggs per dozen	3½	,,	36	,,

[8] Lately Permanent Under-Secretary of State for the Colonies. A high-ranking civil servant.

Nevertheless, following the strike seven trade unionists were sent to prison for having threatened the life of a blackleg.

The same pattern was repeated in 1943. The hub of the movement and co-ordinator in-chief was PSE, the **Pan-Cypriot Trade Unions Committee,** under which the union movement was finally united in 1940. Protest strikes and processions were the rule of the day. One such manifestation occurred on 25 October when there were simultaneous processions in Nicosia, Limassol and Larnaca. Since a permit was not granted these protests were contrary to the law of 1932: 8 persons were arrested in Nicosia, 16 in Larnaca and 12 in Limassol. Some were fined, cautioned or sentenced to terms of imprisonment.

Attempts by the authorities to set up cost-of-living advisory boards, composed of trade union and producers' representatives and government officials, never got off the ground. The chief problem appeared to have been their very limited terms of reference.

The year 1944 also witnessed the same pattern of strikes. On 1 March about 1,800 government labourers and craftsmen employed mainly on military projects, struck for an increase in wages. On 13 March they were joined by 5,000 men who struck in sympathy for one day, thus bringing military and government works almost completely to a standstill. Apart from demonstrations on 19 March in the towns of Larnaca and Famagusta, where it was necessary for the police to use batons and firehoses to disperse the crowds, there was no disorder and there were no prosecutions. However, the so-called *'labourers strike'* ended on 24 May and the men returned to work early next morning following an earlier assurance that the government would carry out an enquiry into the relation between wages and the cost of living and would take into account all available evidence, including the figures which had recently been communicated to the authorities by the trade unions.

The government it may be noted, were arguing that conditions and wages were fair and that strikes during the war, in public works, were simply *'immoral'*. Employers and the Right echoed the governments thinking and were saying that strikes in wartime were not only *'wicked'* but highly *'undesirable'*. A deep-set rift between the left and the right, employers often *'assisted'* by the government, and employees, was beginning to show its ugly face. The beating-up of strike-breakers and the use of hand grenades and other offensive weapons were now in evidence. The unrest that existed was clear for everyone to see.

Even so measures to alleviate poverty were introduced by the government in the 1940s. From 1941 to March 1946 Cyprus received free grants under the Colonial Development and Welfare Act of May 1940 totalling £720.000, to be spent mainly on agriculture and irrigation, medical and education services. Also, during many industrial disputes its conciliation measures were very successful. Back-stage diplomacy also proved rewarding in settling many diputes.

GVI RI

This scroll commemorates
Flying Officer S. C. Haralambide
Royal Air Force

held in honour as one who
served King and Country in
the world war of 1939-1945
and gave his life to save
mankind from tyranny. May
his sacrifice help to bring
the peace and freedom for
which he died.

A Cypriot officer is commemorated for his services during the Second World War.

(V) 1945-1950: Old Problems, New Realities

There was great unrest in the immediate post-war years. Measures by the government to alleviate poverty were not enough. The end of the war not only brought the soldiers home but it put a halt to military employment. Thousands became unemployed and there were no unemployment benefits, old-age pensions or other welfare benefits. If no work was available then only private charity could save them from starvation. Furthermore, taxation was high and unjust and the cost of living soared. Above all, chronic indebtedness and the stranglehold of the money lender were a millstone round the farmer's neck and agriculture, the backbone of the economy, was neglected.

Education suffered the same fate. The figures below show the gravity of the situation:

	Attending
Number of children: elementary school age – 77,000	*46,926*
" " " : secondary " " – 60,000	*4,784*

The low attendances, 61% and 8% respectively, show that the Cypriot youngster, as in the England of Dickens' Oliver Twist, had to find work and receive next to nothing or toil in the fields for ten to fifteen hours a day to supplement the meagre family income. For most peasant families the alternative was starvation.

The figures above relate to 1938 and 1939; for several years during and after the war they were even worse, though the trend was reversed in the 1950s and 1960s.

Understandably therefore, the economic depression in Cyprus, as elsewhere throughout the world, strengthened the elements of discontent amongst the population. It is against this background that we must now examine 4 major incidents which took place in 1945-1946:

(i) The **Lefkoniko incident** of 25 March 1945. The events, which occurred in the village, exacerbated the feelings of discontent even further. It may be added that the precise consequences of this sorry tale have not, as yet, been unfolded. Very briefly, a predominantly leftist procession left the church service where they celebrated Greek Independence Day and proceeded towards the village club where further speeches were on the agenda. The villagers were suddenly stopped at the bridge which was directly opposite the right wing PEK (Pan-Agrarian Federation of Labour) offices and only a short distance from their ultimate destination. The jubilant villagers were then confronted by the police and, following a brief discussion as to whether a permit for the procession was granted or not, they opened fire killing a 28-year-old man, a boy of 11, injuring five seriously, of whom a man of around 45 died on 22 May, and slightly injuring six others.

The disorders as feared, did not spread to other towns or villages. Almost unanimously however, the police action was condemned; severe punishment for the culprits and repeal of legislation controlling assemblies was demanded. Although a commission of enquiry was appointed on the evening of 25 March it was decided on 31 October that the report should not be published and that the police should not be prosecuted. The credibility of the administration suffered another setback. A minute[1] by the Colonial Office dated 6 April recorded that, *"the Lefkoniko incident has unfortunately given all parties an effective stick with which to attack the government..."* The seriousness of the situation alarmed the governor who, in a telegram to his superiors in Whitehall (dated 31 March), pleaded that all possible *"diversions"* should be created so as to concentrate the attention of the public on local affairs rather than on nationalist politics. He pleaded that all grievances which tended to unite the parties *"should be eliminated"*. A programme of economic development and social welfare was urgently needed. The government made a start in 1946 when a ten-year programme of development was announced.

(ii) Within a few hours of the above telegram a second major incident took place — the **armoury theft** of 31 March was viewed with much anxiety. On the night in question, 8 brenguns, 6 pistols, 58 rifles and some 2,300 rounds of ammunition were stolen from the armoury of a Cyprus Volunteer Force station near Nicosia.

Within weeks the arms cache was found in the garden of an AKEL member and recovered almost intact. The Colonial Office immediately remarked that a new and dangerous factor had entered the Cyprus situation. Moreover, it continued, *"there is a risk of violence in the Palestinian sense under the leadership of AKEL"*[2]. This diagnosis proved baseless and utterly misleading. Nevertheless, those arrested were tried by the assizes: one man and one woman were acquitted; two were given 7 year sentences and one was found guilty under the Defence Regulation 34B and imprisoned for 12 years.

---

[1] CO 67/327/16

[2] CO 67/324/5. Minute dated 25 April.

(iii) The **Famagusta Transit Camp** incident of 8 October 1945 also caused a lot of concern. On that day Indian troops were called to the camp to get two reluctant Cypriot companies, due to be taken to either Syria or Palestine, aboard a transporter. There was absolute chaos and shots were fired killing one Cypriot sergeant and wounding six privates and one Indian soldier. The death of **Takis Kythreotis** produced quite a stir in the Island. Protests flowed into the governor from all quarters and many organisations held special meetings to consider the incident and register their disapproval. The official view that *"soft-nosed pistol bullets"* were fired from the crowd, was repudiated. The government moreover, refused to allow a full public enquiry into the incident. The Cypriots protested against further service abroad and demanded the expedition of demobilisation.

(iv) The rift between the government and the governed was widened even further by the **PSE (Pan-Cyprian Trade Unions Committee)** trial of 1945-1946. PSE was the highest directive body and was thus entrusted with the leadership and co-ordination of the activities of all the trade unions throughout Cyprus. The growth of unions can be seen from the table below:[3]

	Registered Unions	Branches	Membership
1939	46	—	2,544
1940	62	—	3,389
1941	68	—	3,854
1942	73	43	9,991
1943	84	68	9,628
1944	122	71	11,865
1945	143	78	13,394 (estimated)

Organized labour was seen as a threat by the authorities. The offices of PSE were raided and a certain amount of literature - books on Marxism etc., - was seized. PSE was procecuted and the trial began on 17 December 1945. Some of the alleged offences were:-

(1) Unlawfully conspiring to overthrow the island's constitution;

(2) Conspiring to overthrow by violence the established government;

---

[3] See Co 69/51. Due to certain variable factors, such as monthly adjustments, the official figures often portrayed a slightly different picture.

(3) Attempting to bring into hatred the lawful government; and

(4) Attempting to excite disaffection against the government.

The defence denied all 17 charges. On 21 January 1946 the trial ended. Twelve of the accused were sentenced to 18 months imprisonment and the other six to 12 months. PSE was found to be an illegal organisation, not because it was a trade union body but because it was *"a conspiracy advocating the overthrow of the government!"*. PSE was replaced by **PEO** (Pan-Cyprian Federation of Labour) in 1946.

The government was denounced as fascist and anti-working class and progressive forces in both Cyprus and Britain vowed to fight for the release of the PSE leaders. Within nine months of their imprisonment they were released. The sentencing of the accused, it may be noted, was followed by a strike on 22 January as a protest against *'unlawful brutality'*. During the so-called *'week of protest'* (September 1946) over 700 meetings were held demanding the annulment of the harsh laws and the release of the prisoners.

In 1946 there was another disturbing factor. On 15 May it was stated in the House of Commons that Cyprus might take 13,000 of the 100,000 Jewish refugees to settle in holdings. The famous **"Palestine Report"** was greeted with great dismay by the Cypriots. In the first place, it was felt that such an influx of refugees, if granted citizenship, would seriously weaken the island's Greek majority. Parallel to the above was the fear that the Zionists who considered Cyprus as being part of the *Land of Israel* were constantly trying to get a footing on the island similar to that which they had already obtained in Palestine. Secondly, at a time when the economy was undergoing a very bad time, it was felt that the provisioning of thousands of Jewish immigrants would lead to acute shortages of supplies and therefore higher prices.

Nevertheless, the attitute of the island's population was throughout the period (1946-1948) one of friendship and assistance. Many Cypriots helped in the escapes, giving shelter to the escapees and aiding them in reaching Palestine. All in all 51,000 Jewish immigrants passed through the Cyprus detention camps (**Karaolos** and **Xylotymbou),** during the $2^1/_2$ years of the camps' existence. Of these, 1,800 internees reached Palestine after escaping from the camps; 110 immigrants, including 49 children, died in Cyprus and were buried in the Jewish cemetery in Margo. Around 2,000 children were born in the camps.

Above: The Haganah ship Exodus 1942 – transporting Jewish settlers from Cyprus to Palestine.
Below: The 1948 miners strike at Mavrovouni-Xero in the Solea valley district.

Cyprus was henceforth entering a new and more difficult era. The government attempted to eliminate the *"authentic grievances"* which tended to unite the inhabitants. On 23 October 1946, Arthur Creech Jones, the Secretary of State for the Colonies, informed his fellow parliamentarians that the government had reviewed its policy on Cyprus. The so-called *"New Deal"* had arrived. He promised 4 "constructive measures":

(1) A more liberal and progressive regime would be established to run the internal affairs of the island;

(2) A vigorous programme of economic development and social welfare. The 10-year development plan estimated to cost around £6,000,000 was the government's promised messiah;

(3) Repeal of the three local laws of 1937 concerning the election of a new archbishop. The repeal was effected by Law No. 20 of 29 October 1946 and the first elections since 1916 took place in 1947; and

(4) Those exiled following the disturbances of 1931 would be allowed to return.

As already mentioned in the previous section measures to alleviate poverty and to reduce rural indebtedness were introduced in the 1940s. These however were not enough. Thus the cost of living index rose by 156% between August 1939 and December 1946 and for the same period taxes collected increased by over 400%. The typical family therefore was faced with frustrated ambitions, inescapable responsibilities and with the ever-growing grind of poverty. The years to 1950 therefore were dominated by bitter strikes:

The **miners' strike** at Mavrovouni-Xero in the Solea Valley district which lasted for 124 days, proved to be the most bitter of the three major strikes of 1948. The others being the Amiandos asbestos mines and builders' strikes. These confrontations revealed the Cypriot working class as a well-organized and militant force.

Apart from the economic issue the authorities were faced with other problems which led to recrimination and ill-feeling. Some general observations will suffice.

(a) The Dodecanese Islands were ceded by Italy to Greece in 1946. The island's Christian inhabitants concluded that they were next in line to join the motherland.

(b) Following the passage of the historic resolution of 28 February 1947, the Greek government had for the first time formally associated itself with the movement for union, though in terms courteous to Britain. Greece it should be noted, depended economically and militarily on Britain in the 1940s. Finding the financial strain too heavy, Britain asked the USA to take over. After 1947 Greece became virtually an American *'protectorate'*. Such dependence necessarily impaired the sovereign actions of the Hellenic government.

(c) By 1948 many parts of the British Empire were being granted independence — Transjordan in 1946, India and Pakistan in 1947, Burma and Ceylon (now Sri Lanka) in 1948. Cypriot hopes were raised once more.

(d) The growth of nationalism in the Middle East had slowly eroded the Anglo-French position there — new sovereign states were springing up.

(e) The Atlantic Charter of 1941 and The Universal Declaration of Human Rights approved by the United Nations General Assembly in 1948, gave new hope to subject peoples. Cypriots constantly quoted them to justify their struggle for ultimate union.

(f) After the war the Cyprus *'movement'* was firmly supported by the Greeks of the diaspora. London, Athens and America provided massive support for the islanders. In the latter country the million or so Greeks, lead by **A.H.E.P.A.** and other organisations, were just as anxious to see Cyprus restored to the motherland as were the Greeks in Europe or the Greek Cypriots themselves.

(g) Apart from relying on emotional factors the Cypriot politicians concentrated on economic and social problems, pointing out to the people that they had nothing to lose materially by ending the British connection.

(h) The Ethnarchic Council was expanded in 1945 to include laymen, and with archiepiscopal elections imminent, a church – dominated national delegation arrived in London at the end of December 1946 to put their case for union with Greece. The delegation travelled by way of Athens arriving there on 16 November; they met most of the Greek political leaders and were received by the King on 4 December. The public and the mass media expressed their unanimous support for the delegations' ideals. In London they met Creech Jones on 7 February 1947. He listened very carefully but in the end he replied that *"no change in the status of the island was contemplated"*. and implied that self-government at that juncture *"will be viewed more favourably"* by the authorities.

(i) Towards the close of the 1940s the forces of the left joined in earnest the rightwing chorus for enosis and for a time took the initiative. The left via the National Co-operation Front, rationalised its support for union with 'Monarcho-Fascist' Greece by stating that this was the first step towards the liberation of the Greek people from Anglo-American imperialism. In furtherance of its objective a memorandum was sent to the Security Council and General Assembly of the United Nations on 21 November 1949 requesting that a plebiscite should be held in Cyprus, under U.N. supervision, if there was the slightest doubt of the entire Greek population's desire for enosis. The mayors of Limassol, Larnaca, Famagusta and Morphou and seven leftist leaders signed this memorandum.

(j) *"Political immaturity"*, *"a weak island unity"*, *"centralisation of power"*, all powerful arguments put forward by the authorities against national self-determination were not present in the late 1940s to the same extent as in earlier years. In fact, power was more fairly shared: the enlargement of the Ethnarchic Council to include laymen was well received; political parties multiplied by the late 1940s; daily and weekly newspapers in Greek, Turkish and English abounded and literary magazines also made their appearance; the most important of which was the monthly **'Kypriaka Grammata'** (Cypriot Letters).

Also of great significance was the formation of the Society of Cypriot Studies in 1936 by leading intellectual figures of the island who vowed to collect, study, preserve and publish historical and linguistic material and study popular art in all its aspects. Its annual publication **'Kypriakai Spoudai'** (Cypriot Studies) has proved invaluable not only to students but to researches as well.

Elementary and secondary education had also shown great strides. According to the census of 1911 only one Cypriot in four could read and write. By 1950 illiteracy was rare even in the remotest

Poverty-stricken Cypriots: The picture shows the interior of a two-roomed village house which was used for cooking, eating and sleeping.

villages. According to Lord Winster *"Cypriots, above all, had great intellectual ability"*. This and other similar statements go a long way in proving that during the entire British administration the Cypriots were not given the opportunity to try their political merits and faculties. They were certainly fully equipped to run their own affairs and decide their own future.

Enough has been said above concerning the enosis upsurge of the late 1940s. Citing six main reasons Whitehall refused to entertain such a union:

(1) Cypriots were not yet ready to run their own affairs. This has already been explained and refuted above.

(2) Greece, which was just recovering from the dual catastrophies of the Second World War and the Civil War, was in no position to administer fresh territories.

(3) The Greek government had not recently asked about Cyprus.

(4) Around 20% of the island's population was Turkish-speaking and their interests and wishes had to be considered.

(5) There was no other territory in the Middle East offering comparative security of tenure which was better situated than Cyprus for use as an advanced air base for the attack of vital strategic targets in southern and eastern Europe.

(6) As a matter of principle, Britain disliked giving up pieces of overseas territories. Churchill warned the House of Commons on 20 December 1946 that, *"the British Empire seems to be running off almost as fast as the American loan...."* He emphasised that this *"process of elimination had to stop"*.

The Turkish attitude over Cyprus also deserves our attention. A paper prepared by the research department of the Foreign Office and dated 3 June 1944[4] observed that since the Turkish government had evinced little interest in the Turks of Cyprus then if Britain proposed the island's cession to Greece — a friendly nation — Ankara would not object. Further references[5] by the Foreign Office confirmed the above analysis.

---

[4] FO 371/44188/9943
[5] In both 1946 and in its survey of Turkish policy in 1949

Above: Olive Oil primitively extracted.

Left: Children enjoying a ride on a donkey, the most sympathetic domestic animal in Cyprus.

Nevertheless, it is correct to say that the situation in the island was complicated by the Turkish Cypriot position which showed a noticeable change in the late 1940s. Following a large Greek demonstration in Nicosia in favour of enosis and autonomy on 3 October 1948, the **National Popular Party** of Turkish Cypriots (the predecessor of the Cyprus is Turkish Party — Kibris Türktür Parti), protested and sent telegrams to Turkey expressing its annoyance. There were student riots in Ankara and the Turkish press, but not the government, warmly supported the cause of their Cypriot brethren. This pleased **KATAK** (the Association of the Turkish Minority in Cyprus), which strongly opposed the possible cession to Greece but demanded instead that if Britain ever decided to relinquish sovereignty the island should go back to Turkey, its previous suzerain and nearest neighbour, which was in a much better position to defend it.

In 1949 the Turkish agitation against enosis grew even more intense and at a press conference in February 1949, J. Sadak the Minister for Foreign Affairs, declared in unequivocal terms that Britain would *"never"* cede Cyprus to Greece. Turkey in fact soon shifted from its role as an uninterested party and then observer and, with British prompting, became especially after 1955, the third interested party when the Cypriot question was discussed.

The period under discussion brings out another interesting observation — the American interest and concern over the Cypriot problem. In the mid-1940s and earlier, the American administration was on the whole in favour of an early and peaceful settlement in favour of Greece. By 1950 and due to the potent and volatile forces (precarious alliances, European involvement, the Communist threat, wide economic interests, the Middle Eastern situation etc.,), prevailing, the Americans revised their policy to one of being *'a benevolent observer and adviser'*. By the mid-1950s the American role was that of behind-the-scenes *'arbitrator'* and finally *'director-general'* of the whole scenario. The guidelines and the overall plans appeared to have been firmly drawn. The three NATO allies (Britain, Greece an Turkey) and finally the Cypriots themselves were left to bargain over the details.

Another observation of the period concerns the military value of the island. The situation, strategic importance and re-enforcement of Cyprus attracted much attention in the early 1940s and 1950s. The *'cold war'* had finally reached the island in 1948. Britain was construct-

The late 1940s brought a new, more cosmopolitan way of life with outings-see left-or with weddings - see above still the most popular event where the whole village is invited.

Left: People henceforth had time for outings.

Below: Family gatherings became synonymous with social occasions.

ing air bases equipped with radar and was transferring to Cyprus from Palestine (where its mandate was due to expire on 15 May 1948) a considerable number of troops, the Middle East radio monitoring service and the Arabic broadcasting station ash-Sharq al-Adna. Thus, in October, the RAF station in Cyprus was raised to the status of Air Headquarters Middle East and there were rumours that Military Headquarters Middle East would also be established there — as it duly was in 1954. In fact, once the decision had been taken to wind up the British base at Suez, Cyprus stock on the British strategic market rose to its original (1878-1882) value. The Cyprus problem therefore, assumed a new dimension. New realities brought fresh and more dangerous problems.

Finally, we must briefly discuss the problems arising out of the constitutional proposals and municipal elections. The abolition of the legislative council in 1931 and the imposition of other restrictive measures resulted in Cyprus being ruled on an undemocratic basis which was certainly repugnant to British ideals. In October 1946, it was announced that a more liberal and progressive regime would be established.

On 9 July 1947, **Lord Winster** (governor from 1946 to 1949) sent invitations to various persons and organisations to take part in a consultative assembly which would make recommendations on the form of constitution to be established. The right, turned down the invitation explaining that the acceptance of a constitution implied a tacit renunciation of their national aims. The left, after some hesitation and a good deal of deliberation decided to accept it — explaining that through self-government the island could more easily march towards enosis.

The assembly had its first meeting on 1 November but almost from the word go there were disagreements as to the interpretation of its terms of reference. Proposals for a constitution providing for self-government were ruled out. The left then submitted a memorandum to the Secretary of State in London on 24 November, requesting a constitution similar to those of Malta or Ceylon. Failure by the Colonial Office to answer the memorandum prompted a leftist deputation to visit London in February 1948. Although the delegation returned empty-handed it discussed the constitutional impasse with members of the influential Fabian Colonial Bureau which incessantly attacked the inequities of the British colonial administration.

In an attempt to break the deadlock, Whitehall issued a statement in the form of a despatch to Lord Winster on 7 May 1948 making certain proposals for constitutional reform. It was made clear at the time that it was open to the constituent assembly to recommend variations in these and other details of the proposed constitution. These proposals were published on 12 May. A limited form of home-rule was provided and proper safeguards for Britain's strategic interests were included in the proposals.

The limitations imposed and the powers reserved for the governor were sufficient to wreck the chance of acceptance by most Cypriot politicians. Nevertheless, a wholly unrepresentative chamber was reconvened on 20 May and on the following day a motion that *"it would be in the best interests of the people of Cyprus that a constitution in the form offered by HMG should be established with the least possible delay"* was carried by 11 votes to 7. Of the majority 6 were Turks, one a Maronite and 4 independent Greeks. The minority was composed of five Greek mayors of the left and two Greek trade union representatives who then announced their intention to withdraw from the constituent assembly. When they did withdraw the assembly finally lost its representative character. The chairman adjourned it *'sine die'* and the governor formally dissolved it on 12 August, stating that these or comparable constitutional proposals would be re-examined and implemented if at any time this was requested by representative leaders of the people. This offer was to remain open for the next six years until Britain announced on 28 July 1954 that a modified constitution was to be introduced. The campaign for *'self government-union'* was continued with even greater vigour. Powerful demonstrations were held in many parts of the island. A peak was reached in October 1948 when an AKEL-sponsored rally attracted a crowd of 25,000 in Nicosia.

The results of the three municipal elections of the 1940s were significant for the future activities of the various groupings. The first elections after the disturbances of 1931 were held on 21 March 1943. A middle-class enosist mayor was returned in Nicosia whilst the left won the mayor's seat and a majority in the municipal councils in Limassol and Famagusta. The elections were significant not only because of the leftist upsurge but because undertakings were freely given by candidates to advance the cause of enosis.

The next elections were held on 26 May 1946. The swing to the left continued. AKEL not only retained its hold on Limassol and Famagusta but won Nicosia and all but two of the principal towns. The following elections were held in different municipalities on four successive Sundays between 8 and 29 May 1949. On the first Sunday AKEL won seven out of the eight seats at Morphou (the largest rural municipality), but the returns of the following three Sundays showed a swing in favour of right wing candidates. The left retained control of its strongholds (the ports of Limassol, Famagusta and Larnaca) by narrow majorities but Nicosia was lost. Dervis triumphed over Clerides amid outbreaks of violence between the two rival groups as a result of which one man was killed, several injured and nearly 200 arrested.

The nationalist groups which polled around 60% of the total votes cast were now in control of 11 out of the 15 municipalities. The left though not routed was decisively beaten. AKEL explained that its failure was due to intimidation of the voters by the right, falsification of the electoral rolls by government officials and significantly, the action taken by the clergy and the Greek consul.[6] However, by 1949 both the nationalists and the leftists were wholly committed to enosis, and by 1950 the Cyprus problem entered a new and decisive phase.

---

[6] CO 67/333/7. Minute by Mary Fisher dated 27 July 1949.

(vi) 1950-1955:
The Cyprus Question is Internationalized.

A new development entered Cypriot politics in 1950. **A Church-organised Plebiscite,** intended to give free expression to the people's wishes for the island's future, was held on 15 and 22 January. Out of the 224,757 Greek Cypriots eligible to vote, 215,108 or 95.7% signed the petition for enosis. Many Turkish Cypriot, Armenian and even English names[1] could be seen alongside the Christian signatures; civil servants and government employees did not take part.

The result of the plebiscite had no effect on the British government. It accused the Church of putting pressure on the people to vote for enosis, pointing out that the archbishop on 8 December 1949 appealed for a unanimous affirmative vote. The Church countered by stating that on 12 December it had challenged the British authorities to conduct the plebiscite themselves. Moreover, leading personalities pleaded for a UN-sponsored referendum.

The archbishop officially reported the results of the plebiscite to the governor on 4 February. Replying on 22 February Sir Andrew B. Wright conveyed the message of his superiors that *"the question of enosis was closed"*. Still on offer however, were the Winster constitutional proposals of 1948. Delegations were sent abroad to enlighten both governments and people on the Cypriot question. The first one from the Ethnarchic Council visited Greece, France and Britain and then went on to Lake Success where it established contacts with delegates to the 5th UNO Assembly. **Alexis Kyrou,** the Greek permanent representative at the UN, gave them valuable assistance. The second delegation, from the AKEL-dominated National Liberation Coalition visited Britain and France and published a pamphlet called *'Cyprus Presents its Case to the World'* in English and French, which it distributed to MPs, private individuals and organizations in both countries. Other European countries were subsequently visited.

Without any shadow of doubt the two acknowledged Greek Cypriot protagonists of enosis were Makarios and Grivas. Brief biographical notes of both are not only desirable but necessary:

George Grivas, born in the Nicosia hospital on 23 May 1898, comes

---

[1] See CO67/370/90580/3.

from the village of Trikomo, around 12 miles north of Famagusta. As a youngster he won both academic and athletic awards at the PanCyprian Gymnasium. In 1916 he was admitted into the so-called *'school of the promising ones'* — the military academy of Athens —and after graduating in 1919 he took part in the ill-fated Greek campaign of Asia Minor. At the age of 26 he was promoted to captain.

During the Second World War, Grivas acquitted himself extremely well and for his services on the Albanian front he was promoted to lieutenant-colonel. During the German occupation of Greece Grivas formed his own secret organization of Royalist offices in 1943 under the name of the Greek letter 'X' *(khi)*[2]. Its twin aims were the return of the king and the neutralization of the communists who controlled the chief resistance movement.

Following a short period of inactivity, the career of Grivas entered a new phase in 1951 when he failed twice to be elected as leader of his own political organization which he founded upon 'X'. He then stood for the Greek Vouli as a populist candidate, but though the populist party and its supporters won the election with a large majority, Grivas failed miserably. Angry and bitter, he then swore that he would give up politics for ever.

Meanwhile, his attention was also focused on Cyprus and during the late 1940s he held regular discussions with people who shared his enosist aspirations. On his first post-war visit in 1951 Grivas made a thorough inspection of the entire island. Two meetings chaired by Makarios were held in Athens on 2 and 21 July 1952. The young Cypriot ethnarch had no confidence in guerrilla tactics but the opposing view prevailed and at a meeting of Grivas, S. Loizides and Archbishop Spyridon of Athens on 11 September, the last declared that *"freedom is never won without bloodshed"*.

In October 1952 Grivas was back in Cyprus and when he returned to Greece on 25 February 1953 he devoted much of his time to drawing up a comprehensive guerrilla plan which he said *"with minor modifications, acted as a general guide to my operations from start to finish of the struggle"*. In March came a fateful meeting in Athens of the political and military leaders of the Cyprus struggle. Makarios, who had just returned from New York presided, and the 12 present took an oath of secrecy and dedicated themselves to the cause of enosis. Makarios explained that only limited sabotage and not full-out

---

[2] Its supporters were called *'Khites'*.

Above: General George Grivas 'Dighenis' leader of EOKA.

Below: Archbishop Makarios Ist President of the Cyprus Republic.

From the 1950s to the time of their deaths in the 1970s, their lives symbolised everything that was Cyprus.

force was needed. Grivas recounts that for the rest of 1953 and during the early months of 1954 he faced opposition not only from Makarios but from the Greek government. However, in March 1954 the first caique (light sailing vessel) arrived from the mainland with arms and ammunition and it was followed by another in October. Grivas also recalls his meeting with Makarios on 15 February 1954, in which he detected that the young ethnarch was then very nearly ready to comply with his plans which the secret liberation committee had decided on 28 January should be put in practice as soon as possible.

Yet the final decision as to what should be done and when, was not at all clear, as was shown by the October meetings in Athens between Grivas and Makarios. The former, in his so- called *'historic mission'* resolved to return to Cyprus but, he had no visa. Consequently, he left his home on 26 October 1954 and with Socrates Loizides set sail for Rhodes. Only seven people knew of their departure. His diary for the day reads: *'God help us ... I depart with faith and courage ... I shall succeed'*.

They reached Rhodes at 3.00 pm on 27 October but bad weather delayed their departure for Cyprus. Grivas however made full use of their 12-day stay and proceeded to organize a centre from which arms could be shipped to Cyprus and made arrangements for the next delivery there. After dark on 7 November that two men boarded a small craft at Callithea Bay and finally set sail at 15 minutes past midnight. At around 8.00 pm on 10 November, the small craft arrived off the west coast of Cyprus at the quiet bay of Khloraka and the home of Azinas was to be Grivas' temporary headquarters. He moved to Nicosia towards the end of the month. At that juncture Grivas not only lacked the unqualified support of Makarios but also that of a proper set-up. He set about his task of forming an organization with unrelenting zeal.

The decisive date was 11 January 1955. Makarios, who had arrived on the previous day from America, summoned Grivas to the house of the bishop of Larnaca and there informed him that he had secured the support of Papagos, the Greek Premier, for their aims, which were still to be sabotage. It was at this meeting, and at Griva's suggestion, that the new secret organization was christened **EOKA (Ethniki Organosis Kyprion Agoniston** — National Organization of Cypriot Fighters). It replaced EMAK — The Cyprus National Liberation Front. Grivas also declared that he would not lay down his arms until Makarios told him to do so. Several days later Grivas was extremely fortunate to meet **Gregorios Afxentiou,** who soon became his trusted second-in-command. In the opinion of many Afxentiou, noted for his honesty and bravery, was to become the most revered hero of the Cypriot struggle.

Grivas was of the opinion that the *'rising'* should commence around the middle of March but Makarios preferred 25 March — the day celebrated as the beginning of the 1821 Greek Revolution. The capture of the **Ayios Georgios**,[3] bringing the third shipload of explosives into the island, meant a brief delay. However, on 29 March, Makarios gave Grivas permission to start his operations. Grivas added *'God is with us'*.

During the early hours of **1 April 1955** a series of bomb explosions wrecked government offices, police stations and military premises throughout the island. On the same day EOKA proclaimed its existence in leaflets signed *'Digenes'*[4]. This was Griva's nom de guerre in his capacity as leader of EOKA. In the course of the struggle he was also called *'Arkhigos'* (leader) and *'Apiastos'* (the one that could not be taken).

So much for Grivas. **Makarios** was born Michael Christodoulos Mouskos in the Paphos village of Panayia near the monastery of Chrysorroyiatissa. The date was 13 August 1913[5] and, while disclaiming any tendency towards superstition, he had always regarded 13 as his lucky number. In 1926 he entered Kykko monastery as a novice and took the name of Kykkotis. He stayed there for 12 years and also, from the age of 20, he attended the three top classes of the Pan-Cyprian Gymnasium. At the age of 26 he was ordained deacon and sent to the University of Athens on a scholarship to study theology and some law. He graduated in 1942 and entered the church of St Irene where he was ordained as a priest on 13 January 1946. Some months later one of the ten scholarships offered by the World Council of Churches was granted to him and in September he departed for the Methodist Theological College at the University of Boston, USA.

---

[3] It was intercepted on the night of 25-26 January by HMS Comet, a British detroyer.

[4] Digenes was a 10th century epic hero of Byzantine Asia Minor.

[5] Grivas was 15 years his senior.

On 13 June 1948 he was consecrated Bishop of Kition and following the death of Makarios II on 28 June 1950 he was elected as **Archbishop Makarios III** on 18 October. He was destined to become internationally known for his leadership of the enosis movement. The *'union with Greece'* campaign was turned by Makarios into a personal crusade. His total involvement was channelled into three main avenues:

(1) Extensive travel abroad. His aim was to win support from as many countries as possible. He visited Greece and other European countries, America and the Middle East and later other Afro-Asian states. Makarios always spoke of the need of world peace.

(2) Systematic preparations at home. Makarios' aim from the outset was to grasp the national liberation struggle initiative from all other groupings. In order to do so several organizations needed to be set up. In 1952 **PEON** *(Pan-Cyprian National Youth Organization)* and **OHEN** *(Organization of Orthodox Christian Youth)*, were set up. Then in 1954 such rightwing associations as **PEK** *(Pan-Agrarian Union of Cyprus)* and **SEK** *(the Cyprus Worker's Confederation)* were reorganized and set on firmer foundations. Moreover, the illustrated monthly magazine, *'Greek Cyprus'* which began publication in 1949 was under the Ethnarchy Bureau — later known as the *'Ministry of the Enlightenment'*.

(3) Conciliation. Like a true Aristotelian Makarios believed in striking a happy medium. Unlike some of his predecessors he did not neglect the sympathies of the left although in the first two years of the 1950s he failed to come to grips with the realities of the Cypriot class system. In fact when the Ethnarchic Council was widened to include laymen it did not form a cross-section of Cypriot society; it simply represented the Church and the higher echelons of the island's Christian community.

Although Makarios's political thinking was still in a formative stage he came to understand that the forces of the left, on both the domestic and the international scene, should not be alienated[6]. As a result of this policy, the first open and official contact took place between the young ethnarch and **AKEL**; the date was August 1954 just twelve days before the Cypriot appeal was lodged to the UN by the Greek government. The participants exchanged views on the best way

---

[6] Yet the policy of the 'national centre' (Athens) was to seek aid only from western powers.

of facing the complexities of the Cypriot problem. Certainly the archbishop could not ignore such a sizeable proportion of the island's population[7]. Although AKEL did not support EOKA's violent tactics, preferring decolonization and full independence to outright political confrontation and enosis, it did not betray its armed struggle for self-determination. Nevertheless, the British colonial administration proscribed the party in 1955.

Very briefly, the agreed strategy of the Greek Cypriots in the early 1950s was as follows:

1. The rejection of any constitutional proposals put forward by Britain.

2. The intensification of the campaign to inform the Greek people about the issues facing the Cypriots.

3. Co-ordination with liberation organizations in Greece and the preparation for an armed struggle. EOKA's campaign eventually opened on 1 April 1955.

4. The solution of the problem by the United Nations with Greek government initiative and help. It was here that Cypriot expectations, as we shall see below, foundered.

Points two and three require no special mention. Points one and four need some explanation:

After the turbulent experiences of the 1940s Greece had no choice but to steer a peaceful course. Hence the problem of the late 1940s and 1950s was that if the government came out openly in favour of enosis it would be accused by its western allies of seeking territorial gains regardless of the defence requirements of the Middle East. Thus the official Greek policy had been to express sympathy with such a desire but, in pressing for a solution, to demand only the human rights of the UN Charter including the right of self-determination. Therefore, the statement by Premier Tsaldaris in 1946 that *'the question of Cyprus is not a demand and it should not be posed in a vindictive manner because it only concerns Greece and her friend GB'* was supported, at least up to 1954, by successive Greek governments. In fact, no Greek administration could ignore the Cypriot demand for enosis. Due mainly to three factors this demand was not pressed:

---

[7] AKEL and its affiliated organizations had the solid support of around 40% of the entire Greek and Turkish electorate.

1. Greece wished to settle it within the framework of Anglo-Hellenic friendship;
2. American economic and military aid to Greece from 1947 to 1951 amounted to around 1,672 million dollars. A government that depends upon such foreign bounty necessarily surrenders its freedom of action[8].
3. From 1945 to the early 1950s Greece suffered from a succession of weak governments. The administrations of Plastiras, Voulgaris, Sophoulis and Tsaldaris soon gave way to the strong Premiership of **Field-Marshal Papagos** who won convincingly in November 1952 as leader of the Greek Rally *('Ellinikos Sinagermos')*.

Papagos was to remain PM of Greece until his death in October 1955. In 1953 he informed Sir Charles Peake (British Ambassador to Athens from 1951 to 1957), that as a solution to the Cyprus problem he proposed the granting of a liberal constitution to the island, with a plebiscite to follow within two years so as to give the people an opportunity to decide their own future. He repeated the offer of bases on Greek territory and he then advised Makarios that Greece would try to solve the Cyprus problem *'within the framework of current realities'* —in essence it was a policy of firmness and compromise best calculated to serve eastern Mediterranean security and Anglo-Greek ties.

However, public pressure and Cypriot insistence prompted Greece to take *'Cyprus to the UN'*. On 15 April 1954 Papagos decided to go ahead with the recourse to the UN and on 3 May he committed himself publicly. On 14 May it may be added, the UK through diplomatic channels again said *'no'* and on 28 July Henry Hopkinson's[9] statement of **'never'** emphatically confirmed it in public. The Greek appeal was transmitted to the UN Secretary-General on 20 August 1954 and despite much opposition from the UK the General Committee examined the Cyprus item on 23 September. For Greece, Alexis Kyrou requested that the principle of equal rights and self-determination, as defined in Article I (2) of the Charter, should be applied to Cyprus. He declared that his government would

---

[8] S. Venizelos admitted to the Greek Vouli on 12 December 1958 that it was the USA which prevented Greece in 1951 and 1952 from taking the Cypriot question to the United Nations.

[9] Minister of State for Colonial Affairs.

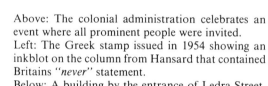

Above: The colonial administration celebrates an event where all prominent people were invited.
Left: The Greek stamp issued in 1954 showing an inkblot on the column from Hansard that contained Britains *"never"* statement.
Below: A building by the entrance of Ledra Street, place of political activities, which was used as a club and hostel.

While strikes (above) were in most cases the only avenue of obtaining better working conditions, the young were taking more interest in education, and schools became naturally, the centres of cultural revival. Below a typical class of children.

bide by the decision taken by the island's population.

Selwyn Lloyd, British Minister of State at the Foreign Office, ccused Greece of seeking to annex British sovereign territory. He ent on to warn of the danger of communal strife arising out of this ction since such a move was opposed by the Turkish community. yprus, moreover, was vital to the discharge of Britain's responsibili- es in the Middle East and under the Atlantic Treaty: *"Leases expire, eaties are whittled away, Greek governments change hence full dministrative control is necessary",* he argued. The Cyprus item was entually discussed at the very end of the Assembly's session in four eetings of the Political Committee on 14 and 15 December. On 17 ecember the General Assembly adopted resolution 814(IX) by 50 otes to none with 8 abstentions. The adopted resolution read:

> *'The General Assembly, considering that, for the time being it does not appear appropriate to adopt a resolution on the question of Cyprus, decides not to consider further the item entitled...'.*

Of vital importance were the words *'for the time being'.* The way as now open for the Cyprus question to be submitted in 1955. The nnual pilgrimage to the UN had began. The problem became an tternational issue and the Greeks were of the opinion that the UN ould deal with it. Opposition leaders however, were of the opinion hat Greece was betrayed by its allies-notably the USA. There were nti-American riots in Athens on 14 December and in Salonica two ays later. Although Papagos declared that Greece was let down by its riends **King Paul** predicted Cyprus' eventual *'reunion'* with the notherland through favourable UN action on self-determination for he islanders.

The British were adamant that they foresaw no change in the sland's status. Repeated public ministerial statements and behind – he scenes diplomatic exchanges were instrumental in projecting the *no change policy'.* Consequently on 28 July 1954 it was announced in he House of Commons that it was proposed to introduce a modified onstitution in the island — based on the 1948 proposals. The fresh nitiative was in essence intended to:

— appease but not please;

— combat the apparent emergence of communism;

— preserve Britain's strategic interests in the area; and

— emphasize once more that no change in the status of the island was contemplated.

It was also at this debate that Henry Hopkinson used the highly undiplomatic phrase ".... **can never expect to be fully independent..**"[10]

The restraint shown by Athens so far was henceforth replaced by increasing antagonism. Amongst other actions a postage stamp showing an inkblot on the column from Hansard that contained Hopkinson's *'never'* statement was hurriedly printed. In Cyprus the proposals were promptly discredited as an obstacle to enosis. On 29 July, Makarios rejected them out of hand and in a message to the people warned that no one should co-operate with the authorities in this *'constitutional conspiracy'* which aimed at prolonging the enslavement of the Cypriot people. Athens radio also called for a flat rejection of the proposed constitution. The government expressed the same view and repeated that the issue of *'self-determination for the Cypriots'* would be taken to the UN.

Opposition was also registered by various non-Greek bodies and organizations. A number of British Labour MPs, seeing that the constitution would provide a legislature made up of an elected minority and a majority composed of colonial officials and appointees, criticized the scheme because it did not allow Cyprus to leave the British Commonwealth if its inhabitants wished it to do so. The Labour Party Conference in October adopted a resolution deploring the policy of the Conservative government and urged its MPs to oppose its Cyprus policy on all occasions. Similarly, a resolution passed by the Liberal Party Council in December also demanded the granting of a more democratic constitution.

Meanwhile in Cyprus protests flowed from all sections; in August the authorities decided to enforce the anti-sedition laws. In turn there were further protests. The government reorganised and strengthened its intelligence services and by a series of local broadcasts, pamphlets and press communiqués tried to counter the enosis agitation. The two C's (confrontation and compromise) were now in direct opposition.

The decision by Greece to bring the Cyprus question before the UN meant that the problem of enosis had entered the most critical phase of its long history. Political ideology and military expedience came into sharp conflict. Even those who viewed the prospect of Greek

---

[10] 531. House of Commons. Debates. 5s Column 508.

le with deep misgivings felt that they could not let the cause down. homas Anthem a distinguished commentator of the time, pointed ut in 1954 that "rightly or wrongly, whether the Cypriots are isguided and foolish in desiring to exchange a rich step father for a oor mother of their own blood, the fact remains that Greeks verywhere, at home and abroad, are solidly behind the enosis ovement". Sir Harold Nicolson another prominent writer, in a letter The Times on 15 July 1954 explained that "even though there are everal arguments against the union of Cyprus with Greece, if tied ghtly together they make a sorry little bundle and if taken separately ey snap at once".

British unwillingness to discuss the Cyprus question with the ireek government and the eventual Greek decision to seek justice at e UN hardened Turkish opinion. The tone of the Turkish press ecame hostile and the dangers posed to NATO's[11] eastern flank ere widely discussed. In his memoirs Eden recalled that it was *'right'* at it should speak in that way *'because it was the truth that the Turks ould never let the Greeks have Cyprus'*. Eden was convinced that the yprus problem would only be resolved between the three allies — ritain, Greece and Turkey. He suggested therefore that the Turkish ress should play up the problem a bit more and thus denounce all ireek moves. In Cyprus, Turkish separatist leaders, alienated by the ireek moves for enosis and supported by the *'mother'* country, were aying that there was *'no Cyprus question'* and that Cyprus would *ever'* be annexed to Greece.

Even so the vast majority of the Moslem population accepted the ct that they were a minority and showed no strong reaction to the oves of their Christian counterparts. Even as late as 5 December 955 Ian Mikardo MP informed the House of Commons that during is visit to Cyprus, the Turks put forward the same sort of views and rguments as were put forward by minority communities living in the idst of people more numerous than themselves. Yet, as the next ction will show the harmonious relations which existed between the wo communities were replaced in the post-1955 period by onfontration and finally by separation.

) In 1952 both Greece and Turkey became members of the North Atlantic Treaty Organization. The 1953 Treaty of Friendship and Co-operation and the 1954 Treaty of Alliance bound the two countries more firmly together.

Two photographs indicative of the years 1955-1958:
Above: Student demonstrators carrying Greek flags are chased by security forces.
Below: Detainees behind barbed wire.

1955-1960:
The National Liberation Struggle and
the Polarization of the two Communities.

The stage was set for a confrontation. EOKA made its first
•pearance on the Cypriot scene with acts of sabotage in the districts
Nicosia, Larnaca and Limassol. Damage to government property
r the first night's incidents (31 March to 1 April) was estimated to be
ound £56,000, most of which was to broadcasting equipment. 21
ople were arrested. For over three years a fierce battle raged
tween EOKA and nearly 30,000 British soldiers for the *control* of
e island.

The guerrilla movement was seen as a chance to fight not only for
itional freedom but for social justice. Although EOKA was almost
tirely a right-wing nationalist-led movement it had a proletarian
ise because it was seen to be carrying on an anti-imperialist struggle.
ence under the banner of national freedom EOKA was able to weld
gether vast sections of the working peasantry with the higher strata
' Greek Cypriot society and the Orthodox Church in a struggle for
itional self-determination. Turkish nationalism however was
·glected. Many Greeks were under the illusion that it was not so
:nuine, passionate or long-standing as theirs but was expressed in the
.treme policies of Dr. **Fazil Kütchük, Rauf Denktash** and a few other
·ehards. Turkish nationalism did exist but it was neither so active nor
· well controlled as its Greek counterpart. Kütchük was chairman of
ıe **'Kibris Türktür Parti** (Cyprus is Turkish Party), which propagated
ιe theory that self-determination for Cyprus would result in the
ınihilation of all Turks, civil war and ultimately total unrest in the
liddle East. EOKA had no reason to attack and antagonize the
loslem inhabitants and in July 1955 issued a Turkish leaflet assuring
ıe island's Turks that it was struggling not against them but against
ritish colonialism, that EOKA's feelings towards them were friendly
ıd that it was expecting them to be its allies. Its fighters had specific
ıstructions not to antagonize them; yet it was short-sighted to ignore
ıe possibility that Britain would encourage such a reaction from
urkey.

These were the realities facing Cyprus in 1955. Alas there were no
atesmen to make the proper appraisal and act accordingly. The
ritish continued to make half-hearted attempts to reach a political
:ttlement while still pursuing their so-called *'primary task of restoring*
tw and order'. Consequently on 15 July 1955 a Detention of Persons

Law, similar to the severe British Defence Regulation 18B, w
decreed. **Kurt Waldheim,** for years Secretary-General of the U
explains the events that followed:

> "To find a way out of the impasse, the British government, in
> June 1955, invited Greece and Turkey to discuss the future of
> the island. Internationalizing the problem, however, led to
> new complications. The Turkish government, under Prime
> Minister Menderes, based its claim to co-determination in
> Cyprus on arguments that are still presented today, namely,
> the security of Turkey, whose coastline is scarcely sixty
> kilometres from Cyprus, and the protection of the Turkish
> Cypriot community. For Menderes, there were only two
> possibilities: maintenance of British rule or partition of the
> island between Turkey and Greece..."[1]

The British invitation of 30 June was accepted by Turkey on
July and by Greece 6 days later. The projected London Conferen
was denounced as *"a trap"* by Makarios. Nevertheless the thr
countries represented by their Foreign Secretaries attended t
conference which opened at Lancaster House on 29 Augu
Immediately the widely differing views of the three allies were broug
sharply into focus. For the Greeks **Stephanos Stephanopoul**
propagated the demand for national self-determination and declar
that Greece had never for a single moment entertained the idea of
"withdrawal from Cyprus of the British Forces". **Harold Macmill**
explained that his government did not *"accept the principle of se
determination as one of universal application"* since, *"exceptions had
be made in view of geographical, traditional, historical and oth
considerations"*. For the Turks **Fatin Zorlu** insisted that his count
looked upon the Cyprus question as a British domestic issue, and t
status quo should be maintained. The Turkish position rested on tv
arguments: firstly the theoretical or juridical thesis that Cyprus w
given to Britain by Turkey in 1878 and hence if she wished
relinquish sovereignty the island should revert to Turkey; second
the practical argument of proximity; Ankara's view being that Cypr
was in fact an extension of the Anatolian peninsula. Thus its long th
promontory which stretches to the northeast is often romantica
described as *'the dagger which points at the heart of Turkey'*. The Tur
borrowed a Churchillian phrase in saying that Cyprus faces their *"sc
underbelly"*. In his diaries Macmillan called the conference *"aborti
but by no means useless"*. In fact the conference underlined the potenti

---

[1] The Challenge of Peace. 1970. Page 62

reek-Turkish antagonism over the problem — a side effect which nthony Eden, the Prime Minister, had deliberately planned when lling it in an effort to disprove the thesis that the Cyprus troubles ere due to old-fashioned British colonialism. Britain the sovereign 'er the island, was thus placed in the position of *'mediator'* in a *ispute'* between Greece and Turkey over the future status of an land that belonged to neither of these states. The novelist **Lawrence urrell** reflected in 1957 that *"the key was finally turned upon Cyprus."*

The British proposals for self-government submitted by acmillan at the conference on 6 September, were subsequently jected by both Athens and Ankara. Meanwhile, news of an xplosion in the grounds of the Turkish consulate at Salonica ormerly Atatürk's house) precipitated murderous anti-Greek riots in myrna and Istanbul on 6-7 September. This night of terror[2] mpleted the *'crucifixion of Christendom'*. The official Turkish view the time was that the riots were simply a communist [3] plot aimed ainst western interests and Greco-Turkish friendship. The incidents fact were undoubtedly connived at, if not directly inspired, by the rkish government and were aimed at putting pressure on the USA oppose the inclusion of the Cyprus item on the agenda of the 10th eneral Assembly. The incidents also provided useful ammunition for rlu in his negotiations with his British and Greek counterparts in ndon.

The truth however was soon to present itself. At the Yassiada ials which opened on 14 October 1960 case number two was listed as eptember 6-7 incidents'. Ten former government officials were tried th inciting riots against the Greek population of Istanbul as a means pressing the Turkish viewpoint on the Cyprus dispute. Evidence s given by defence witnesses that the government had been put up staging a Cyprus demonstration by Harold Macmillan but that the lly, badly mismanaged by **Menderes,** had degenerated into an controllable riot. The court announced its verdicts on 15 September 61 — eleven months and one day after the trials opened.

Suffice to say that F. Zorlu, Hasan Polatkan (Finance Minister) d Menderes were hanged[4] in the prison island of Imrali.

It was estimated that capital goods valued at $150 million were destroyed.
The communist party in Turkey was proscribed!
The first two on 16 September 1961 and Menderes on 17 September. Messages from world leaders pleading for mercy failed to save Menderes.

Above: British Police at a roadblock searching citizens.
Below: A clash between demonstrators and security forces.

Above: Prisoners in a detention camp internment).

Left: Sir John Harding, a militarist appointed governor of Cyprus 1955-1957, failed to bring about a negotiated political settlement.

Below: The Cypriot reply to "Surrender".

Back to 1955 the USA was naturally alarmed by the recent trag
developments. It urged that *'quiet diplomacy'* amongst friends was th
most constructive approach in settling differences. Consequently,
November 1955 Whitehall presented its **Formula for Cyprus** to th
Greek and Turkish governments and to Archbishop Makarios. Th
formula stressed that it was not Britain's position that *'the principle*
self-determination can never be applied to Cyprus' but that accou
should be taken of the *'strategic position of the island'*. As for se
government, *'it is the intention of Britain to work for a solution whic*
will satisfy the wishes of the people of Cyprus'. Britain was assured
the USA's active help over its constitutional plans and was al
confident of the support of **Constantine Karamanlis** [5] over the se
determination formula. The latter's guiding principle, known as th
'policy of the national centre', soon became an irritant in Grec
Cypriot relations. At the inception of this British-American conce
lay the view that the alliance interests of Greece *'must'* prevail over h
interests in Cyprus. The conflict between the national desire f
absolute sovereignty and the pragmatic necessity of retaining powerf
friends was at the root of the long-standing Greek dilemma ov
enosis.

On 3 October meanwhile **Sir John Harding**, the island's ne
governor, arrived in Cyprus and at once Makarios expressed h
willingness to meet him, hinting that a compromise was possibl
Discussions between them proceeded intermittently throughout th
following few months. A final meeting was held in Nicosia on
February 1956 which was also attended by **Alan Lennox-Boyd**, th
Secretary of State for the Colonies. The British assurances based c
the Macmillan proposals were vague and ambiguous, althoug
indirectly the principle of self-determination was recognised.
solution seemed near but differences arose apparently over amnest
public security and the elected majority provisions. [6] Harding wh
was given wider powers than his predecessors in relation to securit
was prompt in building up an intelligence network. After EOKA ha

---

[5] Greek Premier from 1955 to June 1963. He succeeded Papagos as leader of th
Greek Rally, soon to be renamed ERE (National Radical Union). He wa
favoured by the Greek palace and by the USA.

[6] The security of the Middle East, Britain's alliance with Turkey and th
irreconcilable enosist circles in Cyprus and Greece were major problems of th
highest order.

ptured a large consignment of arms transferred from Suez to
magusta, be became personally responsible for the direction of all
curity operations. He requested troop reinforcements and had them
ined in riot-breaking by police methods, and outlying police posts
re given military protection.

Road-blocks and house-to-house searches were intensified.
avelling through the night without lights along narrow mountain
ads, troops usually surrounded suspect villages at dawn. All males
er the age of 12 were taken outside for questioning while the houses
re searched in the presence of woman and children. After many
uitless ventures vast quantities of arms, ammunition and army
iiforms were eventually discovered and, with the help of police dogs,
mmandos found a network of caves in the Troodos mountains. Yet
tensified security operations brought no early results and the last
eek in October saw one of the worst outbreaks of disorder since the
mmencement of hostilities.

In November a state of emergency was declared and under the
:w regulations the unauthorised possession of firearms and
plosives carried a maximum penalty of death. Provision was also
ade for deportation, censorship, the placing of large sums of money
1 the heads of wanted men and collective punishment. Hence, a
llective fine of £2,000 was levied on the villagers of Lefkoniko for
e destruction of the local post office by fire and on the night of 13-14
ecember, security forces arrested 129 leading AKEL and PEO
embers and removed them to a detention camp near Larnaca.
KEL and AON, its youth organisation, were banned under the
nergency regulations as being dangerous associations whose real
ojects were '*to prolong dissension and turbulence on the island*'. But
EO and other communist-oriented organisations affiliated to AKEL
ere not proscribed, apparently because the colonial administration
ished to interfere as little as possible with the trade unions and the
bour movement.

Whitehall's policy in the first 11 months of EOKA's struggle
assed through several distinct and contradictory stages. It had begun
ith a categorical denial that the problem existed at all, or at least that
involved anyone except the U.K. The Greeks were warned in 1954 to
top playing with fire'. The next stage was the attempt to enlarge the
sue by drawing in Greece and Turkey. The British '*domestic*' issue
ad now become an '*international*' problem. When this policy failed it
as restricted to Britain and Makarios and direct negotiations
llowed. When these looked like being successful they were broken
ff because it was felt amongst other things that the whole structure of

middle eastern security would be jeopardized. The unfettered use bases in Cyprus were therefore essential. In his memoirs Ed recorded that he regarded the alliance with Turkey as *'the fi consideration in our policy in that part of the world'*.

The linking of Cyprus with Turkish territorial security was a dire invitation to Turkey to enter the dispute. Another complication w added to the existing difficulties, out of which grew the demand *' taksim ya ölüm* (partition or death), and hence more tension at bloodshed By the second half of 1956, the USA had quietly endorsed t principle of partition, reminding everyone of other *'successful'* partitio such as Trieste. Finally, Britain became the arbiter in what w portrayed as a Greek-Turkish dispute and the protector of the Wes interests in the Middle East. These shifts and turns were constant attacked by the British press. The *Daily Telegraph* demanded on June *'a genuine and positive action'*. The *Spectator* of the same da described the government's policy as *'silly, chaotic and barbaric'*.

Following the breakdown of the Harding-Makarios talks[7] t next policy shift was to banish the archbishop who was hencefor seen as an obstacle to a settlement. According to the highly popul and distinguished diplomat Sir. Evelyn Shuckburgh, Anthony Ed was *"perturbed"* and the Premier remarked that the breakdown of t talks had shown that Makario's sole aim was *"to become King Cyprus"*.

Shuckburgh reveals further than on 5 March the Cabinet talke about Cyprus and its plans to deport Makarios, and *"the other bi Bishop"*. All were agreed on the deportation from Cyprus and the after a long pause Lord Salisbury suggested the Seychelles.[8]. On March 1956, the archbishop, who was on the point of leaving Nicos airport for further talks in Athens was instead ordered to enter a RAF plane. He was sent to the Seychelles where he was to stay for months. With him went **Papastavros Papagathangelou,** chief priest i Phaneromeni Church in Nicosia, **Bishop Kyprianos** of Kyrenia an **Polycarpos Ioannides,** a journalist and secretary of the latter's see. Th four deportees were lodged comfortably in the Sans Souci villa a Mahé, in the middle of the Indian Ocean. Makarios is often quoted a

---

[7] The final meeting on 29 February 1956 was also attended by Lennox Boyd, the Secretary of State for the Colonies. According to N. Kranidiotiš, the Minister then warned the participants by saying "God save your people". See Difficult Years — Cyprus 1950-1960 (Greek edition). 1981. Page 170.

[8] Descent to Suez: Diaries 1951-56. 1986. Pages 340, 343-44.

referring to his exile as *"a great experience and an unforgettable event"*.

The deportation was criticised as being *'insane'* and *'unreasonable'*. Politically, it was a serious miscalculation. Makarios was the one true representative of the island's Greek population, who could not easily be replaced and the only person who could curb acts of violence. The news of his arrest was followed by a week-long general strike. Army units cordoned-off the archbishop's palace and soldiers were posted to guard all government buildings and all the approaches to the capital. Riots also broke out in Greece and on 10 March the government recalled Vasilis Mostras, its ambassador, from London.

In Cyprus meanwhile, violence grew and in April Harding undertook large-scale operations against EOKA in the Troodos mountains. Casualties were certainly far higher in the months following Makarios' banishment. Furthermore, racial strife which started mildly in January 1956 reached a climax in May. Pitched battles were fought between the Greeks and Turks and a barrier was set up in Nicosia to separate the two sides. The creation of an auxiliary police force manned entirely by Turks but under British officers, whose task was to control Greek riots and help the armed forces fight EOKA, served further to polarize the two communities. By February 1957, the mobile reserve of the Cyprus police consisted of 32 officers and 551 men of whom none was Greek but 560 were Turkish Cypriots.

The British government announced on 12 July 1956 that it had appointed as constitutional commissioner the distinguished jurist **Lord Radcliffe,** who was charged with the preparation of proposals for a liberal measure of self-government for Cyprus under British sovereignty, giving the people a wide measure of control over their own affairs while at the same time safeguarding both the interests of the Turkish minority and the UK's strategic requirements. Lord Radcliffe visited Cyprus twice to seek the views of the people. The Greeks demanded however that any meaningful discussions should include Makarios, their acknowledged leader. Nevertheless, his suggestions were published as a White Paper in the UK and Cyprus on 19 December 1956. The report, described as a *'statesmanlike document'* included the following proposals:

(1) A legislative assembly consisting of a speaker, a deputy speaker and 36 other members of which 6 would be elected by members on a Turkish Cypriot communal roll, 24 on a general roll and 6 would be nominated by the governor.

(2) A chief minister to act as head of government in self-

173

governing matters. He would be a prominent person who commanded the largest measure of general support and appointed by the governor.

(3) A minister for Turkish Cypriot affairs would deal with issue of his community, including education. Laws affecting these affairs would require the consent of 2/3 of the assembly's Turkish elected members.

(4) No bill passed by the legislative assembly should become law unless and until the governor had signified assent to it.

Simultaneously with their publication, Whitehall announced that it had accepted Radcliffe's proposals. The Secretary of State for the Colonies (Lennox-Boyd) however referred to another possible solution, that of partition.[9] The proposals were accepted in principle by Ankara and by the Turkish Cypriot community. Athens and the Greek Cypriot inhabitants rejected them mainly for three reasons:

(a) They were neither democratic nor liberal since the elected majority principle was strangled by the almost unlimited powers of the governor.

(b) They did not envisage the right of self-determination for the Cypriot people and were not therefore in accord with the fundamental principles of the UN Charter.

(c) These and other deficiencies precluded therefore the solution of the Cyprus problem.

In the island, acts of violence continued unabated even though security forces scored several successes against Griva's men. Diplomatic activity was also intensified in search of some form of compromise: at the UN a resolution by **Krishna Menon**, the powerful head of the Indian delegation, was adopted by the General Assembly on 26 February 1957 as resolution 1013 (XI)[10] It stated that the solution of the Cyprus problem required an atmosphere of peace and freedom of expression and that a peaceful democratic and just solution would be found in accordance with the purposes and principles of the UN Charter and that negotiations will be resumed and continued to the end.

---

[9] House of Commons Debates 5s. Volume 562 Column 1268.

[10] The vote was 57 in favour, none against with one abstention.

Above: March 1956; The four deportees. From left to right Papastavros Papagathangelou, Archbishop Makarios, Polycarpos Ioannides and bishop Kyprianos of Kyrenia.

Below: The four in a rare picture relaxing in the Seychelles.

Athens was toying with a scheme[11] for a customs union linking Greece, Turkey and Cyprus in the event of enosis. Under this plan Cypriot Turks were to have dual nationality and exemption from conscription. NATO also joined the diplomatic offensive. Lord Ismay, its Secretary-General, announced on 15 March that he was prepared to offer his good offices for promoting a conciliation in the dispute in accordance with the resolution on the peaceful settlement of disputes which was adopted by NATO the previous December. Once more the Greeks were adamant that the problem was outside the competence of NATO and a matter for the UN only.

In March, Britain announced that Makarios and the other deportees could leave the Seychelles but should not return to Cyprus at such an auspicious hour. The archbishop and his co-exiles left San Souci on 6 April 1957 and boarded the Greek ship *Olympic Thunder* bound for Madagascar. They arrived in Athens at 10.00 am on 17 April where they were given a hero's welcome. The Greek capital became the archbishop's new base. He gathered men of real calibre around him and commenced once more his difficult task for keeping world opinion informed of the continuing tragedy of Cyprus. What were Britain's motives for releasing the deportees?

(1) Following the recent Radcliffe proposals, Whitehall was pledged to changes in the island's status.

(2) Britain's middle eastern policy had failed, especially after the Suez misadventure of late 1956 early 1957. Sir Evelyn Shuckburgh was able to record on 28 February 1956 that '*we have no diplomacy at all, no flexibility*'. Of the PM (A. Eden) and Foreign Secretary (Selwyn Lloyd), he recorded in his diaries that the former had "*deteriorated*" and the latter was a rather "*nervous official*" who had neither the "*inclination*" nor the "*courage to take decisions of any kind*". With so much uncertainty and failure on other theatres, military strategists were saying that "*Cyprus should not be abandoned*".

---

[11] Also considered were plans for independence and apparently partition. It appears that the Averoff—Iksel talks of 6 October 1956 were instrumental in the discussion of the last mentioned solution.

(3) The British rightly believed that only Makarios could stem the escalation of violence in the island. Grivas in fact announced a truce on 14 March 1957 to facilitate negotiations as soon as the Cypriot ethnarch was released.

(4) British troops and personnel in the island were becoming highly exasperated due to Whitehall's paralysis in formulating a fair and democratic positive plan for Cyprus.

(5) Britain was bitterly criticised at home and abroad. What was needed was the resumption of meaningful negotiations based on a constructive policy. Whitehall was henceforth saying that in the face of new realities Britain did not need the island as a base but needed only a couple of air strips so that atomic bombers might fly off in pursuance of the West's defence obligations.

(6) Pressure, both official and unofficial, was exerted by the USA. A just and peaceful solution to this so-called *'thorny problem'* was demanded.

(7) For Britain which desired to improve its international image on the Cyprus question, Makarios was proving an embarrassment because there was no recognised leader but himself to conduct any meaningful negotiations.

With Makarios' release a new wave of diplomatic activity began. He wrote to Macmillan on 28 May 1957 recalling the wording of UN resolution 1013 (IX). Yet Macmillan recorded in his diary that *'we still have no clear or positive plan'*. He went on to say that very reluctantly he began to feel that partition *'will be the only way out'*. By July a new scheme was worked out. On the 16th the Cabinet discussed Cyprus and there was wide agreement on the *'tri-dominium'* concept. The governments of Greece and Turkey were sounded out on the possibility of a conference. Meanwhile from late July, the archbishop was orientating himself towards a solution that envisaged independence. Grivas on the other hand was greatly disturbed and urged continued insistence on self-determination.

In November 1957 Harding retired on completion of the two-year tour of service previously agreed. He was replaced by **Sir Hugh Foot,** a liberal colonial civil servant, who arrived on 3 December. He was not new to Cyprus having served as Colonial Secretary from 1943 to 1945. The new governor appeared to have two major objectives: to relax tensions in the island and to work out some plan for settling the Cyprus problem. He visited detention camps, walked through the streets of Nicosia, spoke to leading local personalities, rode through villages and argued in coffee shops. The famous *'honeymoon period'* was in full swing.

Within a month he was back in London with his recommendations. He was very pleased because he had a *'positive policy'* to take to his superiors in London. Within ten days a new initiative was agreed upon. This was immediately rejected by Turkey. However, the failure to find common ground for a settlement induced Britain to introduce its own policy. By May 1958, a draft agreement embodying Foot's plans for internal self-government and the earlier proposals for the external solution of *'tri-dominium'* was agreed upon. The **Foot-Macmillan Partnership Plan** was presented to the Commons on 19 June 1958. Macmillan made it clear that Cyprus was now not a *'colonial problem'* but an *'international one'* — a drastic switch from his attitude three years before when he said at the Tripartite Conference that *'the internal affairs of Her Majesty's possessions cannot be discussed with foreign powers'*. He now suggested an *'adventure in partnership'* between the island's two communities and between the British, Greek and Turkish governments:

(1) For seven years the international status of Cyprus would be unchanged.

(2) The administration of the island as a whole would be directed by a council composed of the British governor, respresentatives of the Greek and Turkish governments and six Cypriot ministers, four elected from the Greek assembly and two from the Turkish.

(3) External affairs, defence and internal security would be matters specifically reserved to the governor acting after consultation with the Greek and Turkish government representatives.

(4) The government said that it would welcome any arrangement which would give Cypriots, Greek or Turkish nationality while enabling them to retain British nationality.

The Greek and Turkish response was disappointing. It was stressed by the Greeks that if applied the proposals would lead to an intense antagonism both between the majority and the minority of the population and between the governments of the countries involved in the island's administration. Thus the plan prejudged the future by preparing the ground for the island's partition. The Turks were also critical. They went as far as to say that the plan was a *'stepping-stone to enosis'*.

In Cyprus the reaction was an increase in violence. EOKA intensified its activities and the British armed forces hit back hard. The problem of racial strife in 1956 and 1957 was not serious. The Turkish underground organization *Volkan* (The Volcano) was simply anti-Greek and was determined to achieve partition. Its *'leader'* was **Rauf Denktash** — an admirer of the Turkish Premier Menderes. Officially proscribed in November 1957 it was succeeded by the *Türk Müdafaa (or Mukavamet) Teskilati* — Turkish Defence or Resistance Organization, known as the **TMT** for short.

The TMT, though cruder, smaller and less well organised, modelled itself on EOKA. Hence the boycott of British goods which EOKA had ordered on 6 March 1958 was now applied by the Turks to Greek produce. Turks caught smoking Greek cigarettes or using Greek shops were beaten up by groups of youths. Any Turk who deviated from the national line that co-existence with the Greeks was impossible was liable to be denounced as a traitor. By mid-1958 pro-partitionist Turks were absolutely sure that soon the tide would turn their way. This confidence stemmed from several related factors:

(i) As in 1955, Ankara was determined to show the world the strength of its feelings on the Cyprus issue. The press and Ankara radio were responsible for whipping-up agitation and building up anti-Greek and anti-British resentment.

(ii) Loss of confidence in Britain's ability to settle the problem without detriment to Turkish interests encouraged the pro-partitionist Turkish Cypriots to step up their agitation for *taksim* (partition).

(iii) Tension was exacerbated by the government's prolonged delay in publishing its new plan for Cyprus. Fearing that the plan, announced on 19 June, would not provide for partition, the Turks, as we shall see below, intensified their activities and serious communal strife broke out on the night of 7 June 1958.

(iv) Such over-confidence was fostered by the firm belief that Turkey would, if necessary, send troops to their assistance. Behind the scenes especially, Ankara certainly made such threats. The fact that in the island the Greeks outnumbered them by four to one was no deterrent. In a fair number of Turkish houses, posters were displayed showing Cyprus partitioned across the figure of a helmeted Turkish soldier.

The year 1958 was very eventful. In January seven Turkish Cypriots were killed by security forces during anti-British demonstrations. Other incidents increased Turkish hostility towards the British. Then in June and July violent clashes broke out between the two communities. A bomb explosion[12] outside Turkey's press office in Nicosia on the night of 7 June marked the beginning of the most acute phase of racial tension the island had seen. Passions reached a climax on 12 June when eight Greeks were massacred by the Turks during a clash near the Turkish village of Guenyeli. A report by the commission of inquiry published in Nicosia on 9 December 1958 found that the Greeks were rounded up by the British security forces and surprisingly released on the same day near Guenyeli, seven miles from where they were arrested and some distance from the nearest Greek villages. The incident has gone down in Cypriot history as the **Guenyeli Massacre** — organised by the British and executed by the Turks.

Arson, murder and destruction continued for two months. In the end 56 Greeks and 53 Turks had died. Sir Hugh Foot ordered an island-wide standstill for 48 hours on 22 July. The TMT was proscribed and around 60 Turks and 2,000 Greeks were arrested. Apart from the actual casualties there was a further disturbing factor: the Turks, with a view to partition, began to withdraw their minorities from predominantly Greek areas and evicted Greeks from areas where Turks formed the majority. In one week alone over 600 families left their homes of which 2/3 were Greek. Suffice to say that many of the Turks who left the Greek areas at this stage did so largely under the pressure of Turkish agitators.

Another highly disturbing factor became more prominent in 1958. When EOKA's campaign opened in April 1955, AKEL was quick to condemn violence, pointing out that armed conflict would lead only to greater complications. The party also expressed its misgivings when it was learnt that Grivas, a fanatical anti-communist, would lead the Cypriot struggle. This uneasy alliance endured many strains. However, during these years armed masked men began to appear in villages seeking out *'undesirables'*. The victims tended to be members of left-wing families which often meant that the workers in them belonged to the *'old'* trade unions dominated by AKEL.

The shooting of left-wingers in Lyssi and Komi tou Yialou by masked men on 21 January 1958 hightened tension. On the following day PEO called a 48-hour strike to be observed throughout the island and there were demonstrations in most of the big towns. A cable to the archbishop in Athens begged him to use his influence to stop such

---

[12] The Yassiada Trials (Turkey) of 1960-61 established that the bomb was planted by Turkish terrorists.

incidents. Makarios's answer, given 48 hours after the murders, was surprisingly a call for unity and not a condemnation of the killings. A few weeks later news leaked out that EOKA had formed a special unit to deal with the communists. AKEL had by now come out openly in favour of independence and Grivas' pamphlet *'The Communist Leadership Against the Cyprus Struggle'* helped to widen the breach between them.

Perhaps the worst flare-up between the two factions was in August 1958 after clashes between Greeks and Turks had already brought the island to the verge of civil war. At Milia (near Famagusta) a so-called *'left-wing home guard'* formed to protect the village against possible Turkish Cypriot attacks was instead ambushed by EOKA. Two people were killed and around twenty injured — nearly all left-wingers. An urgent appeal to Makarios to intervene resulted in another belated call for unity. Similarly, TMT was responsible for the killing of several Turkish Cypriot progressives who spoke out for full co-operation between the island's two communities.

Not surprisingly, the British took advantage of these *'domestic squabbles'* and put forward final proposals for the solution of the Cyprus problem. Macmillan made arrangements to visit both Athens and Ankara. Accompanied by Foot, the British Premier arrived in the Greek capital on 7 August. He pleaded for peace and for a seven year period with provisional solutions but without prejudice to any final settlement. He repeated that *'partnership was a fine and noble ideal'*. The Greeks disliked partnership as a principle since that would have been equivalent to admitting de jure a Turkish presence on the island. Ankara and Nicosia were also visited. As a result of Macmillan's shuttle diplomacy Whitehall concluded that certain modifications to its general policy, announced in June, were needed; in particular, Greek and Turkish government representatives were to have no seats in the central council although they were to be consulted by the governor as envisaged in the original proposals.

Even though agreement was not forthcoming the British planned to put their policy into operation. September 1958 was the month of *'shifts and turns'*. On the 7th Makarios told the Greek government privately that he was now willing to accept independence for Cyprus under UN auspices. On the 16th he made his views known to **Barbara Castle MP** — a senior member of the British Labour Party. She, in common with many others, believed that parts of the Macmillan plan if applied would have regrettable consequences. On 22 September, Makarios authorised Mrs. Castle to give the news to the press. The date coincided with the decision of the UN General Assembly to include the Cyprus question in its agenda.

Under constant pressure from Britain and the USA, Greece decided to seek NATO mediation. On 23 September **Spaak,** the Secretary-General, arrived in Athens. It was agreed that he should submit the following *'personal proposals'* at the NATO council meeting which was to take place within the next few days:

(1) The Macmillan plan to be neutralised.

(2) A seven-point plan to be adopted which included provisions for a single legislative chamber with the future of the island remaining open.

(3) A conference should be held under the aegis of NATO with all interested parties present.

This NATO initiative, once more, failed to secure wide support. The impasse continued and the date for the application of the Macmillan plan - 1 October - was approaching. Back stage diplomacy reached fever point. The stage reverts once more to the UN. Draft Cyprus resolutions were put forward by various countries; eventually an Iranian one which urged something more than the tripartite conference which the British had suggested in 1957 was accepted with several amendments. On 4 December the Political Committee accepted it by 31 votes to 22 with 28 abstentions. The USA, Britain, Turkey and most of the other countries voted in favour while Greece was amongst the opponents. Yet on that same evening an event took place which ultimately led to the **Zürich-London Agreements of 1959** which finally set up the Cyprus Republic.

At the entrance of the Political Committee hall where the vote was taken, Zorlu approached Averoff and congratulated him on the spendid fight he put up in the debate. They agreed to *'meet'*. A compromise motion was upheld by the General Assembly on 5 December. Resolution 1287 (XIII) was adopted by 57 votes to none with one absention. It recalled resolution 1013 (XI) of 26 February 1957 and expressed confidence that continued efforts will be made by the parties to reach a peaceful, democratic and just solution in accordance with the Charter of the UN.

In the delegates' lounge of the UN building on the morning of 6 December, Zorlu and Averoff talked for two hours. The rapproachment between Greece and Turkey led to the Paris talks of 18 December when the two ministers, together with Selwyn Lloyd, their British counterpart, had informal discussions on Cyprus during a

NATO meeting. The two sides met again on the following day and yet again in Paris between 18 and 20 January 1959 during an OEEC (Organisation for European Economic Co-operation) meeting convened to discuss problems connected with the European Common Market. The Turks insisted that at the next top level meeting the Premiers of both countries should be present. Zürich was chosen as the next venue. On 11 February a declaration was initialled by the two countries confirming that Cyprus would become an independent state with a Greek Cypriot president and a Turkish Cypriot vice-president and detailing the *'basic structure of the Republic of Cyprus'*. With the Zürich concordat under their belts the two Foreign Ministers flew to London and conferred on the same evening with Selwyn Lloyd. The London Conference of 17 February 1959 was widened to include two separate delegations headed by Makarios and Kütchük. The purpose of the three governments, which had agreed previously on the plan to be implemented, was to present the Cypriots with a fait accompli which they would be forced to accept. On 19 February the London Agreements were finally initialled at Lancaster House.

The settlement that evolved had two main parts: a draft constitution for Cyprus and three treaties. British rule in the island was to end not later than one year after 19 February 1959. The Republic finally came into being on 16 August 1960. Before it could be established the consitution and the final texts of the three treaties had to be drafted and administrative arrangements to be made for the transfer of power and for the holding of presidential, parliamentary and communal elections.

Three ad hoc committees were immediately set up. The Transitional Committee in Nicosia, composed of the governor and Cypriot members, was responsible for the adaptation of government machinery in preparation for independence. The London Joint Committee, composed of representatives from Britain, Greece and Turkey and from the two Cypriot communities, was charged with drafting the final treaties. The Joint Constitutional Commission, composed of representatives of the two communities and of the Greek and Turkish governments with legal advisers, had the task of drafting the constitution. It was however bound by the 27 articles laid down at Zürich.

The sovereignty of the island was safeguarded by Britain, Greece and Turkey under the Treaty of Guarantee which precluded under Article I either the union of Cyprus with any other state of its partition.

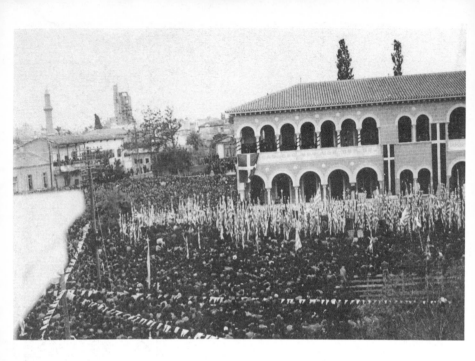

Above: Greek political gathering outside the Archbishopric.
Below: Turkish demonstrators carrying their own flags.

Above: Archbishop Makarios meeting some ex-EOKA fighters.

Left: EOKA fighters return 'home' led here by Polycarpos Georgadjis and Yiannis Matsis.

The Treaty of Alliance provided for co-operation between Greece and Turkey and the Republic in common defence, for the stationing of Greek and Turkish military contingents (950 and 650 respectively) on the island and for the training of a Cypriot army. The Treaty of Establishment concerned the retention of British bases (BSBs) and ancillary facilities on Cypriot territory and problems of finance and nationality arising out of the end of colonial rule.

Hence the turbulent years of 1955-1958 were at an end. Peace was preserved in the south-eastern flank of NATO. In real terms the total British military and internal security expenditure between December 1954 and December 1959 was estimated at £90 million. In human terms lives lost since July 1954, owing to armed action and civil disturbances, were 142 British and 492 Cypriot. However the 18 months prior to independence day were nearly as troubled as the months before the Agreements were signed. The early preparations for independence took place against a background of lawlessness. The archbishop, after an absence of almost three years, returned to Cyprus on 1 March 1959 and was given an overwhelming welcome by a crowd estimated at 200,000. He had the unenviable task of persuading the diverse segments of the Greek Cypriot community to accept the spirit of the Agreements and of convincing the Turkish community that its future on the island could best be served by emphasising the unifying rather than the devisive elements of the compromise settlement.

The Cypriot state was gradually taking shape. On 27 March 1959 agreement had been reached on the allocation of portfolios in the first Cypriot provisional government which was to hold office until the island officially became self-governing. Domestic irritants[13] continued to create problems; however attempts were made by all sides to eradicate the major sources of tension. Hence, polling day on 13 December 1959 went off peacefully. Makarios received 66.82% share of the total vote. Preparations for independence went ahead as scheduled — though postponed several times. The constitution, consisting of 199 articles and 6 annexes, embodying the Zürich-London Agreements and forming the fundamental law of the new state, was taking shape. On 16 August 1960 Makarios was invested as

---

[13] Deep-set emnity between Makarios, Grivas, the Bishops and their supporters; between the various political groupings and finally between the two communities. The interception of the Turkish gun-running motor-boat ('Deniz') on 18 October exacerbated suspicions and tensions even further.

President of Cyprus and Kütchük as Vice-President. Through resolution 1489 (XV) Cyprus became in 1960 the 99th member-state of the United Nations; it became a member in the same year of the Commonwealth and the 16th member-state of the Council of Europe in 1961.

Autonomy however did not entail an independent economy, nor did it entail a sovereign state free from all foreign troops. This in turn implied the impossibility of an independent political line being pursued by the infant state. Ever since 1960 Cyprus has been subjected to the influences and pressures of the respective governments of Greece and Turkey, and the political instability in both these nations has been allowed to spill over and create tenseness within the republic and between its people. Added to the above was the imposition of an unworkable constitution which required only a few flash points to destroy the island's unity completely. In fact, in the first years of independence Cyprus was to pay dearly for the precarious settlement granted her by the allied western powers.

The first decimal coins of Cyprus; the last produced by the British administration.

The signing of the agreements was greeted in London with great relief.

CHAPTER FOUR

THE
INFANT
REPUBLIC

The setting up of the Cyprus Republic meant, in theory at least, that a number of Greeks who had earlier led the struggle for enosis and a number of Turks who had successfully led the resistance to it would come together to collaborate in running the new state. Such co-operation was not easy in view of:

1. the recent enmity between EOKA and TMT;
2. the complexities created by the settlement;
3. the imposed rifts within the two communities which were not conducive to creating harmony or promoting the Cypriot consciousness;

4. more generally, the relationship between the two opposing nationalisms; Cypriots were conscious of their Greekness or Turkishness (their national leaders never stopped reminding them of that), and their first loyalties were to their own communities and leaderships.

It soon transpired that the immediate objective of the Turkish Cypriot leadership was to accept the new contitutional order but its long term policy was to find ways of proving it unworkable and thus to argue that partition was the best solution. In Ankara such an arrangement was seen as the best setting for its declared partitionist policy and even of its *'future'* annexation of the island. To the Greeks the many weaknesses of the constitution produced an imbalance. Governmental dualism and ethnic separatism between Greek and Turkish Cypriots were institutionalized. The constitution had brought into being a state but not a nation.

Conflict, inevitable given the peculiarities of the constitution, intensified as the Greeks tried to show that only a unitary system of government would work in Cyprus, while the Turks took every opportunity to block government business whenever they felt that their rights were infringed or their needs unmet. Soon they were deadlocked on a host of issues including civil service staffing, the army, separation of municipalities[1] and the use of the Turkish veto on central government taxation.

---

[1] The devisive article 173 was probably the greatest source of trouble in the 1960 constitution.

Hence the complex and rigid settlement imposed on the Cypriots by British, Greek and Turkish diplomats, who rejoiced over the triumph of goodwill and international understanding, soon broke down. On paper the constitution was incomprehensible. In application it was a legal monster. Cyprus in fact was given two governments - a majority one and a minority one - functioning together and overlapping. As pointed out by constitutional and legal experts **Cyprus was the first country in the world to be denied majority rule by its own constitution.**

Inevitably, the new state was arrested in infancy. The last attempt to reach a mutually acceptable solution to the so-called *'battle of the five towns'* was made in December 1962. On Christmas Eve, after negotiations lasting late into the night, it looked as if a compromise had miraculously been achieved. A joint communique drafted by Clerides and Denktash was issued announcing an agreement *'in principle'* but within 24 hours Kütchük had repudiated it.

Separation, which became an end in itself bred tension and afforded the opportunity for diehards to plunge the country into strife. Such extremism was shown earlier in the year when two London-educated barristers were murdered by TMT gunmen on 23 April. **Ahmet Gurkan** aged 38 and **Ayhan Hikmet** aged 33 were leaders of the Turkish Cypriot People's Party which was in opposition to the majority NFP[2] led by Kütchük and Denktash. Hikmet was the editor of the weekly newspaper *Cumhuriyet,* founded by Gurkan, which advocated closer association between the two communities. The murders were unreservedly denounced by influential persons of both communities. Especially vociferous in their condemnation were Ali Dana and Emil Dirvana, the Turkish Ambassador in Nicosia. Following Denktash's protests Dirvana was shortly afterwards recalled to Ankara. Thus all the obstacles were now removed to the Turkish Cypriot *'insurgence'* and gradual separation long prepared by Turkish extreme chauvinists both in Cyprus and in Turkey.

The precedents for such terrorism were certainly there. In 1958 progressive Turkish Cypriots were the targets of TMT. The ethnocentric elements who were determined to divide and rule attacked their leading compatriots who were members of AKEL and the united trade unions in order to force around 3,500 Turkish Cypriot

---

[2] National Front Party; successor to the Cyprus is Turkish Party-Kibris Türktür Parti.

workers, organized in the joint Greek and Turkish Cypriot trade unions known as PEO, to leave such all-Cypriot unions and form exclusively Turkish ones. Furthermore, prominent Turkish Cypriot members of AKEL and other democratic Turkish Cypriots were attacked and a number of them murdered in cold blood because they fought for friendship and co-operation between the two communities against colonialism and imperialism and for independence.

Even though acts of violence, arson and destruction of property were a regular occurrence, the British administration reacted by arresting Turkish democrats, politicial and labour leaders instead of the reactionary Turkish Cypriot leaders and their diehard supporters who were responsible for such civil and criminal desobedience. Thus when Francis Noel-Baker MP asked Lennox-Boyd, Secretary of State for the Colonies, on 17 June 1958 what action the authorities of Cyprus intended to take against Kütchük and Denktash in view of their repeated violations of the emergency regulations, the curt reply was *'no proceedings have been taken'*.

During the first months of 1958 relations between the two communities were strained even further. Ankara radio spoke daily in very strong terms of the impossibility of the Turks and Greeks living together in peace. It emphasized that since they had completely different political, religious and cultural backgrounds they could not co-exist under a single political system. The Turkish ruling élite therefore demanded that the island should be partitioned, with Turkey fully controlling financially, politically and militarily *'its'* sector. In such an atmosphere it was easy for their supporters to brand as traitors all those who disagreed with its crazy pro-imperialist policy.

Even so hundreds of Turks joined with their Greek compatriots in the 1958 May Day celebrations, as they had done in previous years. The marchers, shouting anti-imperialist slogans and protesting against the divisions being enforced by the western powers, paraded through the streets of Nicosia with their national flags and vowed to fight for the common ideals of the working class.

The reaction of the fanatical right-wing Turkish leadership was vicious. On that very night TMT activists looted the Turkish sport and cultural club of Nicosia, set fire to it and then accused its members of having been sold to the Greeks. The crime took place under the noses of the security forces, yet no one was arrested. The burning of the club gave the signal for a general attack to exterminate the progressive and peace-loving Turks. The assassins, unbelievably, continued their work unpunished.

16 ΑΥΓΟΥΣΤΟΥ 1960 :

Above: The signing ceremony and proclamation of Cyprus' Independence.

Left: A Greek description: "The Independent Cyprus Republic is born" on 16 August 1960.

Below: The first postage stamp of the Republic.

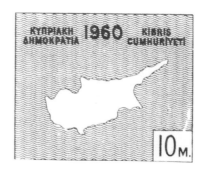

193

Back in 1962 the Greek majority in the House of Representatives rejected in December a Turkish proposal to extend the existing municipal laws for one year from 1 January 1963. On 2 January the council of ministers brought the town councils under the direct control of the central government by setting up development boards to run the main towns. The Greek municipalities surrendered their powers to these boards but the Turkish ones refused to do so; the Turkish communal chamber declaring that the separate municipalities were still legal.

The Turkish Cypriot leaders consulted Ankara and referred the dispute to the Cyprus Constitutional Court, whose neutral president, Dr Ernest Forsthoff (a West German Professor from the University of Heidelberg who later resigned), ruled on 25 April that both moves were illegal. Since the same court had already decided on 8 February that the Turkish veto on the tax laws in 1961 was illegal it meant that the government had no authority to collect customs duties and income tax; both central and local government were henceforth threatened with paralysis.

On 9 April 1963 Makarios explained that the blocking of the taxation laws had caused *'great difficulties'*; that the insistence on separate municipalities in the five main towns was *'unreasonable and wastefully expensive';* and that *'real damage'* had been caused by the Turkish obstruction of proposed legislation for setting up a development bank. Nevertheless the first five-year plan (1962-6) concentrated on developing the economic potential of the island by mobilizing all unemployed resources, thus providing the necessary infrastructure for the diversification of the economy with a view to removing the causes of pre-1960 economic instability. Despite the internal problems of the island the plan succeeded in getting the productive resources moving and restored internal and foreign confidence in the economy. See next chapter for further details.

Yet in 1963 Cyprus was without an income tax law, a customs law and a municipalities law, and the two communities seemed headed for a major confrontation. Convinced by now that the Turks would not consider any change in the constitution by agreement and that their ultimate aim was to partition the island, the Greek Cypriots began to talk of removing the divisive and negative elements of the constitution. At the same time the Turkish Cypriots threatened that any Greek effort to amend the constitution without their approval would meet with Turkish might and would result in *'partition or death'*. A strong Greek Cypriot lobby had even suggested that the government should

Above: A triumphant Makarios accompanied by General Grivas. Between them is Mr. Glafkos Clerides.

Below: The historic signing ceremony. Cyprus becomes an independent country. From the left sitting: Archbishop Makarios; Sir Hugh Foot, last Governor; Dr. F. Kütchük.

use the good offices of the UN to carry through the proposed amendments. Makarios' endorsement of the 1963 **Akritas Plan** — a secret programme to use UN pressure to remove the restrictions on enosis imposed by the Treaty of Guarantee and the Treaty of Alliance — was very unfortunate. The plan was leaked, and with it the suggestion that the Greek Cypriots would use this freedom to conduct an *'enosis referendum',* which by sheer weight of numbers they were bound to win.

On 4 August 1963 Makarios said that he had finally made up his mind that the constitution was in dire need of a change. He would seek this revision since certain provisions of inapplicable character threatened to *'paralyse the state machinery'* In reply Kütchük declared on 22 August that the Turks might resort to civil disobedience if the Greeks attempted a unilateral revision of the constitution which would *'not be binding on the Turkish community'*.

The president however, in his desire to facilitate the smooth functioning of the infant state and remove the causes of intercommunal friction, submitted on 30 November concrete proposals (glossed over by Sir Arthur Clark, the British High Commissioner in Cyprus) for amending the constitution. These were transmitted to Kütchük and copies were sent to the governments of Britain, Greece and Turkey for *'information purposes only'*. These proposals, as set out below, were intended to establish a more unified state and were in logic undeniable:[3]

1. The right of veto of the president and the vice-president was to be abandoned.

2. The vice-president was to deputize for the president in case of temporary absence or incapacity to perform his duties.

3. The Greek president of the House of Representatives and the Turkish vice-president were to be elected by the House as a whole and not, as before, by separate Greek and Turkish majorities within the House.

4. The vice-president of the House of Representatives was to deputize

---

[3] His 13-point plan appeared to have been designed to remove the constitutionally-entrenched minority rights and replace them with expressions of goodwill. They were bound to be rejected by Turkey and the Turkish Cypriots. Makarios had no intention of ever provoking the T··rks.

for the president of the House in case of his temporary absence or incapacity to perform his duties.

5. The constitutional provisions regarding separate majorities for the enactment of certain laws by the House of Representatives were to be abolished.
6. Unified municipalities were to be established.
7. The administration of justice was to be unified.
8. The division of the security forces into police and gendarmerie was to be abolished.
9. The numerical strength of the security forces and of the defence forces was to be determined by law.
10. The proportion of participation of Greek Cypriots and Turkish Cypriots in the composition of the public services (70:30) and the forces of the republic (60:40) was to be modified in proportion to the ratio of the population of Greek to Turkish Cypriots.
11. The number of members of the public service commission was to be reduced from ten to five.
12. All decisions of the public service commission were to be taken by simple majority.
13. The communal chambers would be abolished and a new system devised. Should the Turkish community howerver desire to retain its chamber in the new system, such a course would be open to it.

Meanwhile the two *'mother countries'* were going through a political crisis. Just before Christmas both were left simultaneously with unrepresentative governments. In Greece, the eight-year reign of Karamanlis came to an abrupt end on 11 June 1963. In Turkey, the situation was even worse and after several attempted coups, Inönü's government resigned on 2 December 1963.

It was in the middle of this crisis, and when Greece, after inconclusive elections on 3 November, was also struggling to form a government, that Makarios *'chose'* to make his first formal bid to change the *'Cyprus constitutional oddity'*. Kütchük, to whom the proposals were addressed, failed to reply, although at press interviews he reiterated that the constitution could not be changed. However, on 7 December F.K. Erkin, the Turkish Foreign Minister, announced that Ankara had rejected them and on 16 December Ozkol, the Turkish ambassador, handed to Makarios Turkey's written rejection. Makarios however refused to accept the rejection, pointing out that the proposals had been sent to the Turkish Cypriot vice-president for reply and not to any foreign government.

197

On 20 December the Foreign Ministers of Cyprus, Greece and Turkey met in Paris to discuss the situation. Within a few hours of their first encounter shooting broke out in Nicosia. An initial attempt to bring intercommunal tension to boiling point was averted on 3 December. The government managed to cool tempers after a bomb exploded at the base of the newly erected statue of Markos Drakos, a Greek Cypriot hero during the EOKA campaign.

However, in the early hours of 21 December a police patrol car with Greek Cypriot officers driving down Hermes Street in the old city of Nicosia (the same area which had been the scene of arson and looting by Turkish extremists in 1958) stopped a car for a routine check. Shots were fired and one of the policemen was wounded. The policemen returned the fire. A young Turk was killed and a Turkish woman wounded, dying on her way to hospital. Within minutes shooting broke out in various quarters of the city. By 5 a.m. an angry Turkish crowd started moving into the Greek quarter and by 6 a.m. one Greek and one Turk had been brought to hospital with gunshot wounds. There were further incidents on 22 December and by midday all Turkish Cypriot government employees and policemen had left their posts. The Turks fortified themselves in their own areas; their defences proving to have been well prepared in advance. In order to further their partitioning aims they forced several thousand innocent and contented Turkish peasants to abandon their farms and animals and move into their overcrowded quarter of Nicosia. Thus the aim of partition, camouflaged by Turkish propaganda as *'federation'*, was relentlessly pursued regardless of loss of human life and the human misery created. However, this so-called *'first phase'* of the invasion of Cyprus by Turkey only partly succeeded, since well over half of its brethren refused to obey instructions to abandon their homes for the predetermined enclaves.

The clashes had caught the leadership of the two communities completely unprepared. There is no evidence to suggest that the outbreak of violence had official sanction. In fact Makarios and Kütchük met Greek and Turkish Cypriot ministers at the Paphos Gate police station and there was another call to the public for calm and for the shooting to stop. On 23 December the acting British high commissioner and the USA ambassador called on the president and expressed the grave concern of their governments at the turn of events in Cyprus. They appealed for moderation from both communities. Athens and Ankara also appealed for an end to intercommunal violence. Such pleas were too late.

At 2.25 p.m. on 23 December, Turkish Cypriot extremists moved into the Armenian quarter of Nicosia and forced the inhabitants to leave their houses, shops, church, school and clubs. On the same day some Turkish patients at the Nicosia General Hospital disappeared from their beds - possibly killed. Shortly afterwards British servicemen and civilians were shot at in Larnaca and Lefka by TMT gunmen. A ceasefire was hastily arranged on 24 December. It failed because of clashes on the outskirts of Nicosia, but a new accord was concluded on Christmas Day.

At these discussions between Major-General Peter Young (GOC Cyprus) and the Greek and Turkish army commanders on the island, agreement was reached on the establishment of a headquarters for the joint peace-keeping force. British troops began patrolling Nicosia and Larnaca on the same day and a **'green line'** (reminiscent of EOKA days and regularly likened to the more famous Berlin Wall) was subsequently established on 30 December in Nicosia to separate the Greek from the Turkish Cypriot quarters. The line, guarded by British troops, cut straight across the mixed suburbs of Omorphita and Neapolis and put the entire Armenian quarter as well as the Greek areas of Kermia, Ayios Kasianos and Ayios Iakovos behind Turkish lines.

The renewal of the Cyprus conflict brought Greece and Turkey once again to the brink of war. The joint plea for peace issued by the protecting powers on 23 December was followed the next day by rumours of a Turkish invasion. Late on 24 December the Turkish army contingent in Cyprus marched out of its appointed camp and took positions on the northern outskirts of Nicosia and along the Nicosia-Kyrenia road which leads to the northern coast. On the following day Turkish jets screamed low over the rooftops of Nicosia and Turkish naval units were spotted manoeuvring off the island's coast. Following suit the Greek army contingent also left its barracks and took positions to counter a possible Turkish invasion. Cyprus had become *'the new apple of discord'* between the two countries. In the circumstances the peace-keeping force was composed only of British troops.

For the reasons mentioned below NATO became an interested party and tried to forestall, albeit unsuccessfully, international initiatives:

1. The island's three guarantor powers were integral members of this organization. The western alliance could not simply disregard this

Above: A Greek cartoon showing Britain's involvement in Cyprus being satisfied with obtaining its bases, while Makarios as head of the Republic is left with numerous problems: e.g. economic, "Greek-Turkish Police", dismantling of EOKA etc. etc.

Below: The early years of the peaceful Republic: President Makarios, Vice-President Kütchük and other leading personalities at the Platres festival.

.Above: British soldiers as part of the peacekeeping force.
|Below: UN officers enjoying a chat with locals.

dispute as it had already done other colonial conflicts.

2. There was a real fear at the beginning of the crisis that the Soviet Union might exploit the position of the Cypriot left to acquire a foothold in Cyprus.

3. It was widely believed that if the conflict continued the island might eventually become a *'Mediterranean Cuba'*. Makarios' non-aligned policy was viewed with great concern by the western alliance. The US Pentagon, sensing the coming tensions in the Middle East, considered him too vague and uncertain a quantity and saw that ultimate stability for the bases could be achieved only if the island were brought under NATO control. Alternatively, Makarios and all other opposition should be removed.

While the Cyprus government relied on non-alignment for the removal of its constitutional shackles, the Turkish Cypriot leadership relied on anti-Communist orientation to preserve its rights. There was little internal opposition to this since the Turkish left, as we have already seen, had been suppressed. Thus between 1960 and 1963 Kütchük was particularly opposed to the expansion of trade with the socialist countries and the government's association with the Afro-Asians. After the outbreak of fighting in 1963 he appealed to President Johnson of the USA to prevent Cyprus from being turned into another Cuba by *'Communist armed infiltration'*.

4. Cyprus was of direct strategic interest to NATO and the organization was concerned with the security of the British bases on the island.

The NATO philosophy therefore was that serious inter-member conflicts should be avoided and that if such disputes occurred they should be settled quickly and peacefully. In fact the threat of war between NATO partners was averted by the swift action of the British who arranged, as already noted, a cease-fire. The British desire to safeguard the status quo was instrumental in saving Cyprus from further catastrophe.

Meanwhile on 26 December the Cyprus government requested the intervention of the Security Council. It called for an urgent meeting to consider charges that Turkey had committed aggression and intervened in the internal affairs of Cyprus by violating the island's air space and territorial waters. Turkey denied the charges and the Council adjourned the debate without taking any action. At all times of course the Cyprus government insisted that the UN was the only international forum at which the crisis could be resolved.

Kemal Gürsel, the Turkish president, also cabled a plea to various foreign capitals to *'prevent further acts of genocide'* on the island, and for the second time jet fighters were sent to buzz Nicosia. Although the government had withdrawn its earlier request for UN intervention, the second threat of a Turkish invasion prompted Foreign Minister Spyros Kyprianou to telephone foreign envoys in Nicosia to apprise them of the situation. In the last days of December the Soviet Union consequently denounced any attempt at foreign intervention in Cyprus and President Johnson sent cablegrams to Makarios and Kütchük calling for a peaceful settlement of the dispute.

On 28 December Duncan Sandys, Secretary of State for the Colonies and Commonwealth Relations, arrived in Cyprus and suggested a conference to discuss the island's future government. The conference, with Sandys in the chair, opened at Marlborough House on 15 January 1964. The Greek and Turkish delegations were led by their respective foreign ministers, Palamas and Erkin, and the two Cypriot delegations by Clerides and Denktash. The conference could not suggest a settlement since those who attended it had completely different views on the Cyprus problem. On 10 February it ended in complete failure. Demetris Bitsios, a young Greek diplomat, recalled:

> "The British, and with them the Americans, wanted above all to prevent the internationalization of the problem. They were disturbed also by the support given to the Archbishop by the Soviet Union. Besides, they wished to buy out the Turkish desire to use military force against Cyprus with the promise that no solution would be granted which did not satisfy their views."[4]

Makarios now sought the assistance of the UN. Simultaneously however the USA, pulling strings to make the UN take its time, proposed a NATO solution. An Anglo-American scheme (later termed the *'Sandys-Ball Plan'*) for a NATO force was formally submitted to the parties concerned on 31 January. The scheme involved the landing of 1,200 US combat troops and a NATO mixed force of 10,000 men to be used for peace-keeping duties and a neutral mediator to search for a political solution. Security considerations

---

[4] Krisimes Ores. (Critical Hours). Pages 143—144.

would then make its permanent presence necessary with the island becoming a NATO base; Makarios' neutralist tendencies would be discouraged and a *de facto* condominium of Greece, Turkey and NATO would perpetuate Allied military influence.

The British Labour Party voiced its opposition to such a scheme. During question time in the Commons on 30 January Harold Wilson declared that *'the sooner it is possible to give that force a UN status, the better it will be for peacekeeping and the reputation of the UN'*. However, Turkey and Greece were persuaded to back the Anglo-American initiative. Paraskevopoulos, the Greek caretaker Prime Minister, made some objections which were immediately overruled after a lightning visit to Athens by the NATO Commander in Europe, General Lyman Lemnitzer. Makarios proved adamant. Yet he stated that he would accept an international force under the Security Council. The plan America had in mind was in fact double *enosis* through partition — the whole island thus becoming a NATO base with Britain removed.

George Ball (acting as US Secretary of State in Dean Rusk's absence) was despatched to Cyprus, but even he could not *'bully'* Makarios (they met twice on 12 February) into accepting the plan. Ball visited London, Athens, Ankara and Nicosia between 9 and 14 February. The governments of Britain and of the USA drew up a revised version of their plan which was accepted by Greece on 8 February and by Turkey on the following day. Makarios did not yield an inch. He thus succeeded in sidetracking a trap laid for him to recognize the American position, which was to make Cyprus a NATO responsibility. In this he had the support of the USSR. On 7 February Khrushchev strongly protested in a letter to the heads of government of Britain, Greece, Turkey, France and the USA against the proposals for a NATO force which he described as *'a case of crude encroachment on the sovereignty, independence and freedom of the Republic of Cyprus'*.

Meanwhile a Lemnitzer initiative tried to impose *de facto* partition. He sent telegrams to the governments of Greece and Turkey urging them to disembark troops on the island which would have led to the landing of a NATO mixed force to interpose itself between the two communities and confront Makarios with a *fait accompli*. In the end Makarios' determination prevailed. He was also backed by the strong administration of **George Papandreou,** who was sworn into office on 19 February after a decisive victory at the polls; as far as he could Papandreou resisted American pressure. Hence he sent a message to the archbishop on 25 February assuring him of the solidarity of the Greek nation and government. On 13 April, after a meeting with Makarios in Athens, it was announced that complete agreement had been reached on the handling of the Cyprus problem. At that meeting a critical decision had been made. Papandreou proposed, and Makarios accepted, that troops and arms should be sent to Cyprus to prevent a future Turkish invasion. By midsummer an estimated 10,000 officers and men, fully equipped, were in the island. The bargaining strength of the Greeks and of the Greek Cypriots was greatly reinforced.

Makarios was henceforth assured of the support not only of the USSR and the neutralist world but also of a leading member of the western alliance. Behind Greece, ready to profit from the dissensions of western polycentrism, stood France (the Gaullist notion being that Europe's destiny was not America's concern), unwilling to see the Cyprus crisis taken up by NATO and willing to back Greece in its dispute with the other member (Turkey) of the western alliance.

The archbishop had several motives in seeking refuge at the UN:

1. to secure a guarantee against a possible Turkish invasion;
2. to gather enough support to nullify in due course the treaties of Alliance and Guarantee;
3. to make the UN directly responsible for the solution of the Cyprus problem and thus escape from the straitjacket of new negotiations with the three guarantor powers alone or with NATO: since 1955 Makarios feared all American-backed Anglo-Turkish combinations against Greece and himself;
4. to isolate, as far as possible, the Turks who had evidently fewer friends at the UN than at NATO headquarters;
5. to rule out partition; and
6. to pave the way for a unitary state with majority rule:Makarios, though paying lip-service to *enosis,* desired Cyprus to remain a neutral state.

On 15 February, one hour before Zenon Rossides, the Cypriot ambassador, was to make his appeal to the UN, Britain asked for an early meeting of the Security Council to deal with the *'dangerous situation'* in Cyprus. Two days later U **Thant,** the UN Secretary-General, submitted certain proposals to the Greek Cypriot delegation led by Kyprianou and Clerides. The Cypriots, though pleased with U Thant's initiative, gave no encouragement to proceed further. During the Security Council meeting Kyprianou asked on 25 February whether the Treaty of Guarantee gave the three guarantor powers the right to invade Cyprus. Denktash, on the other hand, three days later expounded the theory that symbiosis between Greeks and Turks was impossible.

However, on 4 March 1964, the Security Council through resolution no. 186 unanimously recommended the establishment of a UN peace-keeping force and the appointment of a mediator *'for the purpose of promoting a peaceful solution and an agreed settlement of the problem confronting Cyprus, in accordance with the Charter of the UN, bearing in mind the well-being of the people of Cyprus as a whole, and the preservation of international peace and security'.* The force was to be stationed in Cyprus for three months and all costs were to be met by the states providing contingents, by the government of the island and by voluntary contributions. In effect the Cypriot authorities accepted an international force funded and manned largely by NATO members but controlled by the Security Council.

On 12 March Turkey rejected Rolz-Bennet of Guatemala as the mediator on Cyprus and on 25 March Sakari Tuomioja of Finland was appointed instead. Following the death of Tuomioja, Señor Galo Lasso Plaza, ex-President of Ecuador, succeeded him on 16 September. On 27 March the UN force became operational and was placed under the command of Lt-General P.S. Gyani of India. By 8 June its strength was 6,411, composed as follows:

Military (UNFICYP)		Police (UNCIVPOL)	
Austria	55	Australia	40
Canada	1,122	Austria	33
Denmark	676	Denmark	40
Finland	1,000	New Zealand	20
Sweden	954	Sweden	40
Ireland	639		
UK	1,792		
	6,238		173

The resolution of 4 March however failed to reduce tension in the island. On the following day Turkish armed bands fired the first shots around the Saint Hilarion fortress and on 6 March a bomb exploded in the building of the Turkish Cypriot communal chamber. The aim, as in 1958, was to put the blame on the Greeks and thus provide an excuse for further strife. Outbursts of shooting and killing continued unabated.

On 13 March Turkey threatened once more to invade Cyprus and demanded that Makarios should put an end to the fighting, release Turkish hostages and restore freedom of movement. Stavros Costopoulos, the Greek Foreign Minister, replied that if Turkey used military force against Cyprus his country would also fight. At 6 p.m. on 13 March the Security Council met and adopted resolution no. 187, calling upon all members to comply with its resolution of 4 March and to refrain from any action which might worsen the situation.

Events now moved very fast in Cyprus. On 4 April Makarios denounced the Treaty of Alliance with Greece and Turkey. On 11 and 26 April heavy fighting was centred around the Saint Hilarion fortress. On the following day U Thant explained that in spite of the presence of UN forces there had been 126 outbursts of shooting in the past month. On 29 April he reported that the UN mission had no hope of succeeding until all the irregulars in the island were disarmed. Nevertheless, in a memorandum to Tuomioja on 14 May, Makarios set out his proposals for a Cypriot unitary state containing wide guarantees for the Turkish minority. Turkish plans on the other hand had previously recommended partition into two cantonal states with a federal government responsible for foreign affairs, finance and defence. It must be noted that, throughout April and May, Lieutenant Commander Martin Packard — a Greek speaking intelligence officer — and others, worked tirelessly for reintegration and had talks with all the island's leaders. He was mysteriously removed from the island and sent back to London!

The month of June was particularly critical. On the first day conscription was introduced and three days later the first recruits were called up. Almost immediately Turkey threatened another invasion. The US again intervened and George Ball undertook his second mission to Athens and Ankara, inviting both Premiers to visit Washington. On 5 June Johnson sent a secret letter to Ismet Inönü that, in the latter's words, *included all the juridical thunderbolts that could be assembled*. The president argued that:

1. The Turkish decision to intervene by military force to occupy a portion of Cyprus was unwise and fraught with far-reaching consequences.

2. The purpose of such intervention would be to effect a form of partition and thus produce a solution which was specifically excluded by the Treaty of Guarantee.

3. Such an invasion would violate a number of international commitments: first, a commitment to complete consultation with the

Boy scouts at the forefront: at work and at orderly processions.

Some of the Republic's new coins.

The early years of independence resulted in a major revival of the Greek arts, culture, history etc.

Above: Kourion theatre hosts a performance of HECUBA (the principal wife of the Trojan King Priam and mother of Hector), by higher education students.

Right: A group of Cypriot students posing under the 'Caryatids' at the Acropolis. Such visits to Greece's classical monuments became the secret desire of every youngster's life.

US before any such action was taken; second, a commitment to consult with the other two Guarantor Powers, which had by no means been exhausted; third, a commitment to NATO not to undermine the strength of that organization or to run the risk of involving the Soviet Union; and fourth, a commitment to the UN to act in a manner consistent with its efforts to bring peace to the island.

4. Under the US-Turkey Agreement of 12 July 1947, American consent was required for the use of military assistance for purposes other than those for which assistance was furnished. *'I must tell you in all candour that the US cannot agree to the use of any US supplied military equipment for a Turkish intervention in Cyprus under present circumstances',* the President continued.

Replying on 14 June, the Turkish Premier stated that *'the necessity of a military intervention in Cyprus has been felt four times since the closing days of 1963'.* Inönü also expressed great concern that the pending report of the Secretary-General to be submitted to the UN on 15 June would result in another defeat for Turkey *'similar to the one we all suffered on 4 March 1964'.*

The Cyprus crisis of 1963-4 marked a watershed in US-Turkish relations. The specific event which triggered the reaction, after a long-simmering discontent, was Johnson's letter. Numerous anti-American demonstrations were staged in Ankara throughout the summer of 1964 and there was strong opposition in the Turkish press to US efforts to restrain Turkey from military intervention. In fact, as in the 1950s, there were guaranteed demonstrations in Greece or Turkey whenever it was seen that American policy was tilting against either country. Thus the US-Turkey honeymoon which had lasted since 1947 was at least temporarily interrupted. This incident in particular disabused the Turks of the belief that their interests were in every respect identical and that they could count on American support in every eventuality.

On 20 June UNFICYP was extended by resolution no. 192 for a further three months. General **Kodendera S. Thimayya,** also of India, succeeded Gyani as commander of the force. Towards the end of the month the USA made mediation moves via its seasoned diplomat **Dean Acheson,** Secretary of State from 1949 to 1953 and then adviser to both Kennedy and Johnson. He went to Geneva where Tuomioja was to be stationed. Before the month was out Tuomioja informed D. Bitsios, the Greek permanent representative at the UN, that the differences between the two sides were virtually unbridgeable, that war between Greece and Turkey was a distinct possibility and that he needed Acheson's help in Geneva to enable him to carry out his task. The Americans had of course stated on several occasions that they viewed with pessimism the role and functions of the UN mediator. **June also witnessed the return of Grivas to Cyprus.** By 15 August he had succeeded General Karayiannis as supreme commander of the Cypriot national guard.

In that climacteric month both Inönü and Papandreou visited the USA. The latter met Johnson at the White House on 24 June and his son Andreas, present at that fateful meeting, recorded that it had not been a discussion but a monologue, which soon became a brain-washing operation with Johnson insisting that what was needed to resolve the crisis were summit-level negotiations between Papandreou and Inönü. Senior officials moreover pointed out that in the event of Turkey attacking Cyprus and or Greece, the Americans would be *"unwilling to lift a finger"*.[5]

US pressure on the Greek government was intensified in July. As early as May, Senator Fulbright, Chairman of the Senate Foreign Affairs Committee, was despatched to Greece and Turkey to convey the sense of urgency felt in the US regarding the restoration of order in the island. On 2 July Johnson sent a letter to Papandreou urging him to come to terms with Turkey. Specifically he appeared to have suggested an exchange of territories under which Cyprus could be united with Greece. But Johnson warned that in the event of war, which Turkey was bound to win, the USA would be obliged to stand aside.

Meanwhile further fighting in Cyprus was used as an excuse for the expulsion of Greeks from Istanbul. On 17 July U Thant warned the Greek, Turkish and Cypriot governments that military preparations in Cyprus were leading to greater risks of a showdown. On the previous day Turkey had gone through the motions of preparing for a landing on the island. Top level Greco-British talks in London on 20 July proved abortive since Whitehall was presenting only a more polished version of the Washington formula. While these talks were under way President Gürsel was threatening to bomb Cyprus. In Athens Makarios agreed with the Greek government on 27 July to take the Cyprus issue to the General Assembly of the UN instead of merely to the Security Council.

---

[5] Democracy at Gunpoint. 1973. Pages 136-137.

In the meantime Acheson was in Geneva where he was in almost daily contact with Tuomioja and the Greek and Turkish representatives. These discussions (in which Ball insisted that no Cypriot should participate) were aimed at the final settlement of the Cyprus problem and were held in the greatest secrecy. The now famous *'Acheson Plan'* was taking shape. Cyprus as an independent state was to be eliminated. The key provisions appeared to have been the following:

1. Cyprus was to be united with Greece, in return for a 30-to 50-year lease of a military base to Turkey. The Turks would have sovereignty over the base, whose size was to be approximately equal to one-fifth of the island, i.e. *'to engulf most of the Turkish Cypriot population'*. Castellorizon, a small island on the Aegean, was also to be ceded to Turkey.

2. Cyprus would be cantonized, creating two parallel governmental structures, one for each of the ethnic groups.

3. A joint military command for Greece and Turkey would be set up.

4. Compensation would be paid to all Turkish Cypriots who wished to leave the island.

The USA's direct and active interest in the dispute was intended to safeguard the south-eastern flank of NATO and to curb Soviet infiltration of the area. In fact Greece was to eliminate AKEL's influence and neutralize Makarios' capability for political action. The return of Grivas in June 1964 was intended to serve as a countervailing force to the President.

The Turkish government accepted the above proposals only as a basis for negotiations. It saw the plan as another variant of partition or double *enosis,* the bargaining being centred on the size of the Turkish area. For exactly the same reason it was rejected by both Athens and Nicosia. Moreover the Greek Cypriot leadership was increasingly identifying itself with a policy favouring independence with neutrality but without *enosis*. It was also believed that greater reliance should be placed on the UN, both for peace-keeping functions and as a guarantor of the independence and territorial integrity of Cyprus. Thus the Acheson proposals of 28 July were found to be inconsistent with existing realities and therefore unacceptable.

In August 1964 the supply of arms by sea from Turkey into the Mansoura-Kokkina Turkish stronghold had reached large proportions and it was felt that an attempt to link up with either Lefka or Polis would be made by the Turks, thus effectively cutting off the western road from Xero to Paphos. A strong national guard contingent directed by Grivas was moved in to cut off any intended armed attack. As the Greeks pushed forward, four Turkish air force jets appeared and fired warning shots out to sea off Polis. By the early hours of 8 August the Turks had been pushed out of Mansoura and Ayios Theodoros and retreated into Kokkina. In the afternoon however 30 Turkish jets appeared and on the following day 64 similar jets machine-gunned everything in sight. Peaceful Cypriot villages and other targets were indiscriminately bombed with napalm bombs. Hospitals were hit and scores of women and children, as well as doctors and nurses, were either killed or wounded.

The irony of this ghastly episode was that the planes and napalm bombs were supplied by the Americans for NATO defensive purposes but were used instead to attack a smaller state, a member of the UN and British Commonwealth. Furthermore, the US Sixth Fleet *('the grey ghost of the Mediterranean'),* which had been in the vicinity for some time, did nothing to prevent the outrage.

At the Security Council the Turkish representative explained on 8 August that Cyprus was being bombed on a *'limited and restricted basis only'.* He told everyone to sleep well since there would be no further action. Yet shortly afterwards napalm bombs were used.

Athens retaliated by warning that if the bombing did not stop *'intervention'* would be the only answer. The Greek telegram, resembling an ultimatum, was delivered at the Security Council; P. Morozov of the Soviet Union supported the Greek demands. Both Johnson and Khruschev, the Soviet leader, once again made it clear to Turkey that they would not approve an invasion. The Turks complied and the Security Council, after denouncing the Turkish action, passed yet another resolution (no. 193) on 9 August calling for a cease-fire. Two days later it noted with satisfaction that *'the cease-fire is being observed throughout Cyprus'.*

On 9 August it was also announced in Nicosia that the Cyprus government had appealed to the USSR and Egypt for military aid to protect the sovereignty and independence of the island. In reply to this appeal the Kremlin emphasized on 15 August that *'if a foreign armed invasion of the island takes place, the Soviet Union will help Cyprus to defend her freedom and independence... and is prepared to begin negotiations on this matter'.* Consequently a joint communiqué was issued in Moscow on 1 October stating that agreement had been reached between the two countries on *'practical measures of assistance'* to be given by the Soviet Union to Cyprus for *'safeguarding the freedom and territorial integrity'* of the latter. The Cypriot Foreign Minister remarked that the Soviet Union's aid was being provided with *'no strings attached and no conditions whatsoever'*.

The Acheson proposals as already shown, were abortive, but the talks were resumed in August and Acheson on the 20th suggested a revised (final) version of his plan. He proposed *enosis* in return for a NATO base in Cyprus under Turkish command. The base would be leased to Turkey for a *'reasonable'* number of years. Both the Turks and Makarios answered *'no'* but a sizeable proportion of the higher Greek establishment believed that the plan should be accepted. Professor Andreas Papandreou, a leading proponent of Cypriot independence, explained: *'The King, in his eagerness to maintain positive relations with the US, took the initiative in promoting this plan, and pressure was put on our government by the Americans to denounce Makarios' policies as a prelude to the execution of the plan'*[6]

At the UN, resolution no. 198 was adopted on 18 December. The Security Council recalled its earlier resolutions and asked members to abide by them; informed members of a marked improvement in the internal condition of the island and, extended UNFICYP for another three months.

The search for a solution was now centred on the UN mediator. On 26 March 1965 the Secretary-General transmitted a report by **Galo Plaza** to members of the Security Council. The report, composed of 173 paragraphs, was a full background investigation into the entire Cyprus problem. After a careful examination of the internal aspects of the Cyprus puzzle and the positions of the parties concerned (Britain, Greece and Turkey), Plaza made specific observations on the prospects of dealing with the situation. In fact the report was intended to serve as the basis for a new solution. Its main points were:

1. Cyprus should remain an independent state, renouncing its right to unite with Greece. The report stressed that *'If Cyprus should become fully independent by being freed from the 1960 treaty obligations, it would automatically acquire at the same time the right of self-determination'*.

2. The island should be *'demilitarized'*. The question of the British bases was set aside for later consideration.

---

[6] Ibid. page 140.

3. There should be *'no partition or physical separation of the two communities'*. Turkish Cypriots *'wished'* to be physically separated from the Greek community, but this separation was utterly unacceptable to the majority community and could not be imposed except by force. Nevertheless, Turkish Cypriot rights should be guaranteed by the UN and supervised by a UN commisioner in Cyprus.
4. A settlement should depend in the first place on agreement between the people of Cyprus themselves and talks should take place between Greek and Turkish Cypriots.

Plaza concluded by reiterating his conviction that *'every endeavour must continue to be made to bring about a peaceful solution and an agreed settlement of the Cyprus problem consistent with the provisions of the UN Charter'*.

The Plaza Report was in general sympathetically received by Greece and the Greek Cypriots. Turkey and the Turkish Cypriots rejected it as *'unacceptable'*. In fact the government of Suat Hayri Urguplu, which had taken over from Inönü, was a caretaker administration formed to fill the gap until the national elections of October 1965. A weak government, conscious of the army in the background, it felt obliged to take a strong line in public over Cyprus. It not only rejected the plan outright but also rejected Plaza himself as a future mediator, proposing instead direct talks between Greece and Turkey. As Plaza himself stated (paragraph 107), the Turks continued to insist that any settlement must contain two elements: *the prohibition of enosis and the geographical separation of the two communities under a federal system of government.*

The Plaza Report was noted by the Political Committee of the General Assembly and so can be said to have been approved to that extent by the UN. Moreover, on 18 December 1965 the Cyprus government succeeded in securing the adoption of resolution 2077 (XX) by the General Assembly which supported its claim for the *'unfettered'* independence of Cyprus and discounted the Turkish claim to the right of intervention based on the Zürich and London treaties. The resolution, carried by 47 votes to 5 with 54 abstentions and 11 nations absent, called on all states to respect the sovereignty, unity, independence and territorial integrity of the island. Surprisingly, the Cyprus government did not demand a Security Council meeting to discuss the actual rejection of the Plaza Report. The five negative

In the late 1960s and 1970s Cyprus developed into a major tourist attraction. Famagusta (above), the "reviera of the Eastern Mediterranean" and "romantic" Kyrenia (below), are now under Turkish occupation.

Light industry and agriculture were encouraged and developed. This led to cultural activities like the Orange Festival of Famagusta and the Wine Festival of Limassol (below) which were well attended.

votes were cast by the USA, Turkey, Iran, Pakistan and Albania.

In Cyprus meanwhile the two communities followed their antithetical directions. The Turkish Cypriot leadership, not content with keeping the two communities apart by persuasion, force, threats and killings, now set up regulations to keep them at a distance. A makeshift administration was set up in the main Nicosia-Kyrenia road enclave with representatives in other areas, a separate civil service, police force (the crescent and star replacing the republic's insignia) and radio station.

Consequently Turkish Cypriots abandoned many of their villages and gathered for *'self-protection'* and the facilitation of partition in the more densely populated areas. According to UN figures around 25,000 so-called *'refugees'* were forced to relocate in this manner. Greek Cypriots were not permitted to enter these areas nor were the Turks allowed to leave without permission from their leaders. Confined in such places without sufficient resources, the Turks survived as a *'separate'* entity only with direct economic aid from Turkey (between £10 and £12 million annually). However, despite harassment from their leaders and pressure from armed gangs which had arrived from Turkey after 1963, a far greater number of Turkish Cypriots remained in government-controlled areas.

The Turkish demand for partition or, as a second best, the geographical separation of the two communities, never wavered. Glafkos Clerides, writing in 1966, explained:

> "Turkey proposes to break up the unitary state by reshuffling the population on the basis of communal criteria to create predominantly Turkish areas, with the apparent intention of creating two federal states; but with the real intention of preparing the ground for partition, which today is physically impossible owing to the fact that the Greeks and Turks live side by side in the same villages and towns of the Island."[7]

Galo Plaza also pointed out in his report that he was reluctant to believe, as the Turkish Cypriot leadership claimed, in the *'impossibility'* of the two communities learning to live together again in peace. He showed that in those parts of the island where movement controls had been relaxed and tensions reduced they were already

---

[7] Middle East Forum. Volume 42. No.1 Page 11.

proving otherwise. In fact a survey conducted on the damage caused to Turkish Cypriot properties induced the government to launch a rebuilding programme to encourage them to return to houses they had left during the fighting. Moreover contacts had already been established where they had been severed: commercial dealings for example had been restarted within days of the fighting. In fact there was in the economic sector an almost total unity and mutual dependence.

However, in order to counter the Turkish separatist moves the Greeks, having secured absolute control over the government, enacted legislation in 1964-65 which incorporated most of Makarios' 13 proposed amendments to the 1960 Constitution. They also offered the Turkish Cypriots a Bill of Minority Rights. In fact the structural and functional changes to the 1960 Constitution had been directed towards establishing a unified state with unfettered independence. There was no intention of reverting to the conditions before December 1963. Plaza also emphasized that the problem of Cyprus could not be resolved by attempting to restore the situation before the outbreak of intercommunal strife, but that a new solution must be found consistent with the provisions of the UN Charter.

In 1965 Henry Labouisse, the new American Ambassador to Greece, 'prepared' a five-point programme for the pacification of Cyprus over a six-month period. The terms were intended to satisfy the pride of the Turks and to improve their relative military position. Petros Garoufalias, The Greek Minister of Defence, who went to Cyprus in mid-March to meet the Cypriot cabinet and present the Labouisse plan, returned empty-handed. Makarios, supported by Papandreou, maintained his unyielding stand and declared that he would never deviate from the line that the Cyprus question was exclusively a matter within the competence of the UN and 'cannot be the object of Greco–Turkish negotiations'.

It was around this time that the first news of an attempt to remove Papandreou appeared in the Press. In early April 1965 the Cypriot media carried the story that the king was searching for a way to overthrow the elected government, to form a cabinet of national unity and to close the Cyprus question on the basis of the Acheson plan. There was in fact such a conspiracy, and it had much to do with the Premier's strong stand on the Cyprus question. A deliberate plot brewing for weeks to oust him succeeded. On 15 July he was forced to resign. According to Andreas Papandreou, 'Cyprus lay at the heart of the tragic political developments that led to the death of democracy in Greece'.

The Greek elections scheduled for 28 May 1967 were never held. On 21 April a small gang of junior army officers, under the leadership of **George Papadopoulos** and closely associated with the intelligence services of Greece and the USA, put into effect a NATO-elaborated contingency plan called *'Prometheus'* and thus plunged the country into a ruthless military dictatorship.

Following the coup many Cypriots feared that the large number of Greek troops in the island might attempt to overthrow Makarios and forcibly achieve enosis. In early August Papadopoulos, then Minister to the Prime Minister, visited Cyprus and tried to concert a plan for *enosis* with the island's government. At the same time the Greek leadership declared that *'Greece and Turkey are bound by the need to confront jointly the common enemy – communism – and to consider all outstanding differences of view as secondary to this primary interest'*. Cyprus was soon to be auctioned, and leading the bidding were the two *'mother'* countries.

On 9 September the Greek and Turkish delegations headed by their two Premiers, Constantine Kollias and Suleyman Demirel, met at Kesan, a small Turkish village about 18 miles from the Greek border, and on the following day at Alexandroupolis in Thrace, Greece. Both countries had agreed that Cyprus must be integrated into the western defensive system, thus preserving the security of the Turkish mainland and of the island's Turkish Cypriots and nullifying the Communist danger from the north. The following issues are not at all clear:

1. what percentage of the island's territory and how many military bases Turkey demanded in return for *enosis;*

2. whether the Greeks offered Turkey the British sovereign base of Akrotiri;

3. whether the Greeks offered territorial concessions in Thrace and elsewhere in return for *enosis;*

4. whether the above proposals were also suggested to the Turks by Stephanopoulos in 1966. He had been premier from September 1965 to December 1966, and had always been at loggerheads with the Cypriot President.

In Cyprus meanwhile, both sides were extending their fortifications and consequently, according to UNFICYP, over 600 shooting incidents took place during 1967. The Ayios Theodoros-Kophinou incidents of 15 November, in which 24 Turkish and 2 Greek Cypriots were killed, have been fully documented by an eye-witness, Brigadier Michael Harbottle, then chief of staff of UNFICYP, in his book *The Impartial Soldier.*

An acute crisis was caused by the incidents in these two villages. In Ankara the Grand Assembly met and decided to fight if necessary. Planes flew over Nicosia and 30 warships stood by in the channel separating the island from Turkey. In Ankara and Constantinople violent anti-Greek riots erupted, and the best units in the Turkish army were rushed to Alexandretta (Iskenderun) on the northeast coast facing Cyprus. In Salonica, the principal port for garrisoning and supplying the Greek army on the island, there were unusual troop movements. Across the Evros river Turkish and Greek armoured units, guns at the port, faced each other.

The build-up by both countries continued. Papadopoulos, who for mainly personal reasons wanted peace, worked tirelessly to avoid such a confrontation. On 21 November he offered bilateral talks, an act contrary to the spirit of the Plaza proposals, but his offer was turned down while an estimated 80,000 people in Constantinople and 30,000 in Izmir demonstrated for war and blood donors volunteered at various hospitals. In Athens air-raid shelters were being cleaned, and according to several reports Greek contingents received sealed battle orders.

Meanwhile peace initiatives to avert a war were forthcoming. U Thant for the UN sent a special envoy, Signor J. Rolz-Bennet, NATO sent Manlio Brosio, its former (1961-64) Secretary-General, and President Johnson sent **Cyrus Vance.** Whilst the last was in Turkey President Sunay warned world leaders on 24 November that his country intended to solve the Cyprus problem *"once and for all".* Yet Demirel informed Kosygin at a Kremlin dinner on 20 September that, *"we are wholly and entirely guided by our desire for a peaceful solution of this problem".*

At midnight on 17 November Turkey delivered an ultimatum to Greece demanding that certain conditions should be agreed to instantly or its troops would land in Cyprus to defend the island's Turks. The five major demands were:

1. General Grivas should be recalled. To lower the temperature the Greeks decided on his immediate recall. He was flown to Athens on 19 November and on the next day resigned his supreme command of the Cyprus forces.

2. All Greek troops stationed in Cyprus since 1964 should be removed. The withdrawal of this estimated 10,000 strong contin-

gent began on 8 December, yet, the admittedly smaller number of Turkish troops that had infiltrated Cyprus since 1963 remained on the island.

3. An indemnity should be paid for the Turks killed and damages for the property destroyed.

4. Greek Cypriot organizations should be disarmed, including the national guard.

5. Pressure on the Turkish Cypriot community should cease.

Agreement on the above conditions and on several other issues was arrived at on 26 November. Cyprus was not invaded. Turkey had triumphed and the agreed withdrawal of the Greek troops meant that Greece and the Greek Cypriots had lost an important bargaining card. In this political climate the Turkish Cypriots instituted on 28 December a separate administration which they named the *'Provisional Turkish Cypriot Administration'*. The UN was not informed until the day after and U Thant expressed his misgivings.

Even though intercommunal tensions eased after the clashes of 1967 the situation on Cyprus remained at an impasse. On the initiative of the island's government the Cyprus question was again brought before the UN, where U Thant offered his good offices by proposing the commencement of direct negotiations between the island's two communities. The *intercommunal talks* began under his auspices in Beirut on 11 June 1968.

Hence the pro-government faction changed its immediate geopolitical goal to independence; other groups continued to seek enosis. Those who sought independence decided to negotiate with the Turkish Cypriots and therefore undertook political and economic actions to facilitate such discussions. Those who continued to seek enosis as an immediate goal decided to continue their *'fight'* not only against the Turkish Cypriots but also to take up arms against Greek Cypriots wanting independence.

For six years the two negotiating teams met regularly. Even though agreement was reached on most matters, considerable differences divided the two sides over the authority to be vested in local government and the international guarantees to be given to the new constitutional order.

The chief stumbling block seems to have been the Turkish insistence on a separatist policy based on a federal state composed of two communities; ie., a state within a state. A breakthrough was very nearly achieved in both 1972 and 1973 but it appears again that Ankara suddenly objected. Partition under the euphemism of federation had been its persistent objective.

Ioannis Christophides, the Cypriot Foreign Minister, informed the UN General Assembly in November 1976 that the Turkish Cypriots had plans to partition the island in 1963. He quoted extracts from a secret document dated September 1963 bearing the signatures of Kütchük and Denktash which revealed planned self-segregation as the first step to partition. In the following year Kemal Satir, a former deputy Prime Minister of Turkey, publicly declared that *"Cyprus will be divided into two sections, one of which will join Turkey"*. A secret document issued on 18 April 1964 by Ismet Inönü, the Turkish Prime Minister, clearly laid out the partitionist plan of his country which was named by him the **'Attila Plan'**. This scheme was proposed in 1965 by Kütchük to the UN mediator and appears in Plaza's report of 26 March 1965 to the UN Secretary-General. The plan covered essentially the area which Turkey occupied following its invasion of Cyprus in July 1974 — the area coveted by Turkey for so many years. Inönü also explained quite emphatically on 17 May 1964 that:

'one day Greece will agree to a peaceful partition of Cyprus with the help of NATO. As long as the Greeks refuse, the battle will go on – Turkey will not recede in any hopeless position – Turkey will use her right of intervention in the island'.

On 8 September 1964 Inönü informed the National Assembly that "officially we promoted the federation concept rather than the partition thesis". In fact geographical federation is simply a disguised form of partition. In June of that year F.C. Erkin, the Turkish Foreign Minister, stated in Athens that "the radical solution would be to cede one part of Cyprus to Greece and the other, closest to the Turkish Asiatic coast, to Turkey".

Turkey's intentions emerged once again on 1 February 1974 when, following a long parliamentary crisis after the elections of the previous autumn, the coalition government under **Bülent Ecevit** signed a protocol in which it declared that only *'Federation'* would be accepted in Cyprus. The call for such a system was repeated with great regularity by Turkish officials.

Such statements thwarted all efforts to reach a settlement in accordance with the previously accepted principles that the solution of the constitutional problem of Cyprus should be on the basis of an independent, sovereign and unitary state. Turkey, seeking a pretext to enforce its plans, set its invasion machine in motion. The opportunity soon appeared in the form of a *coup d' état* by the Greek junta and its proxies against President Makarios on 15 July 1974. Five days later Turkey invaded Cyprus.

The years since 1968 were notable for several other important events. Firstly, Makarios announced on 12 January 1968 that elections would be held during the following month. On 25 February he was re-elected President. He received 220,911 votes (95.45 per cent) and his opponent, a Nicosia psychiatrist Dr Takis Evdokas, within weeks leader of DEK (Democratikon Ethnikon Komma — Democratic National Party), received 8,577 (3.71 per cent). DEK (the **'predecessor'** of EOKA-B and ESEA) was formally set up in March/April 1968 and Evdokas began publishing *Gnomi (Opinion),* a weekly newspaper that sharply criticized the government's policies and advocated *enosis* as the only guarantee against Communism. On 15 February Kütchük was returned unopposed as Vice-President of Cyprus.

A second major event was the attempted assassination of the Greek *'military'* leader. On 13 August 1968 A. Panaghoullis unsuccessfully tried to blow up the car of Papadopoulos. During the enquiries that followed curious links were revealed between Panaghoullis and the Cyprus government which led to the resignation of **Polycarpos Georghadjis,** a former EOKA district leader and at the time Minister of the Interior and Defence. Georghadjis himself was mysteriously assassinated on 16 March 1970.

Thirdly, the Greek Cypriots found themselves plunged into a domestic political crisis. The government's policy of abandoning *'genuine enosis'* for the *'attainable solution'* of a peaceful, independent, sovereign Cyprus was opposed both by the extreme right of the island and by the junta in Greece. Enosis was finally *'buried'* and Makarios was accused of being its 'undertaker par excellence'. By 1972 a new underground organization called EOKA-B was created and quickly infiltrated into the government, civil service, clubs and associations. Its political front ESEA *(Epitropi Sindonismou Enotikou Agonos – Co-ordinating Committee for the Enosis Struggle),* with **Photis Papaphotis,** ex-EOKA district leader, as its general secretary, had regular contacts with the island's senior churchmen and with the Greek embassy. The conspirators were both numerous and well armed.

Plots to assassinate Makarios became frequent. The first assault, coded *'Hermes',* was made on 8 March 1970; power was to be seized by means of a coup. Grivas, reportedly disguised as a priest, returned to Cyprus in September 1971 to direct the anti-Makarios forces. Ankara, which in 1967 was instrumental in removing him from the island, did not raise a murmur in 1971!

In 1973 there were several armed clashes between the *'rebels'* and security forces. After the creation of EOKA-B the government in 1972 formed the Auxiliary Police (or Tactical Reserve) Force. Christos Vakis, the Minister of Justice, was kidnapped on 27 July. Another attempt was made on Makarios' life at Ayios Serghios on 7 October. Earlier, in August, police discovered machine-gun positions on the Nicosia-Troodos road and at Kokkinotrimithia, from which assassination attempts were to be made against Makarios. The president was not the only target. Since 1969 pro-*enosis* groups had embarked on a campaign of terrorism, raiding police stations to steal arms, bombing British military buildings and vehicles, shooting and wounding the chief of police and making several bomb attacks on government ministers and other political leaders. One such attack was outside Papaioannou's house on 14 October 1969. Next day the AKEL leader accused the CIA of preparing a plan which entailed the assassination of progressive Members of Parliament, the arming of Greek and Turkish bands to provoke incidents, the overthrow of Makarios and the imposition of partition.

At the same time the Greek military government, subservient to foreign interests and for the sake of maintaining its power, followed a double policy on Cyprus. Though it officially supported the intercommunal talks it undertook a campaign to corrode the Cyprus state by financing and encouraging elements working to overthrow the island's legitimate government. The Athenian cabal (known popularly as the *'changing of the guard'*, Papadopoulos being replaced following the *'popular'* rising of 16 November 1973 by the hidden strong man **Brigadier Ioannides** on 25 November) worked conscientiously for the virtual partition of Cyprus. Thus Papadopoulos told a Turkish reporter on 31 May 1971 that if Greece and Turkey came to a mutual agreement *'our children in Cyprus would also consent to bury their differences'*

As early as November 1967 the Pipinelis-Cyrus Vance talks seem to have proposed to partition the island[8]. At the June 1971 NATO

---

[8] In December 1966, the talks in Paris between the Foreign Ministers of Greece and Turkey — Admiral J. Toumbas and I.S. Caglayangil — appeared to have had the same double enosis content.

Foreign Ministers' Conference at Lisbon, the two countries by all accounts, promised to split their differences and divide Cyprus. Relations between Papadopoulos and Makarios deteriorated and their meetings on 3-4 September 1971 proved futile. The Greek dictator was furious because the Cypriot president had visited the Soviet Union between 2 and 9 June of that year.

Makarios therefore had been under constant pressure from the mainland clique. Athens now insisted that he should dismiss ministers considered hostile to Greece. A provocative note dated 11 February 1972 demanded that a government of national unity should be formed and should include moderate representatives of Grivas. The president did not resist the pressure for long. A coup *'scheduled'* for 14 February was averted but on 5 May Spyros Kyprianou, the Foreign Minister, who had been the main target of the junta's hostility resigned (his dismissal having been demanded since 1971), together with two other ministers. In June the cabinet was reorganised.

After 1973 *enosis* adherents prepared such plans as *'Apollo'*, *'Gronthos'* and *'Aphrodite 3'*. The conspiracy was in full swing. In the spring and summer of 1974 EOKA-B intensified its activities. Police stations were raided and there were hundreds of bomb explosions. When Grivas died on 27 January George Karousos assumed command of the organization. However, by the end of February control of the movement appeared to have passed to Kikis Constantinou and Lefteris Papadopoullos. In reality it was directed from Athens and financed at the rate of C£1 million a year. On 25 April it was declared unlawful. Makarios reacted by sending a letter, dated 2 July but delivered the next day, to President Phaidon Ghizikis of Greece demanding, amongst other things, the withdrawal of Greek officers in the Greek contingent and national guard on the ground that they were plotting against the island's legal government. No reply was received.

By this time the plot coded *'Hermes'* was an open secret. On 3 July the Greek Foreign Minister S. Tetenes, his aides and several Greek officers resigned in disgust. On 5 July *Apoyevmatini,* a Nicosia newspaper, printed an account of the plot against Makarios, adding that the Greek officers and their EOKA-B henchmen planned to kill the president and put a puppet in his place. On 7 July Cypriot newspapers published the rchbishop's letter under banner headlines. Surprisingly however nothing was done militarily to prevent it.

On 2 July, at the office of General Gregorios Mbonanos, chief of the Greek armed forces, the coup preparations took their final shape.

Those present were Mbonanos, Ioannides, Georgitsis and Papadakis. The last two[9] were ordered to carry out these plans in Cyprus. In order to confuse the island's government, the political representative of Greece in Cyprus departed for the Greek capital on Friday 12 July[10].

The fateful day was Monday 15 July. The first announcement of the *coup d'état* came from the Cyprus Broadcasting Corporation at around 8 a.m. and it contained the following points:

1. The National Guard intervened on 15 July to stop internecine war between Greeks.

2. The main purpose of the National Guard is to maintain order.

3. The matter is an internal one among Greeks alone.

4. The National Guard is in control of the situation and Makarios is dead.

5. Anyone who puts up resistance will be executed at once.

It's ironic however, that the coup provoked no immediate action by the Security Council or the Cypriot delegate to the UN. **Nicos Sampson,** believed to be the fourth choice, was installed as president. Makarios however escaped and on 15 July confirmed reports that he was alive by broadcasting to his people from Paphos. The message, transmitted by the Free Cyprus Broadcasting Corporation, urged the entire Greek Cypriot population to continue its resistance against the dictatorship. From Paphos he was flown by helicopter to Akrotiri and then by RAF plane to Malta, where he spent the night at Valletta as the guest of the Mintoff government.

On 17 July Makarios arrived at RAF Lyneham, Wiltshire, and proceeded to have talks with Harold Wilson, the British Prime Minister, at 10 Downing Street and then at the Foreign and Commonwealth Office with James Callaghan. He was not only promised unqalified support at the UN but also that Her Majesty's Government would not recognize the island's *'existing'* administration since he and none other was the acknowledged leader and elected President of Cyprus. The archbishop called for the restoration of his

---

[9] Chiefs of the Greek armed contingent and supreme command in Cyprus.

[10] On 13 July, Athens gave the impression that it was going to answer Makarios' letter on Monday the 15th. Such tactics were deceptive and misleading.

The storming of the Presidential Palace by anti-government troops:
Monday 15 July 1974.

country's independence and sovereignty. The Americans however were not so accommodating. On 18 July Makarios was received in New York as archbishop and not as president. By the same title he was received by **Kissinger** in Washington on 22 July. Furthermore, on 19 July the USA fought hard at the Security Council to achieve two objectives:

To allow the representative of the Sampson '*government*' to speak on an equal basis with Makarios; and

to prevent this body from reaching a decision which could have impeded a Turkish invasion.

Kissinger failed on the first but succeeded on the second and far more important issue.

In Turkey meanwhile there was a news black-out in its eastern regions and on 17 July two journalists were arrested in Mersin for trying to send out news of troop movements. Troop activity in the Mersin-Alexandretta districts had been evident since early June. Whitehall received a request from Turkey on 16 July for consultation with the government under the terms of Article 4 of the Treaty of Guarantee. Bülent Ecevit arrived on the following day. Ecevit appears to have proposed joint action by Anglo-Turkish forces to restore the status ante bellum. The British Premier refused to use force, hoping that the crisis would be resolved diplomatically. Wilson reveals[11] that the object of Ecevit's visit was to seek British approval for a Turkish invasion, to protect the Turkish minority there. *"To this end, he asked us to allow him to use the sovereign base at Akrotiri for the purpose. He received a courteous but declaratory 'no'...".*

---

[11] Final Term. The Labour Government, 1974-76. 1979. Page 62.

Turkish forces landing in Kyrenia above top and a Turkish tank consolidates
Turkish occupation.

Top: Turkish forces landing unopposed in Kyrenia.

Below: A tank 'consolidates' the Turkish presence.

CHAPTER FIVE

THE TURKISH INVASION OF 1974 and its effects on Cypriot Society

On the early morning of 20 July Turkey invaded Cyprus; the decision to launch the attack had already been taken on 15 July. Ecevit recalled that **"the coup was the green light for our invasion"**. For this operation the full might of the Turkish military machine, supplied by America and NATO, ostensibly to defend the country's and Allied interests, was used against Cyprus. A country with an estimated population of 50 million and an army of well over $\frac{1}{2}$ a million invaded an unprepared island, member of the United Nations, Commonwealth and Council of Europe, with 630,000 inhabitants and an army comprising around 10,000 national guardsmen, the 1,000 Greek contingent and approximately 5,000 others – all it may be added, armed with outdated weapons.

Turkey landed its troops in Kyrenia and its paratroopers inside the Nicosia-Kyrenia road enclave and then bombed the capital and Famagusta. Following strong protests and a warning from Britain the Turks desisted from attacking Nicosia airport because, as Harold Wilson explained, there would have been casualties among the UN forces of which the biggest component was the British, including the 16th/5th Lancers; moreover had Ecevit *proceeded with his design we should not hesitate to order our fighters to shoot down his aircraft..*[1] Even more revealing is the fact that in the aftermath of C.I.D. (Coup, Invasion, Disaster), Britain was willing to withdraw from Cyprus and abandon its military bases. The idea was supported by the chiefs of the defence staff but vetoed by Henry Kissinger, Secretary of State in the Nixon administration.[2] It was later explained by Whitehall officials that such a willingness to quit was *"a temporary aberration, and that the Cyprus bases were as much a part of Britain as Devon and Cornwall"*. In fact under the 1959-60 Agreements, Britain maintained, and does to this day, two Sovereign Base Areas (SBAs) of around 99 sq miles, or 2.5% of Cypriot territory, and a GCHQ listening post on the Troodos Mountains (in addition to other training sites etc.,) which eavesdrops on the Soviet Union, Eastern Europe and the Middle East and feeds information into America's National Security Agency. Whatever their significance now, contemporary military literature describe the bases and other *'retained sites'* on the island as *"the UK's most important interest"*.

---

[1] Final Term. The Labour Government, 1974-76. 1979. Pages 63-64.
[2] The Guardian. 2 April 1988. Page 1.

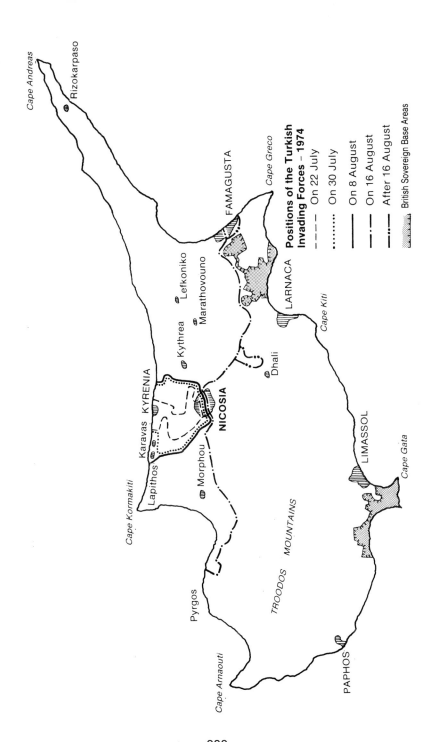

Positions of the Turkish
Invading Forces – 1974

On 22 July
On 30 July
On 8 August
On 16 August
After 16 August
British Sovereign Base Areas

Cape Andreas

Rizokarpaso

Cape Greco

FAMAGUSTA

Lefkoniko

Marathovouno

LARNACA

Kythrea

Cape Kiti

KYRENIA

Dhali

Karavas

NICOSIA

Lapithos

Morphou

LIMASSOL

Cape Kormakiti

Cape Gata

TROODOS MOUNTAINS

Pyrgos

PAPHOS

Cape Arnaouti

What were the new Cypriot realities and new developments?

1. Around 37.5% of the island's territory is still under Turkish occupation and approximately 200,000 Greek Cypriots were ousted from their ancestral homes — less than 700 now remain in the occupied north. By any international standards, the volume of refugees proportional to the ethnic population was enormous — some 40%. This has made the problems of absorbtion, rehousing and perhaps eventual resettlement correspondingly complex. By contrast, the 40,000-odd Turkish Cypriot refugees did not face such problems of shelter provision. The Turkish occupied sector is trying through various means – renaming settlements, comprehensive dehellenisation, erection of monuments to the 1974 *'liberation'* etc., – to convey the message of permanent separation and independence. For the Greek Cypriots a contrasting ideology exists: such permanency is not accepted.

2. Following the invasion, $\frac{1}{3}$ of the Greek population became completely dependent on state aid. Around 15% of the island's employed force and 10% self-employed persons were left without a job. The government was faced not only with a massive rehousing problem but with the added unprecedented difficulty of *'finding'* jobs for the *'unemployed, displaced and dispirited refugees'*. In a series of Emergency Action Plans (1975-1986) the government successfully rebuilt the shattered economy. Within a few years after the events of 1974, economic activity returned to the pre-invasion levels with unemployment virtually eliminated, productive resources replaced, refugees rehoused and confidence in the economic future restored. This upsurge has been described by independent observers as an "economic miracle". Per capita income in 1987 was well over US$6,000

GNP[3] per capita at current prices.

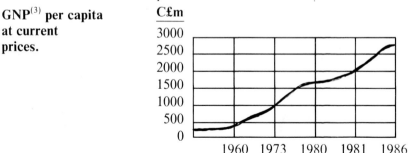

---

[3] Gross National Product is the annual total value of goods produced and services provided in a country.

234

(at a rate of C£1 — US$2), certainly one of the highest in the Middle East and Southern Europe. A quick glance at the diagram opposite will make easier understanding of this rapid growth:

Three further remarks must be brought to the notice of readers:

Firstly, it must be remembered that tourism played a major role in the island's economy. The main tourist centres of northern Cyprus are now under Turkish control. Kyrenia became an occupied place and Famagusta *'the reviera of the Eastern Mediterranean'* became an empty *'ghost'* town. To make up for the loss of tourist accommodation, new hotels, apartments and various other *'attractions'* have been built in many coastal centres. An entirely new tourist town is **Ayia Napa.** On land sloping down to first class beaches, Ayia Napa is built round a small fishing village and an old, high-walled monastery near the southeastern corner of the island.

Together with the friendly hospitality of the people, the excellent and healthy climate, the beauty of the countryside, the beaches and the blue sea, the long and rich history, Cyprus attracts many visitors – many of them returning year after year. Two new airports at Larnaca and Paphos were built to cater for this upsurge and for the Republic's other needs.

Secondly, it must be stressed that in 1972 Cyprus signed an Association Agreement with the European Economic Community (E.E.C.) for the establishment, through two successive stages, of a Customs Union between the two parties. The first stage of the Association Agreement expired at the end of 1987. The second stage became effective in January 1988. This stage consists of two phases, the first is of a duration of ten years and the second of four or five years. These provisions will lead in the near future to a Customs Union and to a free movement of goods between the two parties; this will undoubtedly open new prospects for the use of Cyprus as a base for the production and export of goods by enterprises based on the island.

The *third* related issue that needs brief comment is the one of state involvement. Cyprus will continue to operate a mixed economic system with the government supplementing private initiative. It will continue to promote and maintain favourable investment conditions that will permit entrepreneurs to participate directly in the process of economic development. The broad goals of this policy during the period 1987-1991 may be summarised as follows:

1. Maintenance of a high rate of economic growth.

Above: Mr Eagleton an American Senator visits the Lefkaritis refugee camp.
Below: Refugee women engrossed in making the traditional Cypriot lace – popularly known as 'Lefkaritika'.

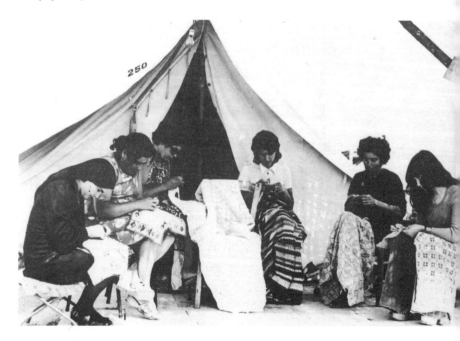

Two photos showing the destruction and misery caused by the Turkish invasion.

2. Diversification of the productive base of the economy.[4]

3. Maintenance of full employment and price stability.

4. Promotion of exports and improvement in the balance of payments.

The ultimate national economic goal remains the improvement of the quality of life and the welfare of the population.

3. In simple economic terms therefore, the total assets under Turkish control in 1974 were as follows:

70% of the gross output.
65% ” ” tourist accommodation.
87% ” ” hotel beds under construction.
83% ” ” general cargo handling (Famagusta).
56% ” ” mining and quarrying output.
41% ” ” livestock production.
48% ” ” agricultural exports.
46% ” ” plant production.
etc., etc., etc.,

4. The Turkish invasion also cost the island 3,000 dead; 2,192 'missing' and 20,000 Greek Cypriots enclaved in various parts of the north. Due to a wave of expulsions only around 700 remain today (1989). Furthermore, and with the intention of changing the demographic character of the island large numbers of Turkish settlers — totalling approximately 64,000 in the Spring of 1989 — have been uprooted from their homes and transferred to Cyprus. Correspondingly however the indigenous Turkish Cypriot population has decreased by around 20% — from 100.000 to 80,000 —with Australia and Britain being the chief emigration destinations.

5. The impact on the lives of the refugees has been dramatic. The pain and a long list of problems — adjusting to a new environment and very often with a depleted family, developing a new local status and new family guidelines (behavioural and workwise) etc., — have tested extensively the virtues and stamina of this large section of the island's inhabitants. Thus, whilst the intention has been, through the housing and economic programmes, to integrate and reactivate, at the same time the distinctiveness of the refugees who are still committed to repatriation, has been accentuated.

---

[4] Prior to 1974 agriculture engaged 36% of the working population but only 21% in 1984.

Above: A set of postage stamps depicting an atmosphere of destruction and reconstruction.
Below: Life in a refugee camp was always difficult.

Also the massive propertylessness which such refugee status had generated, greatly unbalanced the structure of Cypriot society. In the island property ownership plays a crucial role in the family life-cycle, setting parametres for family patterns and helping in the solution of urban problems of adaptation.

6. Of particular importance — and often forgotten — is the impact of the invasion on Greek Cypriot women. Apart from the moral degradation faced by them when trapped by undisciplined soldiery, it has since been calculated that out of every 100 married women at least three lost a husband (male protector and breadwinner), brother or child, either dead or missing. This is a frightening statistic and one that has had dramatic effects on the renowned Cypriot close family unit. Whether its a sign of the times or simply due (or accelerated) to the effects of the new situation the age-long supportive family unit has shown signs of cracking — and, at times, directly from the centre.

7. On the cultural, educational and social fields, Cyprus once more, has not stood still. In relation to population, Cyprus ranks among the first countries in the world in terms of university degree holders. The establishment of the planned university will give a further boost to the educational standards of the islanders.

The state encourages all worthwhile intellectual creativity — an activity which is a fundamental element in any country's existence. Cypriots in fact have survived as a people through so many adversities in the course of time because they created a culture, an identity, and preserved it. Poets, literary writers and others are essential to the preservation of a culture as blood is to the continued functioning of the human body. Creativity, courage, determination and initiative are all deep-set aspects of the proud inhabitants of Cyprus. Worldwide, the islanders have excelled themselves in many fields.

Two other social phenomena must be added. Cyprus is a law-abiding society and a safe place to live and operate from. INTERPOL statistics for 1986 reveal that the volume of crime per 100,000 Cypriots stood at the impressively low level of 698. For the same year, the average figure for European countries was 4,000 or about six times as much as that of Cyprus.

Secondly, it must be emphasised that Cyprus is an epidemic-free country with first class medical and health care facilities. There are general hospitals in all the towns and also a good number of clinics. Life expectancy currently stands at around 77 years for women and 73 years for men.

8. Also of great significance is the fact that a large part of Cyprus' centuries-old cultural heritage, represented by archaeological sites, monuments and museums, are now either damaged or destroyed and thus in great need of preservation and care. Listed below is a very brief description of some of the major monuments of this inestimable archaeological wealth, which has formed the basis of the cultural existence and heritage of the island and the chief factor of its tourist development:

'Salamis' the illustrious kingdom of Evagoras, Onesilos and Nicocreon and the glorious and cosmopolitan capital of the island during the Classical, Hellenistic and Early Byzantine periods with its unique treasures — theatres, gymnasium and baths, forum and temples — is perhaps the greatest casualty of the Turkish invasion.

'Enkomi-Alasia' one of the most significant commercial centres of the period 1,600 to 1,050 BC, is another area rich in archaeological monuments and now inaccessible to the island's inhabitants.

'Medieval Famagusta' the unrivalled commercial and cultural centre of the Eastern Mediterranean in Frankish and Venetian times, is another casualty. The Venetian walls, which are preserved in their entirety, Othello Tower and the stately Gothic cathedral of St Nicholas are among the most important medieval monuments of the island.

'Bellapais Abbey' is the only Frankish monastic establishment preserved in the island and together with the Cathedral of St. Sophia at Nicosia and St. Nicholas at Famagusta, they represent Gothic monastic and church architecture in the island.

'The Medieval Castles' of Kyrenia, St. Hilarion, Buffavento and Kantara, so important in the defence of the island in years gone by, are also behind Turkish lines.

'Soloi', the kingdom of Philokypros and Pasikrates was one of the most famous cities of Classical, Hellenistic and Roman Cyprus.

'Vouni Palace', the 'Temple of Athena' and scores of other Byzantine monasteries and churches, with their superb exhibits and monuments are also in the Turkish-occupied north.

9. Lastly, it must be emphasised that in spite of the political and other hurdles, Cyprus has transformed itself from a relatively poor agricultural society into one with an enviable living standard, a growing export-oriented industry, a modernising agricultural sector, an attractive base for offshore operations and an internationally recognized tourist centre. Moreover, the island has become an ideal place for business conferences, international seminars and special organizations' annual meetings. A conference of unique importance was the Foreign Ministers Non-Aligned Movement one, held in Nicosia on 7-10 September 1988. Cyprus' ideal geographical position and excellent conference facilities are certainly factors which sway decisions in its favour.

So much for the effects on and present realities of the Cypriot scene. On the political field we must mention the following:

Turkey had at last realised its long-standing objective. Ecevit, hailed as the *'second Ataturk',* at one time alleged that such intervention was made to protect the independence of the Republic of Cyprus and restore its constitutional order. On another occasion, through Osman Olcay, its permanent representative at the UN, Ankara supported the view that the aim of the invasion was to protect and liberate the island's oppressed Turkish minority.

It is by now universally accepted that the coup was not directed against the Turkish community, nor did Turkey bring to Cyprus peace other than *'the peace of the grave'.* But as this naked act of aggression was bound to offend international public opinion, Turkey attempted to cover up her aims by invoking the *'legal fiction'* that her armies came to Cyprus in exercise of her rights under **Article IV of the Treaty of Guarantee.** This reads as follows:

> In the event of a breach of the provisions of the present Treaty, Greece, Turkey and the UK undertake to consult together with respect to the representations or measures necessary to ensure observance to those provisions.

> In so far as common concerted action may not prove possible, each of the guaranteeing Powers reserves the right to take action with the sole aim of re-establishing the state of affairs created by the present Treaty.

Thus Article IV is clear and unambiguous. Turkey could not intervene unilaterally unless common or concerted action proved impossible after consultation among the three countries. Even then

Left: Diamantis, to some the father of modern Cypriot Painting, has established a new artistic movement in the island.

The picture in oil is entitled "Two figures".

Below: Many modern Cypriot Artists looked back to the good old days of the past.

Hatzisoteriou brings to real life a typical Cypriot "panygiris" (a fair).

243

Above: Hambis, an artist-engraver, depicts the tragedy of Cyprus.

Right: A woman by Stass Paraskos – an artist who has established Cyprus' school of Art in Paphos.

Above: A painting showing Locals at a Kafenion.

Left: Two stamps showing folklore events; highly popular with locals and tourists alike.

Cyprus has witnessed a great revival in cultural activity and intellectual creativity. Poets, literary writers, painters and musicians etc., have scaled new heights of excellence and have rightly achieved international recognition. Solon Michaelides (right) typifies this trend.

European Music Year Solon Michaelides 1905-1979

15c

ΚΥΠΡΟΣ · CYPRUS · KIBRIS

Together with the "artistic revival" an "economic miracle" followed the tragic events of 1974: Reforrestration, new roads (see above) new industries, new airports and new harbours (new Limassol harbour – below), etc.

200,000 turned up to greet Makarios when he returned to Cyprus on 7 December 1974.

intervention should be limited to the sole aim of *'re-establishing the state of affairs created by the Treaty',* which is the constitutional order of 1960 and nothing else. Not only did Turkey, in furtherance of her ulterior motives, avoid meaningful consultations but she also spared no effort to dismember Cyprus and destroy what she herself had guaranteed.

In the face of this gross breach of an international treaty, Britain and Greece avoided taking any action to protect the island. To quote the words of the House of Commons Select Committee on Cyprus which reported in 1976:

> "Britain had the legal right, a moral obligation, and the military capacity to intervene in Cyprus during July and August 1974. She did not intervene for reasons which the Government refuses to give ..."

Yet in other situations like the Falklands in April 1982, Britain engaged in a war with Argentina for the sake of around 1,800 islanders situated in the South Atlantic and approximately 13,000 km from the UK. In the case of Cyprus, the British Foreign Secretary suggested that there was no moral obligation to intervene because the Treaty of Guarantee, though not formally abrogated, was in practice *'a dead letter'*. The fact remains however that Britain had not honoured its signature and its obligations as a guarantor of the independence and territorial intergrity of Cyprus. Furthermore, all its actions point to collusion with and even capitulation to US foreign policy. Lord Caradon (formerly Sir Hugh Foot and last Governor of Cyprus) wrote in *The Times* on 17 April 1975 that,

> "... it is not possible to uncover or detect any British influence or initiative other than we should follow Dr Kissinger. We have followed him with devastating and shameful results and failed to honour the British obligation as guarantor of the Cyprus people..."

It must not be forgotten that as long ago as 1964 Acheson had attempted to partition the island. The double annexation of Cyprus would have meant the establishment of American and NATO bases there to serve the large western interests in the area. This solution would have filled the vacuum left by Britain in the Middle East. It was, as we have seen, rejected. Yet Acheson and others still perservered. Thus, in a speech at Salem College in North Carolina on 27 October 1966 he declared that a solution could be imposed on Cyprus by the use of superior arms. Furthermore, in November 1973, at a well-attended seminar in Rome, that seasoned US diplomat **Cyrus Vance** warned that if there was another crisis in Cyprus his country would not attempt to stop the Turks. Those present included Averoff, Bitsios, Glafkos Clerides, Rauf Denktash and other leading politicians and scholars. In 1964 and 1967 however, the USA managed to hold back the Turks after they had planned to invade Cyprus. Why not in 1974? Several possible reasons can be discerned:

1. The Cyprus question was dragging on for far too long and Turkey was growing impatient over the impasse. In 1974, Ecevit was able to tell Sisco, the American intermediary that *"this time Sir, we will decide what to do"*.

2. Cyprus' move towards the non-aligned camp and the fear of a possible leftist advance in the island.

3. The Greek military government's policy inconsistencies were surfacing more and more. Popular resistance was certainly making a comeback.

4. The ill-prepared Cypriot forces were not capable of resisting a Turkish invasion.

5. The unsettled and insecure Middle East situation was made more dangerous by the so-called Yom Kippur War, between the Israelis and the Arabs, which broke out in October 1973.

6. The Soviet Union appeared to have taken a *'non-active stance'* over Cyprus during the crucial few months before the coup and invasion.

Hence the USA decided not to prevent the Turkish invasion. Although the Americans thought that the Greek Cypriots had a fair case their regional and international strategic policy dictated that they should support Turkey. The USA knew of the pending coup and invasion through the CIA and through its orbiting satellites, but allowed it to happen and so can be accused of manipulating the whole Cyprus tragedy. Its indecision and obsession with not antagonizing Ankara only served to give Turkey a free hand in Cyprus. An American study mission report concluded in September 1974 that *'US policy towards Cyprus seems to have been one of hasty improvisation which failed badly'*. Congressional debates and the American press also condemned the White House's ill-considered and short-sighted Cyprus policy.

Although the crisis of 1974 was only one in a series in the history of this tragic island, it was the greatest and most crucial because it threatened the destruction of the island as a viable and independent state. From the beginning of the invasion Turkey followed its pre-arranged and well-organized '**Attila**[5] **Plan**'. The aim of this plan was to remove the Greek population in the Turkish occupied areas; to alter the demographic status of Cyprus by the importation of Turks from the mainland; to ruin or usurp the sources of livelihood of the Greek Cypriots and to create such faits accomplis as would influence the solution of the Cyprus problem in favour of Turkey's objective. This objective is a *de facto* partition of the island under the guise of a loose federation, which would enable her for the present to exercise political and military control of the *'whole'* territory but would lay the foundations for the possible annexation of the entire island.

Four other events are worth noting at this juncture: *Firstly,* the junta in Greece, under the pressure of public indignation, was forced to resign. After seven years democracy had returned to Greece. Karamanlis was recalled from Paris and on the following morning he was sworn in as Prime Minister. This transition however, on top of the other domestic and foreign difficulties, resulted in a brief period of complete inaction. Meanwhile Cyprus was burning.

Secondly, on the same day as the above, the illegal government in Cyprus established by the coup found itself unable to stay in office and Sampson was replaced by Glafkos Clerides, the President of the House of Representatives. He in turn was replaced by Makarios when he returned in December 1974.

Thirdly, after the 20th the UN limited itself to the passage of resolutions which Turkey completely ignored. It refused to comply either with resolution 353 of 20 July or with resolution 354 of 23 July of the Security Council, which among other things called for an immediate cease-fire, urged an end to foreign intervention and the withdrawal of all foreign troops and finally requested the three guarantor powers to start negotiations for a setlement. The Greek Cypriots complied with the cease-fire demand of 20 July but the Turks did not. Meeting no resistance they repeatedly violated it, thus realizing their objective of occupying about 37 per cent of Cyprus.

---

[5] Attila was the notorious King of the Huns c. 406-53 and is remembered for his savagery, murder and arson.

Fourthly, a preliminary cease-fire was reached on 22 July, leading to the first Geneva Conference. The Foreign Ministers of the UK, Turkey and Greece held lengthy negotiations from 25 to 30 July. Even though several ideas and suggestions were discussed, the cease-fire was continuously broken by the advancing Turkish troops. Nevertheless, the three delegations recognized the importance of setting in motion measures to regularize the situation in the island, having regard to the international agreement signed at Nicosia on 16 August 1960 and to resolution 353 of 20 July approved by the Security Council. The participants declared that in order to stabilize the situation the areas controlled by opposing armed forces on 30 July at 22.00 hours Geneva time should not be extended. They called on all forces, including irregular ones, to desist from all hostile activities. A new meeting in which representatives of the two Cypriot communities would participate was also outlined. However, the Geneva Declaration signed at 9.00pm on 30 July proved to be worthless.

The second Geneva Conference attended by the three Foreign Secretaries and on the following day by Clerides and Denktash, duly met on 8 August. Following heated arguments over the existence or non-existence of the 1960 constitution (Callaghan explained that he recognized only that of 1960) specific proposals for the settlement of the Cyprus problem were tabled by Clerides, Denktash and Günes. It became clear that Turkey had not gone to Geneva to negotiate but to issue an ultimatum — the acceptance immediately of either of its two plans, both based on Turkish administration of 34% of the island's territory: in one case a single area in the north running from Limnitis on the west coast through Lefka, Morphou, the old city of Nicosia and ending at the old city of Famagusta, and in the other a smaller area in the north and five areas around the main towns. The second plan put forward by Günes had to be accepted by Greece and Cyprus on the spot. At 8 pm, on 13 August Mavros and Clerides asked for 36 hours to consult their governments. Günes refused.

Callaghan explained that 36 hours' grace was justifiable and that all diplomatic avenues had not been fully explored. He accused his Turkish counterpart of being unreasonable. Günes not only disagreed but remarked later that Gallaghan was no more that a *'perfect telephone receptionist'*. The Conference broke down at 3 a.m. on 14 August. At 4.30 a.m. Turkish forces began operations which included the bombing of towns. Turkey's prearranged tactics had triumphed. Its forces had occupied that area defined at Geneva plus another 3% bringing it to 37%, thus instituting the *'Attila'* or *'Sahin'* (Falcon) line, an artificial boundary separating the Greeks and Turks of Cyprus. The Attila II operation was thus completed.

On 14, 15, 16 and 30 August the Security Council issued new resolutions (making 8 since 20 July), calling for the immediate termination of military operations, the withdrawal of all foreign troops and the resumption of talks. These recommendations were once more wholly disregarded by Turkey. A General Assembly resolution 3212 (XXIX) adopted by 117 votes, none against and no abstentions, which was of similar content, was also ignored by the Turks. In fact the only agreement reached between the cease-fire of 16 August and the end of September was the one between Clerides and Denktash for the release of all prisoners of war. The agreement was signed on 20 September.

However, the second phase of the Cyprus operation strained Turkey's relations with the UK, the USSR and finally the USA. On 22 August Turkey rejected Soviet proposals for a wider international conference. The USA Congress voted repeatedly to cut off military aid to Turkey without however inducing it to make any concessions of substance.

On 7 December 1974, Makarios returned to Cyprus. Almost half the Greek population gathered in Nicosia on that day to welcome him. Addressing his people from the archbishopric, he declared a general amnesty for those who were involved in the July coup by saying *"I forgive them all for their sins"* and also extended a hand of friendship to the Turkish community by repeating that talks were wanted *"for the bridging of our differences, for the finding of a solution to the Cyprus problem"*.

Even though the intercommunal talks were resumed on 14 January 1975 the Turks used them as a pretext to gain time and bring about new faits accomplis. The divergencies in the views of the two sides on settling the problem have been described as being *'wider than the Aegean Sea'* — another Greco-Turkish irritant.

A comparison of the first two proposals by each side (taken from the abortive meetings of January-February 1975) will suffice to illustrate this contention.

Where the Greeks spoke of Cyprus being an *'independent sovereign republic'*, the Turks desired to see an *'independent and secular republic'*. The Greeks wished that the *'constitution shall be that of a bicommunal multi-regional federal state'*, but the Turks demanded that *'there shall be made a constitution for a bicommunal and biregional federal state'*. Thus from the Turkish point of view the only realistic solution was a federation composed of two ethnic groups. In their opinion the future political settlement of the Cyprus problem should be based on three principles:

1. A bizonal federation;
2. The establishment of a central government with limited powers;
3. The participation of the two national communities in central government on an equal footing.

And in furtherance of their set policies the Turks proceeded to proclaim a *'Turkish Federated State of Cyprus'* (TFSC) in the occupied area of the island on 13 February 1975. The Security Council met on 20 February to take up the complaint of the Republic's government about the illegal declaration. Resolution 367 adopted by consensus (without a vote) on 12 March expressed regret at this unilateral declaration. It also requested the UN Secretary-General to convene new discussions under his personal auspices.

Accordingly, talks took place in Vienna between 28 April and 3 May, as well as between 5 and 9 June 1975. There was no progress. However, the *third* and *'fourth'* round of talks once more took place in the Austrian capital between 31 July and 2 August and in New York from 8 to 10 September. At the third round it was agreed that 9,000 Turkish Cypriots from the Greek-controlled southern part of the island should be allowed to join their compatriots in the northern area and that the 10,000 Greek Cypriots already in the north should be allowed to stay and be joined by 800 of their relatives from the south. Other issues discussed included the jurisdiction of a federal government of the island. Clerides told a press conference on 3 August that the Turkish Cypriot side had committed itself to produce by the end of August a comprehensive plan for solving all aspects of the Cyprus problem. However, no such plan having been submitted, the fourth round of talks in New York was adjourned on 10 September after a brief formal session, no date being set for future negotiations.

Further talks were held in Vienna from 17 to 21 February 1976. The communiqué issued at their conclusion stated that:

1. Clerides and Denktash had held 'substantive discussions on the territorial and constitutional issues'.

2. It had been agreed that an exchange of written proposals on both these issues would take place in Cyprus within the next six weeks.

3. The two negotiators would meet again in May 'with a view of establishing a common basis prior to referring the matter to mixed committees in Cyprus'.

It seemed therefore that some progress towards a negotiated solution was achieved. The *fifth* round of talks were '*good, constructive and helpful*' according to Denktash. However, Clerides resigned on 7 April, after appearing to have made a secret '*procedural agreement*' with his co-negotiator without informing any member of the Greek Cypriot leadership.

The '*procedural agreement*' reached at the February discussions laid down that the Greek side would be the first to submit recommendations for a settlement and that the Turks would then have ten days in which to consider them before submitting their own proposals. But when Clerides tried to fulfil the agreement by handing Denktash a secret draft of the Greek proposals on 24 March, the latter reacted by disclosing publicly that he had received the draft and that he could not accept it. On the behaviour of the shrewd but highly unprincipled Turkish leader, a London-based newspaper recorded the following:

> "There can be little doubt that his real aim in behaving as he did was to cause disarray on the Greek side and thus further delay any serious negotiation. He has already indicated that the replacement of Mr Clerides as negotiator by Mr Tasos Papadopoulos will entail a corresponding replacement of himself by a person with the same status"[6]

The person chosen was Umit Suleyman Onan, then speaker of the TFSC constituent assembly. The first meeting between these two London-trained lawyers took place on 27 May when they discussed humanitarian matters, principally the question of Greek Cypriots missing or living in the Turkish-controlled north. At the time around 2,200 people were unaccounted for.

An event of much greater importance was to follow. More by design than by chance, Makarios received a letter from Denktash dated 9 January 1977 suggesting a meeting between them. They had not met since December 1963. The discussions took place on UN

---

[6] The Times. 15 April 1976. Page 15.

Above: The highly popular President and Archbishop of Cyprus at a Commonwealth Conference. Seen here seated to the right of Queen Elizabeth II.

Below: February 1977: High level (summit) meeting between Makarios, Waldheim, Denktash and their negotiating teams.

neutral ground on 27 January. Makarios stated later that the objective was *'to find common ground for a package deal'*. Denktash announced after this historic event that such fundamental aspects of the Cyprus question as the central administration, a federal system and the territorial issue[7] were discussed. In fact the overall atmosphere had been friendly and a step had been taken towards the resumption of the intercommunal talks deadlocked for about a year. The meeting was thus described as a *'breakthrough'*.

A second meeting between them, attended by Waldheim, took place again in Nicosia) on 12 February 1977. It was agreed that the intercommunal talks should be resumed. It appears that agreement was reached on *four key guidelines:*

1. The aim was to establish an independent, non-aligned, bi-communal federal Republic.

2. The size of the territory under the administration of each community would be negotiated in the light of economic viability, productivity and property rights.

3. Questions of principle such as freedom of movement, freedom of settlement and property rights would be open to discussion, taking into account the fundamental principle of a bi-communal federal system and certain practical difficulties which might arise for the Turkish Cypriot community.

4. The powers and functions of the central federal government would be such as to safeguard the unity of the country having regard to its bi-communal character.

It was certainly a breakthrough and there was much optimism. In another effort to make further progress President Carter of the USA despatched Clark Clifford, a veteran White House confidant, on a nine day exploratory fact-finding trip to Europe beginning on 16 February 1977. On his return Clifford informed the international relations committee of the House of Representatives on 10 March that *'with good faith on both sides a Cyprus settlement is definitely possible before the end of 1977'*.

---

[7] For the first time the Turks voluntarily brought the territorial question under discussion which in the eyes of the Greeks was a matter of cardinal importance to any future settlement.

Vienna again hosted the *sixth* round of the intercommunal talks. According to the map presented by Papadopoulos, 20% of the total area of Cyprus would remain under Turkish Cypriot administration. In the preparation of the map account was taken of the guidelines agreed between Makarios and Denktash in February on population, viability, productivity and land ownership. The Turks on the other hand, were talking of a weak central government to rule a strong bi-communal Cyprus and there were no territorial concessions. Although some progress had been made in clarifying positions, there was no hope of bridging the gap between the two sides in that round of negotiations. In accordance with the communiqué issued at the end of the talks (7 April) Papadopoulos and Onan met again in Nicosia on 26 May and 3 June, but without making any further headway.

Meanwhile the embittered Cypriots went through another ordeal. Archbishop Makarios died of a heart attack on 3 August 1977 at the age of 64. He was buried after five days on a mountain peak overlooking the Kykko monastery after a funeral service in Nicosia attended by nearly 200 representatives from more than 50 countries. His premature death revived fears of renewed conflict in Cyprus. These fears however have not materialised. Spyros Kyprianou who succeeded the Cypriot Ethnarch declared that he would *'stay on the same course'* on all fields. In fact, Cyprus was making advances everywhere. Culturally, economically and socially it achieved new heights — and the trend is still upwards.

The long-awaited Turkish *'proposals'* were handed to Waldheim on 13 April 1978 in Vienna. The procedural agreement reached when he met Kyprianou and Denktash in January was that detailed and comprehensive proposals should be given to him and that he should then hold consultations with both sides to establish whether or not they formed a basis on which he would be justified in recommending the resumption of the intercommunal talks — suspended since April 1977. Instead, the UN Secretary-General was given a 34-page outline of the *'main aspects'* of the Turkish proposals and told that the full text would not be made available until the talks were reconvened. The Cyprus government rejected these proposals as *'completely unacceptable'* since they in no way formed a basis for the resumption of the intercommunal talks. Kyprianou said at a press conference on 19 April that they amounted to an attempt to 'legalize and consolidate the faits accomplis and that their acceptance would mean a decision to commit suicide'.

Above: The "Great Father and Maker" of Modern Cyprus died in August 1977. The roads leading to Kykko Monastery, his final resting place, were lined by 1000s of grieving Cypriots.

Below: May 1979: Summit talks between Kyprianou, Waldheim, Denktash and their advisers.

Once again the USA attempted to get some movement in the talks. Its so-called *'Framework for a Cyprus Settlement'*[8] was a 12-point plan, prepared jointly by the USA, UK and Canada. Although the document included several positive elements it was riddled with inconsistencies and it therefore failed to make any progress.

However, UN initiatives resulted in a Kyprianou-Denktash meeting at which a *ten-point agreement* was reached on 19 May 1979.

1. The intercommunal talks should resume on 15 June.
2. The basis of the talks would be the Makarios-Denktash guidelines of 12 February 1977 and the UN resolutions relevant to the Cyprus question.
3. There should be respect for the human rights and fundamental freedoms of all citizens of the Republic.
4. The talks would deal with the territorial and constitutional aspects.
5. Priority would be given to reaching agreement on the resettlement of Varosha under UN auspices.
6. All should abstain from any action which might jeopardize the outcome of the talks, and special importance would be given to initial practical measures by both sides to promote goodwill, mutual confidence and the return to normal conditions.
7. The demilitarization of the Republic of Cyprus was envisaged, and matters relating thereto would be discussed.
8. The independence, sovereignty, territorial integrity and non-alignment of the Republic should be adequately guaranteed against union in whole or in part with any other country and against any form of partition or secession.
9. The intercommunal talks would be carried out in a continuing and sustained manner, avoiding delay.
10. The intercommunal talks would take place in Nicosia.

The talks which resumed on the agreed date foundered on two major sticking points: the acceptance or rejection of a bizonal or bicommunal federal state and the Varosha issue. In an effort to break the deadlock Waldheim in 1980 proposed various *alternative formulae* for the resumption of the talks. These were eventually held on 9 August but again they proved abortive.

---

[8] It was submitted to the two communities in November 1978.

In 1981, expectations that during the summer there might at last be a step forward in the negotiations had been fuelled both by official statements and by press speculation. Firstly, a new cycle of discussions which began on 6 May gave the impression that they would be fruitful. Secondly, a report in the British *Sunday Times* on 24 May hinted that a solution envisaging two autonomous zones in loose confederation and the return of Famagusta, at first under temporary UN control, was on the cards.

Once more, nothing transpired. However on the same day that the above article was published, the people of the Republic went to the polls to elect a new House of Representatives. The election was contested by seven parties and six independent candidates. In a turnout of 95%[9] there were no surprises. The election was dominated by AKEL, DESY, DEKO and EDEK parties. Between them they took over 93% of the total votes cast and all the 35 seats in the Chamber. The electorate totalled 308,511 of which 1,505 were Maronites, 1,114 Armenians and 256 Latins.

Elections were also held on 28 June in the Turkish-occupied north. Comparing the results with those of the previous election we find:

	1976.	1981.
For Denktash as 'president'	76%	51.7%
For the 'assembly' of the TFSC and Denktash's National Unity Party	53%	42.6%

The parties which increased their power at the expense of the NUP were the Communal Liberation Party (CLP) and the Republican Turkish Party (RTP), which stood against economic or political integration of the occupied areas with Turkey and Denktash's partitionist policy and called for a solution of real federation which would safeguard the unity of Cyprus. Omitting the votes of the mainland settlers, who constituted then around 25% of the population, it becomes evident that the overwhelming majority of the native Turkish Cypriot electorate voted against Denktash and his policies.

---

[9] Voting is compulsory in Cyprus.

There was yet another election in 1981. After 50 years of mainly conservative, and at times ultra-right rule, Greece elected on 18 October an unmistakably left-wing government. The long-awaited *'allaghi'* (change) had arrived. The Panhellenic Socialist Movement (PASOK) took 48.06% of the votes cast and 172 out of the 300 seats in the Vouli. The new government headed by **Andreas Papandreou** pledged its support for the territorial integrity and unity of the island. There was a complete identity of views between the Cypriot and Greek governments.

In 1982 an *'evaluation'* was prepared by Waldheim and was presented formally at the intercommunal talks of 18 November. As reported, this evaluation involved a negotiating basis allocating 70% of the area of the island (excluding a federal district) to the Greek Cypriots and 30% to the Turkish Cypriots, but with the Turkish Cypriots taking some 40% of the jobs in the public sector. It was also understood that the presidency would rotate between the two communities on an annual basis and there would be a six-member federal council in which four seats would be reserved for the Greek Cypriots and two for the Turkish Cypriots. Moreover, each community would retain a large degree of veto power over major legislative and constitutional changes.

Nothing transpired from these *'proposals'*. On 13 May 1983, the UN General Assembly passed a resolution calling, once more, for the withdrawal of all occupation forces from Cyprus and endorsed Kyprianou's call for a complete demilitarization of the island. The resolution was endorsed by a vote of 103 to 5 with 20 abstentions. Joining Turkey in opposing the measure were Pakistan, Somalia, Malaysia and Bangladesh. Denktash responded three days later by indicating that he would declare the northern part of the island an independent state. As we shall see below, he carried out this threat on 15 November.

A further *'initiative'* was undertaken by the new UN Secretary-General, **Perez de Cuellar** on 8 August when he submitted a document to the Cyprus government and the Turkish Cypriot leadership. He had undertaken to make a series of *'soundings'* in order to facilitate further discussion of the Cyprus problem. Again all efforts were thwarted. On 15 November, the occupied part of Cyprus was declared an independent state. This move was in contravention of all UN resolutions and was duly greeted with world-wide condemnation. Three days later, UN resolution 541/83 urged the international

Above: The British Prime Minister meets and reassures Spyros Kyprianou that Britain only recognizes the legally elected government of the Republic of Cyprus.

Below: The Greek Prime Minister Andreas Papandreou visits Cyprus. There to meet him were political, church and other prominent persons. He is seen here being greeted by the Mayor of Nicosia, Lellos Demetriades.

community not to recognize any Cypriot state other than the Republic of Cyprus. The resolution was adopted with 13 votes in favour, one against (Pakistan) and one abstention (Jordan).

The year 1984 opened very briskly. On 11 January a *'framework'* for a comprehensive settlement of the Cyprus problem had been submitted by Kyprianou to Perez de Cuellar. It was also explained to **Mrs Thatcher,** the British Premier, on 18 January. Again all efforts proved abortive. Denktash proposed instead measures to legalize his *'illegal'* state. On 11 May 1984 the United Nations adopted resolution 550 on Cyprus by a vote of 13 in favour to one against (Pakistan) and one abstention (United States) and urged all states to condemn secessionist actions and requested that no one should recognize the purported state of the *'Turkish Republic of Northern Cyprus'*.

Perez de Cuellar continued his initiative with a series of *'proximity'* talks. It appeared that the Turkish Cypriots had agreed to reduce the area under their control to about 29% and to waive their claim to a rotating presidency. The Greek Cypriots also appeared to have accepted the principle of the equal representation of the two communities in the upper house of a bi-cameral legislature.

Summit talks opened in January 1985. The UN was very active with its draft plans. The Secretary-General had several meetings with Kyprianou and Denktash. Yet the Cyprus question remained at an impasse. Hopes however, were raised by two events:

1. While attending the World Economic Forum at Davos, Switzerland on 30-31 January 1988, Papandreou and Ozal (the Greek and Turkish Premiers) held two days of talks on bilateral relations. It was the first substantive meeting between the leaders of the two countries for ten years. Furthermore in June Ozal paid the first visit to Greece by a Turkish Premier since 1952. It was said by officials that in the case of both Cyprus and the Aegean, a mechanism had been set up to begin resolving both issues.

This thaw in the relations between the two countries plus Turkey's desire to join the Common Market[10] has raised hopes for an early solution. *If* Turkey is serious in joining and *if* the other European Community countries stick to their founding Charter and insist on

---

[10] Greece as a member can veto any Turkish (or other) application.

admitting only states with a clear-cut commitment to freedom, justice and democracy, then the world can rest assured that the islanders will celebrate a demilitarized and united Cyprus. Two big *ifs* but history has shown that more difficult and delicate issues were resolved when willingness, tact, courage and fairness prevailed over petty-mindedness, economic and military considerations.

2. On 21 February 1988, George Vassiliou was elected President of Cyprus for a 5-year term — securing 51.63% of the votes in one of the closest run-off elections in the island's history. At once Vassiliou announced that he would revive the National Council, as originally set up by Archbishop Makarios, which would function as a permanent institution and aim to chart *"a collective policy and planning for the joint laying down of the strategy and tactics of the struggle for the salvation of Cyprus"*.

He also announced that he was willing to meet Denktash and or Ozal to study ways of approaching the island's problems thus leading to a final solution. Meeting in Geneva on 24 August, at a working luncheon given by Perez de Cuellar, Vassiliou and Denktash agreed to resume intercommunal talks in Nicosia on 15 September. In a statement issued after the luncheon de Cuellar announced that both had expressed their willingness to negotiate without preconditions and to attempt to achieve a negotiated settlement on all aspects of the Cyprus problem by *"1 June 1989"*.

Talks have continued since August under the new procedure that had been agreed in New York last November. According to this new formula a wide range of options are being considered on a non-commital basis in an effort to find common ground. Thus the proposals of the Greek Cypriots were submitted on 30 January 1989 to the Turkish Cypriot leader Denktash. The proposals which take into account the concerns of the island's inhabitants, aim at establishing an independent, sovereign, territorially-integral, non-aligned, federal republic. The document approved by the Republic's National Council, is entitled *'Outline Proposals for the Establishment of a Federal Republic and for a Solution of the Cyprus Problem'*.

Thus the present round of intercommunal talks – designed to produce a lasting settlement of the Cyprus problem – began in August 1988. In a series of meetings since then, culminating at the session in New York (28-29 June 1989), President Vassiliou and the Turkish Cypriot leader Denktash, in the presence of Oscar Camilion and or Perez de Cuellar, have examined various *options* or *alternatives,* for all aspects of the problem.

1988-1989: New initiatives, further talks, fresh hopes. Above: George Vassiliou at the centre of the negotiating table. To his right Denktash and to his left Oscar Camilion, the special Representative of the UN Secretary-General in Cyprus. Below: A firm handshake and smiles all round. A publicity stunt or can Cypriots expect a rosier future?

Cypriots and the world can only wait. It is important to note however that towards the end of May 1989 a decisive step was taken to reduce tension in Cyprus' divided capital. Twenty-four military posts along Nicosia's demarcation *(green line)* were *unmanned.*

Can this be a pointer towards a settlement? Hopes, however were dashed once more. On 23 August, the 'assembly' of the pseudostate in the Turkish-occupied part approved a resolution imposing conditions for the resumption of talks—the 4th round of which was due to begin in July. This is an attempt, one year after the commencement of talks, to change the basis and procedure of the talks by imposing new and unacceptable conditions. Nevertheless, the UN Secretary-General is continuing his efforts to find common ground for meaningful negotiations. The Non-Aligned Movement and other countries, such as the UK, are throwing their weight behind the Secretary-General's activities.

The dramatic changes towards more open societies and freedom of movement in Eastern Europe and the destruction of the *"Berlin Wall"* in November brought new hopes to the Cypriots that 1990 will bring the desired solution. Nicosia must not remain the *only* divided city in Europe.

APPENDIX -A-

Personalities involved with the Cyprus Question: 1950s to Date.

Archbishop MAKARIOS III 1913-1977

For his earlier career etc, please refer to section vi.

In the early 1950s Makarios travelled extensively abroad and successfully gathered support for Cyprus' independence claim. Following the commencement of the armed struggle for national self-determination on 1 April 1955, and the break up of talks between Makarios and the British colonial administration, the Cypriot ethnarch was exiled to the Seychelles in March 1956 – only to be released a year later.

After protracted negotiations, Britain agreed to grant Cyprus its independence. On 13 December 1959, Makarios was elected as the First President of the Infant Republic and he assumed his duties on 16 August 1960. Cyprus became the 99th member-state of the United Nations.

From 1960 to 1977 he went through many trials and tribulations culminating in four attempts on his life and in July 1974 came the fateful coup and Turkish invasion.

Without any shadow of doubt the Archbishop had great natural dignity: he was very accessible, courteous and considerate even to the least important visitor who went to see him. He had a teasing but not unkind sense of humour and few could resist the charm and twinkling smile that was never far away.

The Cypriot Ethnarch was a dynamic and great leader. From the time he became Archbishop (1950) to the time of his death (5.15 am, 3 August 1977), he held the trust and worship of the Cypriot people. Makarios had a unique multi-layered authority: spiritually as Archbishop, communally as Ethnarch, nationally as unchallenged President and internationally as an acknowledged leader of the Commonwealth and the Third World and an apostle of non-alignment and world peace.

From 1950 Makarios had symbolised everything that was Cyprus. His life was simply the history of the island – *The Great Father and Maker of Modern Cyprus:* certainly a wise and apt description of the island's first President.

George GRIVAS 1898-1974

For his early career etc, please refer to section vi. In the 1950s Grivas focused his attention on Cyprus — he planned guerrilla tactics to oust the colonial regime and achieve enosis.

During the early hours of 1 April 1955 a series of bomb explosions inaugurated the commencement of the national liberation struggle. On the same day EOKA proclaimed its existence in leaflets signed *'Digenes'*. This was Grivas' nom de guerre in his capacity as leader of EOKA. In the course of the struggle he was also called *'arkhigos'* (leader) and *'apiastos'* (the one that could not be captured).

After the Cyprus settlement (Feb. 1959), Grivas left Cyprus and, acclaimed as a national hero by the Greeks, he was promoted to General in the Greek army.

From 1964 to 1967, he returned to the island and commanded the Cyprus National Guard.

In 1967 Turkey demanded his recall but in 1971 he returned secretly to Cyprus and was in opposition to Makarios. He died in 1974.

As a military strategist he was admired and feared by all.

Spyros KYPRIANOU

Born in Limassol in 1932. Graduating from the Greek Gymnasium he proceeded to study economics and commerce and then law in London.

During his student days in the British capital, he founded the Cypriot Students Union (EFEKA) of which he was the first president during the period 1952-54.

In February 1952 he was appointed *'London Secretary'* to Archbishop Makarios and in 1954 he took the office of *'Secretary of the Cyprus Ethnarchy in London'* and was responsible for enlightening British public opinion on the rights of Cyprus.

From London he went to Athens in 1956 and from August 1956 to March 1957 he represented once more the Cyprus Ethnarchy in New York. From there he went back to Athens and then back to London.

On declaration of Cyprus's Independence on 16 August 1960, he was first appointed Minister of Justice but within a few days he was given the Ministry of Foreign Affairs. In this capacity he represented Cyprus in many international conferences, meetings etc, and accompanied President Makarios on his state and other visits.

On 5 May 1972 he resigned following a serious dispute with the military leaders in Athens.

In May 1976 he announced the establishment of the Democratic Party (DEKO) and from 1976 to 1977 he was President of the House of Representatives.

On the death of Makarios on 3 August 1977 he became, under the Constitution, Acting President of the Republic and on 3 September he was unanimously elected President. He was subsequently re-elected and he held his position until February 1988.

In the face of many difficulties, he served his country with dignity and courage.

Glafkos CLERIDES

Born in Nicosia 1919, he proceeded to study law at Grays Inn and Kings College, London.

He served in the Royal Air Force during the Second World War and in 1942 his plane was shot down; he remained in a German prisoner of war camp until the end of hostilities.

He returned to Cyprus in 1951 and became a practising lawyer. In that capacity and as a member of EOKA (known by the pseudonym of *'Eperides'),* he successfully represented many Cypriots during the EOKA years of 1955-1959.

From 1960 he was the first President of the House of Representatives — a post he held for 16 years. In that capacity he performed the duties of 'Acting President' during Makarios' absence.

From 1968 to 1974 he was the chief GreekCypriot negotiator in the intercommunal talks.

In 1976 he formed DESY ('Democraticos Sinagermos'), and continues to play a leading part in the political affairs of Cyprus. His party commands around $1/_3$ of the island's Greek Cypriot electorate.

An astute politician with in-depth knowledge of Cyprus' history and current affairs.

George VASSILIOU

Born in Famagusta May 1931. He completed his secondary education in Cyprus and later he studied at the universities of Geneva, Vienna, Budapest and London.

Returning to Cyprus in 1962, he established the Middle East Marketing Research Bureau which at present is probably the largest research and consultancy organization in the region.

After victory at the polls he assumed, on 28 February 1988, Cyprus' highest office as its 3rd elected President. His election, coupled with the recent thaw in Greco-Turkish relations, gave rise to new hopes for a solution to the Cyprus question.

A highly-principled, open-minded, hardworking and sincere person; certainly a leader who could unite and bring peace to the island.

TURKISH CYPRIOTS
Fazil KÜTCHÜK

Born in 1906 he proceeded to study at the Universities of Istanbul and Lausanne.

From the 1940s he was acknowledged as one of the leading Turkish Cypriot personalities. Although he led the Cyprus is Turkish Party and later the National Front Party, he was for most of his career a moderate and not an out-and-out extremist.

He served as the first Vice-President of Cyprus when the Republic was established in 1960.

Rauf DENKTASH

Born 1924, he was educated at Lincolns Inn in London. He went on to practice law and from 1949 to 1958 he served in the Cyprus Legal Department, Attorney – General's Office.

A key pro-partitionist and shrewd political figure of the post -mid-1950's period.An admirer of Adnan Menderes the Turkish PM of those years.

He was president of the Turkish Communal Chamber 1960-1973 and at present he is *'president'* of the illegal Turkish Federal State of Cyprus.

At all times (except where shown in the main text) he had been the chief Turkish Cypriot negotiator at the intercommunal talks. Seen by many as the stumbling-block to a negotiated settlement.

GREEKS
Alexandros PAPAGOS 1883-1955

A distinguished soldier and statesman. He took part in the Balkan Wars of 1912-13, Asia Minor adventure of 1919-1922 and fought the Italians and the Germans during the 2nd World War. He was taken to Germany as a hostage. Liberated in 1945, he directed postwar operations in Greece against the communist resistance fighters and was appointed Field-Marshal in 1949.

In May 1951, Papagos resigned as military commander-in-chief to form a new political party, the Greek Rally (Ellinikos Sinagermos), which soon became the strongest political force in Greece.

Enjoying wide popularity and modelling himself after Charles de Gaulle, Papagos led his party to a decisive victory in the elections of November 1952 and became Premier. He died in office.

Papagos holds the distinction of being the first Greek Premier to take the Cypriot question to the United Nations — in 1954.

Constantinos KARAMANLIS

Born in 1907 at Próti, near Serres in Macedonia. The oldest of seven children of a poor schoolmaster, Karamanlis was able, with the help of local benefactors, to attend secondary school and the University of Athens, receiving a law degree in 1932 and practicing law in the capital.

Launched into politics by the Populist Party, he was elected to Parliament in 1935 for Serres, which continued to re-elect him. In 1952, he entered the government of Papagos as Minister of Public Works and when Papagos died in October 1955, Karamanlis was chosen by King Paul to succeed him.

He formed his own party (The National Radical Union — ERE) and served Greece as Premier for many years.

In July 1974 he was recalled from Paris to head the National Emergency Government. He founded the New Democracy Party which won the elections of November 1974. He served as PM to 1980 and as President of the Greek Republic from 1980 to 1985.

Following acute pressure from the Greek Palace and the USA, Karamanlis decided to disentangle the awkward Cyprus problem and was instrumental in setting up the Cyprus Republic in 1959-1960.

Evangelos AVEROFF-TOSSITZA

Born in 1910 he was educated at the University of Lausanne, Switzerland.

He was active in the resistance movement 1939-45; imprisoned in Italy he escaped and continued the fight until the end of the War.

Elected MP in 1946 he served successively as Minister of Supply, Minister of National Economy and Commerce and then as Foreign Secretary from 1956-62.

He was active in the resistance against the Greek dictatorship 1967-74 and was twice imprisoned. With the return of civilian government he served as Minister of National Defence 1974-81, Deputy Premier June-October 1981 and then leader of the New Democracy Party 1981-84.

On the Cyprus problem Averoff, like Karamanlis, was constantly functioning within the restrictive dictates of NATO and the USA. He appeared to want enosis and later independence but his country which depended economically on the USA had a limited range of options. He was unable to withstand the pressure too long; he was instrumental in guiding through the highly restrictive Zürich-London Agreements of 1959, which finally set up the Cyprus Republic in 1960.

His two-volume work in Greek entitled *'A History of Missed Opportunities'* published in 1981 records the chances which were available to close the Cypriot chapter before the catastrophic coup and Turkish invasion of 1974.

George PAPANDREOU 1888-1968

Born at Kaléntzi Greece, Papandreou served his country well in several positions. He headed a Greek government in exile 1944, and then was leader of the national administration, 1944-45. He was again Premier, as head of the reformist Union Party in 1963 and 1964-65.

Papandreou was arrested following the military coup of 1967 but his son, the celebrated economist **Andreas Papandreou,** went into exile and continued criticism of the dictators after his father's death. Following the fall of the junta in 1974 and the return of civilian government, A. Papandreou was elected Premier in October 1981 as head of PASOK — the Panhellenic Socialist Party. He was re-elected for a second term in 1985 but lost the elections of June 1989.

As far as he could George Papandreou supported the legally -elected government of Archbishop Makarios and did everything he could to prevent the subjugation and placing of Cyprus under the American and NATO military umbrella. Thus, he was instrumental in rejecting the Acheson proposals of 1964. Papandreou is referred to as the grand old man *(o geros)* of Greek democracy.

TURKS
Adnan MENDERES 1899-1961

Born near Aydin he was educated in law but became a fairly successful farmer.

He entered politics in 1932,at first in opposition but later with the party in power under Kemal Atätürk.

In 1945 he became one of the leaders of the Democratic Party and became Prime Minister in 1950. He was re-elected in 1954 and 1957 but in May 1960 he was deposed and superseded by General Cemal Gürsel after an army coup.

He repeated more than once that Turkey would *'never'* accept a *'Greek Cyprus'*. He demanded federation and/or partition, depending on what suited his country best.

For the *'crimes'* of the 1950s he was hanged at Imrali in September 1961. Pleas by world leaders failed to save him.

General ISMET INÖNÜ 1884-1973

Turkish soldier and politician born in Izmir, Asia Minor.

The first Premier of Kemal Atätürk's new Republic 1923-1924, 1925-1937. He introduced many political reforms transforming Turkey into a modern state. He was unanimously elected President in 1938 on Atätürks death and he served in that capacity until 1950.

From 1950 he was leader of the Opposition but in 1961 he became Premier with General Gürsel as President. In 1965 he resigned after failing to govern effectively with minority support.

With Venizelos and Atätürk, Inönü was one of the architects of Greco-Turkish friendship in the 1930s.

In the 1960s however, and conscious of the army in the backround, the ageing Inönü was forced to seek the geographical separation of the two communities in Cyprus and his premiership was responsible for repeatedly violating the air space of the island. In his reply to President Johnson's letter on 14 June 1964 Inönü stated that the necessity of a military intervention in Cyprus had been felt *"four times since the closing days of 1963"*. Ten years later that became a reality.

Bület ECEVIT

Born in 1925 he was educated in Istanbul, Ankara, London and Harvard.

A celebrated columnist, poet, scholar and politician. He was elected MP for the centre-left Republican People's Party in 1957 and served as such to 1980.

From 1961 to 1965 he was Minister of Labour and Secretary – General of the RPP from 1966 to 1971.

He served as Prime Minister for 9 months in 1974, 1 month in 1977 and from January 1978 to October 1979.

Conscious of the army and the partitionist policies of his country, NATO and the USA behind him, he ordered the invasion of Cyprus in 1974.

Following the military coup of 1980 he was detained and barred from political life and then imprisoned for a short period of time.

Sir Antony EDEN 1897-1977

Educated at Eton and Christ Church Oxford. Elected MP for Warwick and Leamington in 1923, he held his seat till his resignation in 1957.

He was Foreign Secretary in the 1950s and on 6 April 1955 he succeeded Winston Churchill as Prime Minister.

Failing health coupled with the effects of the Suez fiasco of 1956 resulted in Eden resigning the premiership on 9 January 1957. He was created 1st Earl of Avon in 1961.

Over Cyprus and during such troubled times he had no positive policy and due to his prompting, Turkey was pleasantly hijacked into the Cyprus question as the third interested party.

Sir Maurice Harold MACMILLAN

Born in 1894, he was educated at Eton and Balliol College, Oxford. In the 1950s he served as Minister of Housing 1951-54 and as Minister of Defence 1954-55 and thereafter Foreign Secretary to the end of 1955 when he was appointed Chancellor of the Exchequer.

Macmillan succeeded Eden as PM in 1957. Like his predecessor his Cyprus policy was riddled with inconsistencies. It was a *non-policy* dictated by Middle East strategic and economic interests and by the belief of a firm alliance with Turkey. Both leaders unashamedly played the *Turkish card to the detriment by Cyprus' unity. Partition,* as a way out of the Cyprus impasse, was always high on their list of priorities. Both Eden and Macmillan must have been aware of the dictum that *diplomacy* is *a multi-million pound business.* They practised it to its fullest capacity! Over Cyprus morality, justice and fairness were way down their list of political perceptions.

James CALLAGHAN

Born in 1912 he was elected Labour MP for South Cardiff in 1945. In 1964 he was appointed Chancellor of the Exchequer in Harold Wilson's government and from 1967 to 1970 he served as Home Secretary.

As Foreign Secretary from 1974 to 1976 he worked tirelessly at Geneva with his Greek and Turkish counterparts (Mavros and Günes) to bring about a cease-fire and thus prevent further destruction following the Turkish invasion. As far as he could Callaghan supported the unity and territorial integrity of Cyprus. For this he had to bear the wrath of the Americans and the Turks. He served as Prime Minister from 1976 to 1979.

Sir John HARDING 1896-1989

Born in 1896 he rose to the position of Chief of Staff of the Allied Army in Italy in 1944.

From 1955 to 1957 he was Governor-General of Cyprus during the first two years of the National Liberation Struggle.

He re-organised the security forces to combat EOKA, re-established order through the imposition of martial law and press control, banished Makarios to the Seychelles and although he failed to bring about a political settlement he was widely respected and feared for his straight forward soldierly approach.

He was created a Peer in 1958 and has taken the title of Ist Baron of Petherton.

Sir Hugh FOOT

Born in 1907 he was educated at Cambridge. He held many government administrative posts abroad — in Palestine, Transjordan, Jamaica and Cyprus.

He was the island's last Governor from 1957 to the time it achieved full statehood. A man of peace and great international understanding he was instrumental in bringing an end to the hostilities in Cyprus. From February 1959 he successfully guided the interim Cypriot administration to become a republic in August 1960.

He was awarded a life peerage in 1964 and assumed the title of Baron Caradon.

AMERICANS

Dean ACHESON 1893-1971

A law graduate from Yale and Harvard.

Under-Secretary of State from 1945 to 1947 and Secretary of State from 1949 to January 1953. He acted as adviser to 4 Presidents. He became the principal creator of US foreign policy in the Cold War period following the 2nd World War. He helped to create the Western Alliance (NATO, was the first peacetime defensive alliance entered by the USA), in opposition to the Soviet Union and other Communist Nations.

After leaving office he returned to private law practice but continued to serve as foreign policy adviser to successive Presidents.

His partitionist policies regarding Cyprus had a profound effect on the island's survival. The famous *'Acheson Plans'* of 1964-65 were intended to lead to double enosis which would have meant the establishment of American and NATO bases there to serve the large western interests of the area. Although rejected at the time, Acheson perservered and he declared in 1966 that a solution could be imposed on Cyprus by the use of superior and more sophisticated arms. Such a policy was *'approved'* and achieved in 1974.

John F. KENNEDY 1917 - 1963

Born in Massachusetts on 29 May 1917, he graduated from Harvard in 1940 and then served with great gallantry during the Second World War.

In January 1961 he was inaugurated 35th President of the USA —the youngest man and the first Roman Catholic to be so elected.

As Senator and then President until he was mysteriously assassinated on 22 November 1963, Kennedy earned the gratitude of the world for his constant reminders that all should fight against the common enemies of man: tyranny, poverty, disease and war itself.

During his three-year presidency, relations between the USA and Cyprus were very cordial. In fact, Kennedy treated Makarios with the utmost respect and when the latter heard of Kennedy's assassination he openly wept because as he said *"Cyprus had lost a dear friend"*.

Henry Alfred KISSINGER

Born on 27 May 1923 in Fürth, now in West Germany. His family emigrated to the USA in 1938 to escape the Nazi persecution of the Jews.

He obtained his Ph. D. in government from Harvard University, became a professor there and served as a consultant on security matters to various US agencies during 1955-1968, spanning the administrations of Eisenhower, Kennedy and Lyndon. B. Johnson.

From 1969 to 1976 he was a major force in World diplomacy and served as Secretary of State from 1973 to 1977.

In 1973 he shared the Nobel Peace Prize.

Over Cyprus he took the view that US interests and global commitments dictated that the island should remain under NATO control and supervision and within the USA's sphere of influence. Therefore, attempts by Cyprus to follow a non-aligned policy were resisted and in 1974 when Turkey invaded the island the USA did not raise a finger to stop her. America had achieved its aim by proxy. Its Cyprus policy was ill-considered, short-sighted and hopelessly dominated by military considerations. Its partitionist policies appear to have succeeded and it now has a large military base in the Turkish-controlled northern part of Cyprus.

UNITED NATIONS

U THANT 1909-1974

Burmese diplomat. When his country became independent in 1948 he took up government work and after holding several appointments he became permanent UN representative for Burma in 1957.

In 1962 he was elected Secretary-General of the UN and proceeded to play a major diplomatic and peaceful role during many crises and disputes.

In 1964 he was instrumental in mobilizing a UN peace-keeping force for Cyprus and a mediator for the purpose of promoting a peaceful solution and an agreed settlement for the island.

Kurt WALDHEIM

Austrian statesman born in 1918 near Vienna.

In 1972 he succeeded U Thant as Secretary-General of the UN; a post which he held until 1981.

He worked tirelessly to get the two Cypriot sides round the negotiating table. He believes strongly in the unity and territorial integrity of the island.

At present he is President of his native Austria.

Javier PÉREZ DE CUÉLLAR

Peruvian diplomat born in 1920.

He served as a UN Under-Secretary-General for special political affairs for many years. In this capacity he was instrumental in trying to secure a peaceful solution to the Cyprus problem.

Appointed Secretary-General in 1982 he has continued to urge and encourage the intercommunal talks in Cyprus.

He has been associated with the Cyprus issue for years; he believes in the co-existence, harmony and unity of all peoples.

Map showing the pre-1974
distribution of Greek and Turkish
population over the island
● = Greek inhabitants
○ = Turkish inhabitants

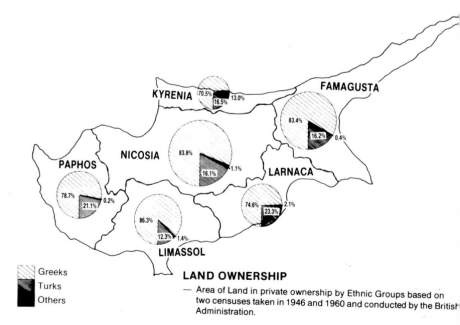

Greeks
Turks
Others

LAND OWNERSHIP

— Area of Land in private ownership by Ethnic Groups based on
two censuses taken in 1946 and 1960 and conducted by the British
Administration.

278

APPENDIX -B-

ORTHODOX ARCHBISHOPS OF CYPRUS 1570s-1989

Timotheos	1575 —
Athanasios	1600-1602
Benjamin	1602-1609
Christodoulos	1609-1631
Nikiforos	1660-1673
Hilarion Kigala	1674-1678
James I	1679-1689
Germanos II	1690-1705
James II	1710 -
Silvestros	1718-1731
Philotheos	1734-1759
Païsios	1759-1766
Chrysanthos	1767-1810
Kyprianos	1810-1821
Joakim	1821-1824
Damaskinos	1824-1827
Panaretos	1827-1840
Joannikios II	1840-1849
Kyrillos	1849-1854
Makarios I	1854-1865
Sofronios II	1865-1900
'Vacancy'	1900-1909
Kyrillos II	1909-1916
Kyrillos III	1916-1933
'Vacancy'	1933-1947
Leontios Leontiou	1947 (June/July)
Makarios II	1947-1950
Makarios III	1950-1977
Chrysostomos I	1977 —

NB: The dates, shown above for the Turkish Supremacy (1571-1878), are not always accurate.

APPENDIX -C-

OTTOMAN SULTANS 1566-1924

Selim II	1566-1574
Murad III	1574-1595
Mohammed III	1595-1603
Ahmed I	1603-1617
Mustapha I	1617
Osman II	1618-1622
Mustapha I	1622-1623
Murad IV	1623-1640
Ibrahim	1640-1648
Mohammed IV	1648-1687
Suleiman II	1687-1691
Ahmed II	1691-1695
Mustapha II	1695-1703
Ahmed III	1703-1730
Mahmoud I	1730-1754
Osman III	1754-1757
Mustapha III	1757-1774
Abdul Hamid I	1774-1789
Selim III	1789-1807
Mustapha IV	1807-1808
Mahmoud II	1808-1839
Abdul Mejid I	1839-1861
Abdul Aziz	1861-1876
Murad V	1876
Abdul Hamid II	1876-1909
Mohammed V	1909-1918
Mohammed VI	1918-1922
Abdul Mejid II	1922-1924 (caliph only)

NB: The sultanate was abolished and Turkey became a Republic in October 1923. The Moslem religion was disestablished and the caliphate abolished in March 1924.

APPENDIX -E-

BRITISH PERSONNEL
1878-1960

Administrators:-

1878: Garnet Wolseley
1879: Robert Biddulph
1886: Henry Bulwer
1892: Walter Sendall
1898: William Haynes Smith

High Commissioners:-

1900: William Haynes Smith
1904: Charles King-Harman
1911: Hamilton Goold-Adams
1915: John Clauson
1920: Malcolm Stevenson

Governors:-

1925: Malcolm Stevenson
1926: Ronald Storrs
1932: Reginald Stubbs
1933: Herbert Palmer
1939: William Battershill
1941: Charles Woolley
1946: Reginald Fletcher,
     Lord Winster
1949: Andrew Wright
1954: Robert Armitage
1955: John Harding
1957: Hugh Foot, later
     Lord Caradon

APPENDIX -E-

GREEK MONARCHS 1833-1967

1833-1862 Otto, Prince Otto of Bavaria
1863-1913 George I, Prince William of Denmark
1913-1917 Constantine I
1917-1920 Alexander
1920-1922 Constantine I
1922-1923 George II
1924-1935 'Republic'
1935-1944 George II
1944-1946 'Regency'
1946-1947 George II
1947-1964 Paul I
1964-1967 Constantine II

NB: Following a referendum, the monarchy was abolished in 1967.

APPENDIX -F-

POPULATION STATISTICS

1. Actual Population: 1881-1983 (to the nearest 1,000)

1881	186,000	1946	450,000
1901	237,000	1960	578,000
1921	311,000	1983	652,000

2. Comparative table (%): 1881-1983

	1881	1931	1946	1960	1973	1983
Greek Cypriots	73.4	79.5	80.2	76.6	78.9	80.1
Turkish »	24.9	18.4	17.9	18.1	18.4	18.6
Others	1.7	2.1	1.9	5.3	2.7	1.3

3. 1881 Census by Religion

136,629	Greek Orthodox
46,389	Mahommedan
3,066	Various Religious sects
186,084	(the majority being Roman Catholic and Church of England)

4. 1960 Census by Nationality

442,521	:	Greek
104,350	:	Turkish
3,628	:	Armenian
2,708	:	Maronites
3,351	:	British
2,796	:	Latins
18,261	:	Others
577,615		

NB: For all population figures (1-4) allow for counting, non-registration and other statistical errors.

APPENDIX -G-

Other Personalities "involved" in the Making of Modern Cyprus

Creativity, courage, determination and initiative are all deep-set aspects of the proud inhabitants of Cyprus. Worldwide, the islanders have excelled themselves in many fields.

The arts in Cyprus have benefited from the growing interest on the part of the government which has established an art gallery, a public library, a state theatre and a state orchestra At this level Cyprus has also profited from the activities of the British Council, the Goethe Institute, the French Cultural Centre and the American Centre.

Frequent visits by internationally-known artists, orchestras, ballet and theatrical companies have stimulated public awareness. A useful contribution is also made by the TV network which makes generous use of imported educational and cultural film material.

Some talented local artists have emerged and their work has appeared in many European exhibitions. For example, *Angelos Makrides,* who represented Cyprus at the prestigious Biennale of Art in Venice 1989, is noted for the mastery of his inspiration and materials. Everything is measured and has an inner rhythm; and in this lies the expressive power and imposing presence of his compositions — works of art which are tender and poetic in their expression of the tragic.

Other artists, just as expressive have made their name in international forums. Among them are **Stass Paraskos** who has established the first school of painting in Paphos, and **Diamantis** who is regarded by many as the *"father of modern Cypriot painting"* Other artists include: **Charalambides, Kanthos, Kotsonis, Skoteinos,** etc., etc.

In the field of poetry and prose-writing, the Cypriots have again made great strides. **Manos Kralis** born in Nicosia 1914, is talked of as being one of the *'rejuvenators'* of Cyprus' poetry. His collection of poems called *'Taste of Freedom'* published in 1974 have as a central theme the tragic events of the Turkish invasion — a subject that has been explored by many others.

Undoubtedly, **Vasilis Michaelides** is the undisputed *'Cypriot National Poet'* yet, others have contributed immensely to the islands' cultural development. **Azinos, Germasiotis, Kakolis, Liasides, Paleshis,**

Tziapouras, Charalambides, Chrysanthes and Loukis Akritas whose work *'The Plain' (o kambos)*, should be set amongst the two or three best prose-writings left to us by the generation of the 1930s.

Local Cypriots and those in the diaspora have also excelled in other fields and have received worldwide recognition and fame:

V. **Karageorghis** is an eminent scholar and archaeologist; **G. Cacoyiannis** has excelled as a film critic and producer. In the realm of business and international finance **Sir Reo Stakis** has achieved worldwide success; other Cypriots have also achieved prominence in this field. Cyprus also boasts probably the largest research and consultancy organization in the eastern Mediterranean region; called the *'Middle East Marketing Research Bureau'* it was established in the early 1960s. The largest Contruction Company of the Middle East is "J&P", established by the energetic **Joannou** and **Paraskevaides** and Cyprus is still its headquarters.

Cypriots have also made great strides in medicine and the other sciences and arts. The talented and hardworking islanders are to be seen in leading hospitals, universities and research organizations all over the world. **A.K. Emilianides** was a leading constitutional jurist and historian; **Th. Papadopoulos** is a historian and scholar with few equals. In medicine Professor **A. Nicolaides** is a leading heart surgeon; **Ch. Theophanides** is one of the world's leading sugar diabetes specialists and **G. Christofinis** is a microbiologist with many authoritative research papers to his name.

In music, talent is again plentiful. **Michalis Violaris, Marios Tokas** and **Anna Vissi** are highly successful artists of popular Greek songs. **George Michael** is one of the great mega-stars of the world's pop scene. **Solon Michaelides** is a talented conductor and **Marios Papadopoulos** is a young conductor and soloist of great international standing.

Michael Kakoyiannis, the creator of *'Zorba the Greek'* is one of the world's great film directors.

The list is large and the space does not allow to mention them all. New talent is emerging from the younger generations.

BIBLIOGRAPHY
A short selection of easily obtainable books in English

M.A. Attalides (Ed) — Cyprus: National & International Politics. 1979

A.C. Brown & H.W.
Catting — Ancient Cyprus. 1975

S. Casson — Ancient Cyprus. 1937

V. Coufoudakis (Ed) — Essays on the Cyprus Conflict. 1976

N. Crawshaw — The Cyprus Revolt: An Account of the struggle for union with Greece. 1978

L.G. Durrell — Bitter Lemons. 1959

C.M. Foley — Legacy of Strife: Cyprus from Rebellion to Civil War. 1964

H.M. Foot — A Start in Freedom. 1964

M. Harbottle — The Impartial Soldier. 1970

M. Harbottle — The Blue Berets. 1971

D. Hunt (Ed) — Footprints in Cyprus. An illustrated history. 1982

V. Karageorghis — The Ancient Civilisation of Cyprus. 1970

V. Karageorghis — Cyprus: From Stone Age to the Romans. 1982

S. Kyriakides — Cyprus: Constitutionalism & Crisis Government. 1968

H. Luke — Cyprus under the Turks, 1571-1878. 1921

H. Luke — Cyprus: A Portrait & an Appreciation. 1965

P. Loizos — The Greek Gift: Politics in a changing Cypriot Village. 1975

K.C. Markides — The Rise and Fall of the Cyprus Republic. 1977

S. Mayes — Makarios: A Biography. 1981

L.C. Moseley (Ed.) — Research for Social Welfare. Six case studies in Cyprus. 1979

S. Panteli — A New History of Cyprus. From the Earliest times to the present day. 1984

Th. Papadopoullos — Social and Historical data on Population, 1570-1881. 1965

A. Papandreou — Democracy at Gunpoint: The Greek Front. 1970

P.G. Polyviou — Cyprus: Conflict & Negotiation 1960-1980. 1980

K. Spyridakis — A Brief History of Cyprus. 1974

R. Stephens — Cyprus, a place of arms. 1966

C.G. Tornaritis — Cyprus and its Constitutional and Other Legal Problems. 1980

J. Triseliotis — Social Welfare in Cyprus. 1977

P.N. Vanezis — Makarios: Life and Leadership. 1979

K. Waldheim — The Challenge of Peace. 1980

C.M. Woodhouse — Karamanlis: The Restorer of Greek Democracy. 1982

C.M. Woodhouse — The Rise and Fall of the Greek Colonels. 1985

S.G. Xydis — Cyprus: Reluctant Republic. 1973

INDEX